Second G
Phonics & R

Teacher's Manual *(Part 2)*
Lessons 81 to 160

Visit **McRuffy.com** for helpful resources to teach this curriculum!

Teacher's Manual *(Part 2)*
ISBN 9781592693153

A part of the **McRuffy Press Second Grade Phonics & Reading Curriculum** ISBN 978159269-2057

Written and illustrated by
Brian Davis M. A. Ed.

Graphic Design by
Sherylynn Davis

McRuffy Press, LLC
P.O. Box 212
Raymore, MO 64083

816-331-7831

sales@mcruffy.com

www.McRuffy.com

Puppy Place Game

Play games and rescue puppies on the back of the Language and Reading (LAR) workbook!

All games: Use the reading book for the week to create questions for the games. Players answer a question or complete a task before earning a roll. Players will get a point for each correct answer or completed task. If a player lands on a puppy space, rescue the puppy and take it home (move to the center of the board). On the next turn, the player will roll and move from the start space.

Players earn a point for each task completed successfully. Players earn an extra point for each puppy they rescue. Players also earn a point for completing the path when they cross the start space (not from the doghouse). Players may keep track of points using small objects such as counters, beans, or coins. Points can also be kept on paper as a scorecard. The first player to score 10 points wins.

Use a die, spinner, or draw numbers to move on the board with game pieces (small objects or game pawns).

Games (tasks to complete before moving)

Word List Reading Game: Read a word from the list. You may limit it to words that are also a part of the week's phonics theme.

Word List Meaning Game: This game would most likely require an adult to create questions or clues. Direct questions to a player on their turn to find a word on the word list according to the meaning. It does not need to be a formal clue. Find a word that means ___. or What is something that ___?

Word List Rhyme Game: Find a word on the list that rhymes with ____.

Word List Sentence Game: Use the word ______ in a sentence.

Find A Word Story Game: Find the word ______ on page ____.

Read A Sentence Game: Read the (first, second, third...) sentence on page _____.

Answer Sentence Game: Find a sentence on this page that tells _________.

Finish the Sentence Game: One player or the teacher reads part of a sentence. The player taking the turn finishes the sentence. You may tell the player the page the sentence is on or a choice of two pages.

Answer a Question Game: Make up questions to ask about the story that a player must answer before moving on the board.

Skate Spelling

Play a game on the back of the Spelling and Phonics workbook!

Move to spaces to collect the letters needed to spell words from the weekly spelling lists. Players can use a die, spinner, or draw numbers from a container to move around the board. Players can move in any direction on the board and even change directions in a turn, but players cannot move diagonally. They can only move along the lines behind the spaces. Use game pawns or small objects for playing pieces.

If a player's playing piece is on a space, another player cannot move to the same space. The player must choose another direction to move. If the same letter is used more than once in a spelling word or spelling word list, the player must visit that letter space once for each time it is used.

Players can start on any penguin space in the corners of the board. On other turns, players can move to a penguin space and jump to any other penguin space and keep moving. For example, if a player is two spaces away from the penguin on the bottom left and rolls a five, the player can move to that penguin space and jump to the top right penguin and then move three more spaces.

Players will write the letters they capture to spell the words on a piece of paper or students can write the words first leaving space between letters so they may be circled as they are captured on the board.

Games: *Choose the rules for playing the game.*

Choose one:

Same Words Rule: All players race to spell the same spelling word.

Different Words Rule: Players choose different words from the spelling list. If a player chooses a word that has more letters than another player's word, the player with the longer word may automatically fill in enough letters so that both players are moving to get the same number of letters.

Choose one:

Letter Order Rule: Letters must by moved to in the order they are used in the words.

Letter Scramble Rule: Letters can be moved to in any order.

Choose the number of words: You may play a shorter game and only spell one word or a longer game and spell more words, such as a list of three words. You may write the words before the game with spaces between letters and then circle the letters as you move to them and land on them.

Word Lists

Lesson 81: dew, few, hew, Jew, knew, new, pew, blew, brew, chew, crew, flew, grew, screw, skew, stew, threw, you, youth, group, soup, mousse

Lesson 86: buy, by, cry, dye, dry, eye, fly, fry, guy, lye, my, ply, pry, rye, shy, sky, sly, spy, spry, sty, thy, try, why, brier, crier, die, dried, drier, flier, flies, fries, fried, lie, pie, spied, tie, vie

Lesson 91: wad, waddle, waffle, wahoo, walk, wall, wallaby, wallet, wallop, wallow, walnut, walrus, Walter, waltz, wand, Wanda, wander, want, war, warble, ward, warden, wardrobe, warfare, warm, warmth, warn, warning, warp, warpath, warrant, warship, wart, warthog, was, wash, washtub, washy, wasp, watch, water, watt, what

Lesson 96: because, caught, cause, daughter, daunt, fault, flaunt, fraud, fraught, gaunt, gauze, haul, haunt, jaunt, launch, Maud, maul, naught, naughty, Paul, paunch, pause, Saul, slaughter, staunch, taught, vault, bought, brought, fought, ought, sought, thought

Lesson 101: unaware, unbolt, unbutton, unbuckle, unchain, unclean, uncoil, uncover, uncut, underfoot, undergo, underground, underline, undermine, undershirt, understand, understood, undertake, undo, undress, unfair, unfold, unforgiving, unfriendly, unglued, unhappy, unhitch, unjust, unkind, unknown, unlatch, unless, unlike, unload, unlock, unpack, unplug, unquiet, unreal, unrest, unroll, unscrew, unselfish, unskilled, unsnap, unsound, unstop, unstring, unstuck, untidy, untie, until, unto, untold, untrue, untwist, unwilling, unwind, unwise, unwrap, unzip

Lesson 106: cough, enough, laugh, rough, tough, trough
Alphabet, elephant, dolphin, gopher, graph, orphan, pamphlet, phantom, phase, Phillip, phone, phonics, phonograph, photograph, phrase, physical, physics, telegraph, telephone

Lesson 111: ahead, bread, breakfast, breast, breath, cleanse, dead, deaf, death, dread, feather, head, headache, health, heavy, instead, lead, meadow, measure, peasant, pheasant, pleasant, pleasure, read, ready, realm, spread, stead, steady, stealth, sweat, thread, threat, threaten, tread, treasure, unhealthy, unpleasant, unread, unsteady, wealth, wealthy, weapon, weather

Lesson 121: above, another, become, beloved, blood, collide, color, come, comfort, comfortable, commend, community, company, compass, compare, compete, complain, complete, computer, conclude, confuse, connect, consider, control, cover, done, dove, falcon, from, front, glove, love, lovely, mammoth, month, mother, none, nothing, of, onion, other, oven, shove, shovel, some, somewhat, somewhere, someone, sometime, something, son, ton, undone, welcome

Lesson 126: action, affection, attention, auction, carnation, caution, celebration, commotion, condition, decoration, direction, emotion, formation, fraction, hesitation, information, instruction, irritation, lotion, mention, motion, nation, notion, occupation, portion, position, proportion, question, relation, relaxation, sensation, station, vacation

Word Lists

Lesson 131: angrily, boldly, bravely, bubbly, carefully, carelessly, certainly, closely, coldly, completely, constantly, happily, harshly, jointly, joyfully, kindly, lately, lightly, likely, loosely, lovely, meanly, merrily, mildly, monthly, noisily, oddly, pleasantly, powerfully, proudly, quickly, quietly, rarely, really, sadly, scraggly, secretly, selfishly, Shelly, shortly, shyly, simply, sleepily, slightly, slowly, softly, strangely, suddenly, sweetly, swiftly, terribly, tightly, unkindly, unlikely, unselfishly, weakly, wobbly, yearly

Lesson 136: react, recall, recess, reclaim, recline, record, recount, recover, recruit, redecorate, redeem, redouble, reduce, reduction, refill, refinish, reflect, reflex, refresh, refrigerate, refund, refuse, regain, regret, rehearse, rejoice, rejoin, relate, relax, relay, release, relief, relieve, relive, rely, remain, remake, remark, remember, remote, remove, renew, renumber, repair, repay, repeat, repent, rephrase, replace, replant, replay, reply, report, reprint, request, require, resign, respect, respond, result, resume, retell, retire, retrace, retreat, return, reveal, revenge, reverse, review, revue, reward, rewind

Lesson 141: Agent, agreement, announcement, apartment, basement, cement, comment, compliment, content, department, different, element, enjoyment, excitement, experiment, garment, instrument, lament, moment, monument, movement, ornament, parent, payment, present, prevent, repent, silent, statement, treatment

Lesson 146: Barnyard, hoedown, sidewalk, sidekick, skateboard, homework, schoolwork, grown-up, handcuffs, himself, herself, keyboard, playground, quicksand, someday, sixteen, somewhere, themselves, therefore, without, bagpipe, bedroom, blackboard, footstool, footstep, know-how, punchbowl, haystack, bedtime, nighttime, hayloft, pitchfork, washtub, horseshoe, hushpuppies, cornbread, hayride, applesauce, background, backwoods, blacksmith, blackbird, campfire, catfish, crawfish, doorway, earthworm, homestead, friendship, greyhound, hardship, homework, lighthouse, livestock, pinecone, playground, raindrops, withdraw, yourself, buckshot, bug-eyed, bullfrog, bull's-eye, icehouse

Lesson 151: Anything, anyway, anywhere, applesauce, arrowhead, automobile, basketball, blackberry, blueberry, bumblebee, buttercup, butterfly, buttermilk, cowpuncher, everyone, everything, everywhere, eyeglasses, fingernail, fingerprint, firecracker, freshwater, gingerbread, gooseberry, granddaughter, grandfather, grandmother, grasshopper, lumberjack, handkerchief, hamburger, headquarters, honeysuckle, housekeeper, however, huckleberry, hushpuppies, jellybean, jellyfish, microphone, microscope, marshmallow, mulberry, neighborhood, nevertheless, newspaper, nonetheless, peppermint, petticoat, pineapple, policeman, rattlesnake, screwdriver, seventeen, shoemaker, skyrocket, somebody, strawberry, tablecloth, tablespoon, troublemaker, typewriter, understand, undertaking, waterfall, watermelon, woodpecker

build, builder, building, built, disguise, guarantee, guard, guardrail, guess, guesswork, guest, guide, guidebook, guideline, guidepost, guilt, guiltless, guilty, guinea hen, guinea pig, guitar

Writing Skills Workbook Instruction

Lesson numbers are the suggested lesson to present the activity. The lesson numbers refer to the lesson numbers of the overall Second Grade SE Phonics and Reading Curriculum. Generally, you may shift the day for the activities for anytime during that week of lessons. Reading book related writing is usually presented after students have read the entire book. Students usually finish reading the book in the third lesson of the week. This would be lessons that end with 3 or 8. Some pages are labeled story planning pages. These work with the creative writing assignments in the Teacher's Manual. Creative Writing assignments generally appear in the fourth lesson plan of the week. These are lessons that end with 4 or 9. If you use these, this will be the first step in the writing process. You can spread the completion of the writing assignment of several days, even extending into the next week. Some writing lessons refer back to these daily lesson plans in the teacher's manual.

As with other lessons in this manual, bold print usally indicates instruction that can be directly read to the student.Answers to questions are in parenthesis. Some Writing Skills Workbook pages ask questions using question words. You may want to make sure students are familiar with these words (who, what, where, when, why, how). There is a Question Words poster in the Resource Pack.

Lesson 81

Students will arrange a poem into two different rhyming patterns. This activity can be done during any lesson from 81 to 85, but probably not Lesson 84. The LAR workbook page for Lesson 84 features a stew recipe writing activity, so no other writing activity for this week is in this workbook.

Introduce the activity.

The lines in poems do not have to rhyme, but they often do. Usually those rhymes will fit a pattern. For lines in a poem to rhyme, only the last word in the line has to rhyme. We can label these patterns with letters. Each time a line doesn't end with a word that doesn't rhyme with the ending word of the last sentence, a new letter labels that word in the rhyming pattern. When any other ending word rhymes with that word, it is labeled with the same letter.

For example, listen to this poem. (Read the complete poem, then discuss.)

There was a little frog
It waited for a fly
It sat upon a log
When will a lunch zip by?

The four ending words are frog, fly, log, and by. The first label will be A. The first rhyming word is frog. All words that rhyme with *frog* will be labeled with the letter A. The next ending word is *fly*. Does the word *fly* rhyme with *frog?* (no) So words that rhyme with fly will be labeled B. Does the next ending word, log, rhyme with frog or fly? (Yes, it rhymes with frog.) **Words that rhyme with frog are labeled A in this poem. So our pattern so far is ABA. Now test the next ending word, by. Does it rhyme with frog and be labeled A, or fly and be labeled B? If it doesn't rhyme with either it will be labeled w letter C.** (It rhymes with fly. It is labeled B) **So this poem has a rhyme pattern of A, B, A, B.** (Continued on the next page)

Lesson 81 Continued

I'm going to change the order of the sentences in the poem. Tell me the new rhyme pattern:

There was a little frog
It sat upon a log
It waited for a fly
When will a lunch zip by?

What is the new rhyme pattern? (AABB). ***Frog*** **and** ***log*** **are the first two ending words. They rhyme, so they are both labeled A. The next ending word is** ***fly*****. It doesn't rhyme with** ***log*** **and** ***frog*****. It is labeled B. The final ending word is** ***by*****. It rhymes with** ***fly*****.** ***Fly*** **was labeled B, so** ***by*** **is also labeled B.**

On the workbook page are 4 lines of a poem that are mixed up. Put them into two different orders to makc a poem. Match the patterns above the writing lines. First write it with an ABAB pattern. Next, change the order of sentences to make it an AABB rhyming pattern poem.

The expected answers are as follows, but you may accept any answers that follow the rhyming letter patterns:

ABAB Pattern Poem

I made something new
It fed a hungry group
It was so easy to chew
All liked the yummy soup

AABB Pattern Poem

I made something new
It was so easy to chew
It fed a hungry group
All liked the yummy soup

Lesson 86

This lesson can be done during any lesson from Lesson 86 to 90. Students will research the four stages in a fly's lifecycle. Students will write a brief description of each stage and draw or print, cut, and paste a picture on the lifecycle diagram.

Lesson 89

This page will be used to help develop the creative writing assignment presented in Lesson 89 of the Teacher's Manual. This page is for notes, so students do not have to write in complete sentences. The *What happens next* section can include several events in the story. The questions about Violet and Tom can refer to their actions or feelings.

Lesson 93

This lesson can be done during any lesson from Lesson 91 to 95, but students will have more background information for warthogs and walruses in Lesson 93. The LAR workbook page for Lesson 94 is also dedicated to creative writing. Therefore, this is the only writing assignment for this week in this workbook.

Write your own opinions to answer the questions. Don't just write your choice. Write about why that is your choice. Try to write in a way to convince someone else that your choice is best. Even if you don't like either choice, pick one and write to try to convince it is the best choice.

Lesson 96

This activity can begin in Lesson 96, but it can be completed over a number of days. You may allow students to write one statement a day if they can't think of three in one lesson.

Write four or more sentences with this format: I once thought _________ because __________________. The sentences can be about real experiences or made up.

Examples: I once wolves would make good pets because they look like dogs. I once thought the moon was made of cheese because it had holes like Swiss cheese. I once thought pineapples grew on pine trees because pineapple begins with pine. I once thought Dr. Pepper was good to drink when I was sick because it had doctor in it.

Lesson 98

Write captions for the pictures from *A Jewell for Paula.*

Lesson 101

This lesson can be done anytime during the week. Students will write sentences to answer questions with the words that contain the prefix un-. You may also require that the answer have different words with the prefix un-. The Resource Pack has a reference sheet of words that begin with the prefix un-.

Answers should be complete sentences. Answers can be more than one sentence.

Lesson 102

This lesson can be done anytime during the week. The word list on the page contains nonsense words beginning with the prefix un-. Students will make creative definitions for five words from the list. Students can choose any of the words to write about. They may also make up an "un-word" formed by adding the prefix un- to their names.

The Un-dictionary needs to add new unreal un-words. You've been chosen to write definitions for five words. Since these are not real words yet, you will have to make up the definitions.

In another lesson, you may have students write example sentences for their un-words.

Lesson 106

Students will write sentences and then translate them into Morse Code. This can be done anytime during the week. The Resource Pack also contains a copy of the Morse Code. You may have students write and encode other sentences throughout the week.

Before people had telephones, they could send messages using a system called a telegraph. You couldn't hear other people talk. Instead a code was sent made up of dots and dashes. It was sent by electricity over wires. A man named Samuel Morse was one of the inventors of the telegraph. The code is named after him.

Each letter is formed using a series of dots and dashes. Today you will write sentences using Morse Code.

The first word from the example sentence, did, has been translated for you. When you translate the next word, be sure to leave space between the code for each letter. Also add a vertical line at the end of each word.

Next, write your own sentence. Use a subject that is spelled with a ph making the f sound, since you are learning those words this week. Write about a dolphin or a gopher.

Lesson 108

Write captions for the pictures from *The Elephant and the Alphabet.*

Lesson 111

This lesson can be done anytime throughout the week.

Pretend you found a treasure chest. Write about it. Answer the three questions. Use at least one e-a word in each answer.

Lesson 112

This lesson can be done anytime during the week.

Plan a healthy breakfast. Choose at least one item from each food group. Draw a picture of that food. Don't just write the food item. Write something about each food. For example, you could tell why you choose that, who in your family likes it the most, ways to prepare or cook it, or anything else.

Lesson 121

This lesson can be done anytime during the week. Students will write about being considerate to three different people. One person a day can be chosen, or all in one lesson. Students will include at least one of the words in the word list at the top of the page.

Students should identify the person. They can then write to answer general questions. Students can choose to answer one or more.

Why should you be considerate to that person? When will you or when are you considerate to that person? How do you show you are being considerate?

Lesson 124

This sheet can be used for students to show the story elements after they have completed the writing assignment in the Teacher's Manual.

Students are to write a story based on the book, *Lovey Dove and the Falcon*. It is to be about Lovey Dove and Sonny the Bear. The LAR workbook page for Lesson 124 is an exercise that matches story elements to statements about the story.

Students will do a similar thing for the story they write. Students will write statements to match the story elements like on the LAR workbook page.

Lesson 126

This lesson can be done anytime throughout the week. Students will answer questions to tell about their favorite celebration. It can be the celebration in general or one specific celebration. For example a general description of holiday such as Christmas. It can be a specific celebration such as "my fifth birthday".

Lesson 127

This lesson can be done anytime throughout the week. This page may also be used for brainstorming the creative writing assignment in Lesson 129. Students may choose to change the name of their creatures in their story.

In this story this week, students will read about an imaginary people (or creatures similar to people) called Foozles. Students will create their own creature/people called Doozles. Students will answer questions and write descriptions for Doozles. Students should use -tion words in their descriptions.

Students will draw a picture of their Doozle. Students will answer the questions about Dozzles. They should include words that end with -tion in their answers.

Celebrations can include holidays or things Doozles do on celebrations such as birthdays.

Competitions can include sports or games Doozles like to play.

Occupations can include different kinds of jobs Doozles have.

All of these can be creative, made-up celebrations, competitions, and occupations.

Lesson 131

This lesson can be done anytime throughout the week. Students will answer questions to develop a paragraph with a main idea, supporting sentences, and a concluding sentence. Students will write answers to the questions or develop other supporting sentences to write the paragraph.

Students should start the next sentence at the end of the previous sentence instead of on a new line to write a paragraph of four sentences. The paragraphs begin with the main idea sentence, so students do not need to write it. Students will only write the sentences they create.

Lesson 133

Write captions for the pictures from *What is Blizzy?*

Lesson 136

This lesson can be done anytime throughout the week. Students will write steps to tell how to repair something. Students should use words from the re- word list. They should also use words to show order.

Students should write 4 to 6 steps. The steps can be to repair anything. The steps do not need to be researched. They do not need to be accurate. Students can be creative with their repairs, they can even be creative in what needs to be repaired.

Some ideas include:

Restringing your shoe, repairing a musical instrument, airplane, car, favorite toy, time machine, robot, appliance, refrigerator, spaceship, bicycle tire, telephone, light bulb, television, computer, treehouse, chair, pen, backpack, clothes, famous painting.

Lesson 137

This lesson is like Lesson 131. It can be done anytime throughout the week. Students will answer questions to develop a paragraph with a main idea, supporting sentences, and a concluding sentence. Students will write answers to the questions or develop other supporting sentences to write the paragraph.

Students should start the next sentence at the end of the previous sentence instead of on a new line to write a paragraph of four sentences. The paragraphs begin with the main idea sentence, so students do not need to write it. Students will only write the sentences they create.

Students should use the words with the prefixes re- from the questions in the supporting sentences and concluding sentence.

For example, It was recovered when ________ or It was recovered by ________

Lesson 141

This lesson can be done anytime throughout the week. This can be done in one lesson or questions can be answered over multiple lessons. The workbook page has eight questions. Students will choose four questions to answer. Each question has a word that ends with -ent. Students should use that word in their answers.

Lesson 143

Write captions for the pictures from *Jonathan's Musical Instrument.*

Lesson 146

This lesson can be done anytime throughout the week. Puns are often formed by using homophones or taking parts of words literally. Students will choose three compound words to turn into puns. Three examples are at the top of the page.

Students will draw pictures and write a brief explanation like the examples. A selection of words from this week's list is given at the top of the page. Students are not limited to the compound words on the page, but they should use a compound word for the pun.

Lesson 148

Students will list 3 facts about several of the characters from *Hound Dog Hoedown*. Students may use thc rcading book to help them. The facts can be characteristics and/or things they did in the story.

Lesson 151

This lesson can be done anytime throughout the week. **In the story, The Bobcat Cowboy Jellybean Train Robbery, Bubba offers a free Rowdent Gulch guidebook. Help him create a guidebook.**

You can make places to see, things to do, places to stay, and places or things to eat. Use words from this week's word list. It is printed on the page. You don't have to answer with place in Rowdent Gulch that you've read about, but you can if you would like. You can make-up places.

Remember the travelers will be small animals. Don't just name a place or thing, give helpful information to a traveler. For example you can tell the best foods at a place to eat, why a place might be a good place to stay, why the traveler would want to see or do something.

Lesson 154

Students will add information to the Not Wanted poster for the Bobcat Cowboys.

Lesson A
Special Unit

The Special Unit has been added to update the curriculum to current standards. It consists of ten additional lessons. Student and support materials are located in the Resource Pack. The lessons are labeled from A to J instead of numbers. Reading material is centered on fables and folktales.

Lesson Objectives

1. Students will write collective nouns. (L)
2. Students will recognize reflexive pronouns. (L)
3. Students will read and recount fables. (R)

Materials (Resource Pack)

Special Unit Lesson A worksheet (LAR workbook)
Collective Nouns poster
Collective Nouns Animal Group Names sheet
Reflexive Pronouns Poster
Fable *The Lion and the Mouse* (2 pages)
Fable and Folktale Outline Sheet

Teaching

1. Use the Collective Nouns poster. **What is a noun?** A person, place, or thing. **Do you have any collections of things like coins or cards? Your collection is a group of things. Today we're going to learn about another kind of noun. It is called a collective noun. A collective noun is a noun that describes a group of things. Look at the poster. What are the examples of collective nouns on the poster?** (A flock of sheep, a school of fish, a rookery of penguins, a litter of puppies) **The blue words in the examples are the actual collective nouns. The collective nouns *are flock, school, rookery*, and *litter*.**

   Use the Animal Group Names sheet and the top section of the Special Unit Lesson A worksheet. **Add a collective noun to each blank on the top section of the worksheet. Use the Animal Groups Names Sheet to find answers. Sometimes you have a choice of more than one answer. Choose one to write in the blank.**

   Display the poster where students can reference it in future lessons.

2. Use the Reflexive Pronouns Poster. **What are some examples of pronouns?** (you, me, I, he, she, it, them, etc.) **A reflexive pronoun is a pronoun that refers to another pronoun or noun in a sentence. Reflexive pronouns are compound words that end with *self* or *selves*. If the reflexive pronoun describes a singular noun, one person, place, or thing, it will end with the word *self*. If it is plural, describing two or more nouns, it will end with selves.**

   Use the bottom section of the Special Unit Lesson A worksheet. **Circle the reflexive pronouns in each sentence.**

   Display the poster where students can reference it in future lessons.

3. Have students read both versions of *The Lion and the Mouse*. Ask the following questions:

How is the structure of the two fables different? (One is a story. One is a poem.)
Which one do you think told the story the best? (Answers vary)
How are the stories alike? (They both tell about the lion and the mouse.)
What are some details that are different? (Examples: the story gave more details and different dialogue.)
Which told you the most about what happened? (Answers vary)
Many poems have rhymes. What are some rhymes in this poem? (Answers vary)
The syllables in the lines of a poem form a rhythm. Does this poem have any kind of a rhythm? How can it help you read the poem? (Answers vary)
What is the lesson taught by the fable? (Little friends may prove great friends)
What does that mean? (Any friend can be helpful. Don't think less of someone because of some characteristic such as size, or age.)
What did the lion think of the mouse in the beginning? (He was too small.)
What did the mouse think of himself in the beginning? (He felt he could be a good friend to the lion.)
Whose view changed in the story? (The lion's)
What caused the change? (The mouse saved the lion.)
Tell me the story of the lion and the mouse in your own words.
How is this story like *The Kindness of Gnatty*? (Examples: Both had a mouse rescue another character. The cat was stuck like the lion.)
How is it different? (Examples: The cat didn't save the mouse first. The mouse became a king. The unkind characters were punished. It had a different lesson.)

Have students outline the story. Write the words *Beginning*, *Middle*, and *End* or use a copy of the *Fable and Folktale Outline Sheet*. Have students write details describing each part of the story.

Worksheet Answers

Top Section

Write a collective noun for each group of animals.

1. A band, troop of gorillas
2. A kindle, litter of kittens
3. A flock, paddling, raft, waddling of ducks
4. A flight, flutter of butterflies
5. A gaze of raccoons

Bottom Section

Circle the reflexive pronouns in the sentences.

1. My friends made a pizza by (themselves.)
2. I rode a horse by (myself) on the trail.
3. You can go fishing by (yourselves.)
4. The bird hurt (itself) when it crashed into the window.
5. The little girl tied her shoelace by (herself) for the first time.

Lesson B

Lesson Objectives

1. Students will recognize collective nouns. (L)
2. Students will write reflexive pronouns. (L)
3. Students will read and recount fables. (R)

Materials (Resource Pack)

Special Unit Lesson B worksheet (LAR workbook)
Collective Nouns poster
Collective Nouns Animal Group Names sheet
Reflexive Pronouns Poster
Fable *The Fox and the Grapes*
Fable and Folktale Outline Sheet

Teaching

1. Review collective nouns. Use the Collective Nouns poster.

   Top section of Lesson B worksheet: **Read each paragraph. Circle the collective nouns.**

2. **Review reflexive pronouns. Use the Reflexive Pronouns poster. Have students read each reflexive pronoun and think of a matching pronoun. (I – myself, we – ourselves, you – yourself, yourselves, it – itself, she – herself, he –himself, they – themselves)**

   Bottom section of Lesson B worksheet: Complete each sentence with the correct reflexive pronoun. The list is in the box.

3. Have students read both versions of *The Fox and the Grapes*. Ask the following questions:

   How is the structure of the two fables different? (One is a story. One is a poem.)
   Which one do you think told the story the best? (Answers vary)
   How are the stories alike? (They both tell about a fox trying to eat some grapes.)
   What are some details that are different? (Examples: the story gave more details and different dialogue.)
   Which told you the most about what happened? (Answers vary)
   Many poems have rhymes. What are some rhymes in this poem? (Answers vary)
   The syllables in the lines of a poem form a rhythm. Does this poem have any kind of a rhythm? How can it help you read the poem? (Answers vary) Read the poem and have students clap the rhythm.
   What is the lesson taught by the fable? (It is easy to hate what you cannot get.)
   What does that mean? (If we can't have something we really want, we try to believe it isn't really very good.)
   Have you ever felt that way? (Answers vary)
   What did the fox want? (He wanted to eat the grapes.)
   How did he try to get them? (He tried to run and jump.)
   How did the fox's feelings toward the grapes change? (He decided they weren't very good.)
   What caused the change? (He couldn't reach them.)

3. (Continued) Have students outline the story. Write the words *Beginning*, *Middle*, and *End* or use a copy of the *Fable and Folktale Outline Sheet*. Have students write details describing each part of the story.

Tell me the story of the fox and the grapes in your own words.

Worksheet Answers

Circle the collective nouns used in the paragraphs.

A (pride) of lions circled the (dazzle) of zebras. A (wake) of buzzards flew overhead. In the bushes hid a (cackle) of hyenas. The chattering of a (troop) of monkeys alerted the (herd) of zebras. They ran toward a river filled with a (bask) of crocodiles.

The zoo has a new farm area. They have a (brood) of chickens that lay eggs. You can buy food and feed a (herd) of goats. A (drove) of pigs splash in the mud. A (kine) of cows is milked each day. A (paddling) of ducks quack on a pond. They swim above a (troubling) of goldfish.

Complete the sentences with reflexive pronouns.

myself ourselves yourself yourselves itself herself himself themselves

1. We made the tree house by ourselves.
2. Alex didn't like being at home by himself.
3. Can you eat the pizza by yourself?
4. The donkey made a fool of itself.
5. Claire made the dress for herself.

Lesson C

Lesson Objectives

1. Students will match collective nouns to nouns. (L)
2. Students will recognize capitalization of holidays, product names, and geographic names. (L)
3. Students will read and recount fables. (R)

Materials (Resource Pack)

Special Unit Lesson C worksheet (LAR workbook)
Fable *The Mule and the Dog*
Fable and Folktale Outline Sheet

Teaching

1. Review collective nouns. **Tell me some examples of collective nouns. Collective nouns aren't used only for animal groups. They are also used to describe groups or people or things too. For example: a troop of scouts, a bouquet of flowers, or a hill of beans. Lots of collective nouns are commonly used, but anyone can make up new collective nouns.**

   Use the top section of the Lesson C worksheet. **Match the collective nouns to the nouns.**

2. Review proper nouns. **What are proper nouns?** (Names of people, places, or things) **Proper nouns are written a special way. Do you remember how we write proper nouns?** (Write proper nouns using a capital letter for the first letter in the name, even if it is not at the beginning of a sentence.) **Give me some examples of proper nouns. Today we are going to learn about other proper nouns.**

   Names of holidays are also proper nouns. What are some of your favorite holidays? The words in the name of the holidays are capitalized.

   Names of products are proper nouns, for example the brand name of your favorite candy bar would be capitalized. Can you give me some examples of brand names?

   Names of places are also capitalized. Places include states, countries, towns, streets, or even stores. Can you give me some examples?

   Use the bottom section of the Lesson C worksheet. Write the holidays, product names, and place names from the sentences on the lines.

3. Have students read *The Mule and the Dog*. Ask the following questions:

   What is the lesson taught by the fable? (Silly horseplay is no joke.)
   What does that mean? (If you do something dangerous or harmful to others to get attention, it isn't funny.)
   Have you ever done something dangerous just to get attention? (Answers vary)
   Why did the mule act silly? (He wanted to get attention like the dog.)

3. (Continued)

What did the farmer think of the mule at the beginning of the fable? (The mule was his favorite.) **How do you think the farmer felt about the mule at the end of the fable?** (He may not have liked it any longer.)
What caused the change? (The mule acted in a way the farmer didn't expect.)
Why was it ok for the dog to act silly, but not the mule? (The dog was harmless in his actions. It's natural for a dog to be happy around its master. It is expected.)

Have students outline the story. Write the words *Beginning*, *Middle*, and *End* or use a copy of the *Fable and Folktale Outline Sheet*. Have students write details describing each part of the story.

Tell me the story of the mule and the dog in your own words.

Worksheet Answers

Draw lines to match the collective nouns to their matching nouns.

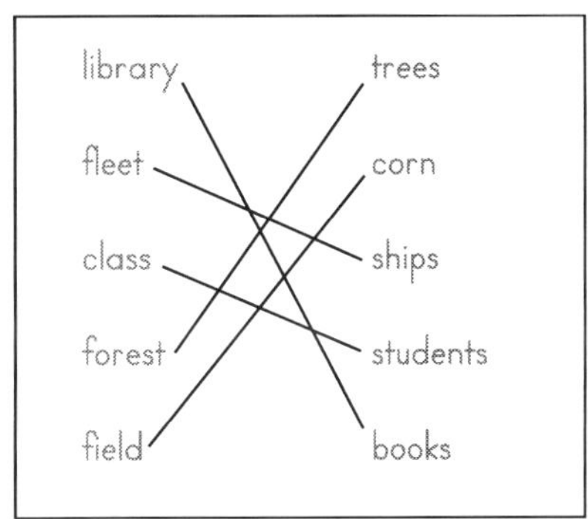

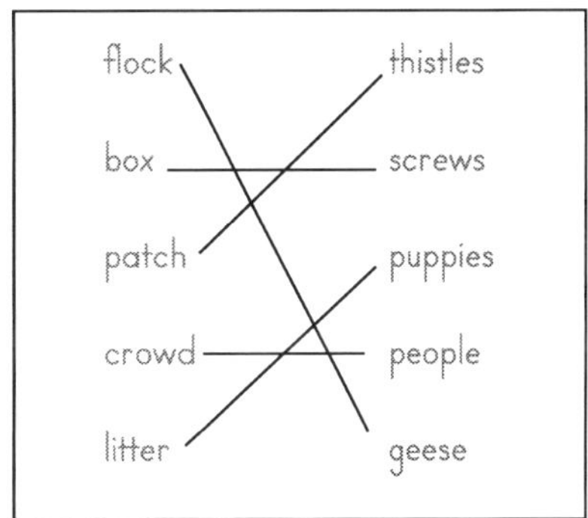

Find the words that are holidays, product names, of names of places. Write them on the lines.

1. Our family likes to eat at Doodles Burgers. Doodles Burgers

2. Is Alaska the largest state? Alaska

3. We ate turkey at our Thanksgiving meal. Thanksgiving

4. The new drink is called Blue Juice. Blue Juice

5. The campground is in Badger Park. Badger Park

6. Sparkle Smile is the name of the toothpaste. Sparkle Smile

Lesson D

Lesson Objectives

1. Students will identify collective nouns in sentences. (L)
2. Students will match reflexive pronouns to matching nouns or pronouns. (L)
3. Students will read and recount fables. (R)

Materials (Resource Pack)

Special Unit Lesson D worksheet (LAR workbook)
Fable *The Ant and the Grasshopper*
Fable and Folktale Outline Sheet

Teaching

1. Use the top section of the Lesson D worksheet. **Most of the collective nouns we've used so far connect to another noun using the word *of*, like a flock *of* sheep. Even if a collective noun doesn't connect to another noun, it is still a collective noun. The flock grazed in the field.**

   Find the collective nouns in the sentences on the worksheet. Write the collective noun on the line at the end of the sentence. Many of the sentences use *of*, but a few do not.

2. Use the bottom section of the lesson D worksheet. **Match the reflexive pronouns to the list of nouns and pronouns. One of the red words will be used twice. Draw straight lines to show the matches.**

3. **Have students read** *The Ant and the Grasshopper*. **Read the fable again. This time use different voices to read what the ant says and what the grasshopper says.**

   Ask the following questions:

   What is the lesson taught by the fable? (It is best to prepare for days of need.)
   What does that mean? (Plan ahead. When you have plenty, save some back for times you might have less.)
   Which character was the wisest? (The ant)
   Why? (It planned for the winter. It didn't starve.)
   What was the grasshopper's attitude toward winter? (It was nothing to worry about.)
   Do you think the grasshopper learned its lesson? (Answers vary.)
   What is something you might need to plan ahead for? (Answers vary, maybe saving money for another time or doing a school project as early as possible.)

   Have students outline the story. Write the words *Beginning*, *Middle*, and *End* or use a copy of the *Fable and Folktale Outline Sheet*. Have students write details describing each part of the story.

   Tell me the story of the ant and the grasshopper in your own words.

Worksheet Answers

Write the collective nouns used in the sentences on the lines.

1. A band of theives robbed the stagecoach. band
2. The dog hid behind a clump of bushes. clump
3. I need a clean pair of socks. pair
4. My family likes to go sailboating. family
5. A basket of fruit is on the table. basket
6. The class rode a bus two hours. class
7. The group enjoyed the field trip. group
8. The carton of eggs fell on the floor. carton
9. The team scored a goal. team
10. The crowd cheered loudly. crowd

Draw lines to match the reflexive pronouns to their matching nouns or pronouns.

myself ourselves yourself itself herself himself themselves yourselves

boy we you I girl they tree

Lesson E

Lesson Objectives

1. Students will create collective nouns in sentences. (L)
2. Students will read and recount fables. (R)
3. Students will write an opinion piece. (W)

Materials (Resource Pack)

Special Unit Lesson E worksheet (LAR workbook)
Fable *The Mountains in Labor* and *The Tree and the Reed*
Fable and Folktale Outline Sheet

Teaching

1. Use the Lesson E worksheet. **There are many common collective nouns, for example group, fleet, flock, herd, and family. Others have been kind of strange such as dazzle, rookery, paddling, and convocation. Sometimes the collective nouns may seem strange, but they actually describe a characteristic of a group. Using collective nouns, especially more creative collective nouns can make writing more interesting. Always using the words *bunch* or *group* to describe groups could get very boring.**

   Look at the examples at the top of the workbook page. Read the first one. How is the word crash descriptive of a group of rhinoceroses? (They are big animals. If a group was moving together they would probably crash into a lot of things.)

   Read the next sentence. What about a pounce of cats? How would that describe the group? (Cats like to pounce on their prey.)

   Discuss the last two sentences. (Ants work together like an army. Sometimes they swarm like an army. Butterflies flutter when they fly.)

   Make up descriptive collective nouns and use them in sentences. Look at the example for ice cream cones. *Freeze* was chosen as a new collective noun. A sentence was written that used the collective noun. Write new collective nouns for clouds, boys, and girls. On the last set of lines, choose your own group, make up a collective noun, then use it in a sentence.

2. Have students read *The Mountains in Labor*. Ask the following questions:
   What is the lesson taught by the fable? (Much outcry, little outcome.)
   What does that mean? (Sometimes a big threat can turn out to be nothing at all to worry about.)
   Many fables teach lessons that can be applied to lots of situations. If something seems like a threat should we just ignore it? (No) **Why or why not?** (Answers vary)
   What if there had been a terrible volcanic explosion instead, were the people prepared for that? (No)

   Read *The Tree and the Reed.* **Read the fable again. This time use different voices to read what the tree says and what the reed says. Use your own voice for the story teller.**

2. (Continued) Ask the following questions:

   Think back to the fable about the Lion and the Mouse. The mouse rescued the lion. How is this fable like that one? (There was a strong character and a small character. The small character was successful.)
   Which character understood itself the best? (The reed)
   Why did the tree think it was strong? (It had deep roots and was tall.)
   The last paragraph of the fable begins: *But it soon had to repent of its boasting.* What do you think that phrase means? (It had to realize what it said about being so strong was false.)
   Why did the reed survive the hurricane? (It could bend with the wind instead of breaking.)
   What is the lesson that is being taught? (Humility often brings safety.)
   What does humility mean? Look it up in a dictionary if you are not sure.
   How could humility bring safety? (Answers vary)

   Have students choose one of the fables and outline the story. Write the words *Beginning*, *Middle*, and *End* or use a copy of the *Fable and Folktale Outline Sheet*. Have students write details describing each part of the story.

3. Writing assignment: **Which of the fables have you liked the best or do you think has the best lesson? Write your opinion. Introduce the fable by stating its name and a summary of a sentence or two. Give reasons for supporting your opinion. Use linking words such as *because, and, also* to connect your opinions and reasons. The opinion should end with at least one concluding sentence.**

Worksheet Answers: Answers vary

Lesson F

Lesson Objectives

1. Students will capitalize holidays, product names, and place names. (L)
2. Students will write the plural form of irregular nouns. (L)
3. Students will read and recount fables. (R)

Materials (Resource Pack)

Special Unit Lesson F worksheet (LAR workbook)
Irregular Nouns Poster
Dictionary
Fable *The Rabbits and Frogs* and *The Lion and the Statue*
Fable and Folktale Outline Sheet

Teaching

1. Use the top section of the Lesson F worksheet. **What should you do when you write the name of a holiday, a product's brand name, or the name of a place such as a state or street in a sentence?** (You capitalize the words.)

   Proofread the sentences. Correct the capitalization in the sentences on the worksheet. Look at the example. First find the words that need to be capitalized. Cross out the lower case beginning letter. Write the capital letter above it.

2. **When a noun refers to one single thing, it is in its singular form. When a noun refers to more than one thing, it is in its plural form. The regular way to change a noun from singular to plural is to add an *s* at the end of the word. *Dog* is singular, referring to one dog. *Dogs* is plural, referring to more than one dog.**

   Nouns that form their plural form in some other way other than adding an *s* is an irregular noun: one goose, two geese.

   Use the irregular nouns poster. **The poster shows some examples of how irregular nouns form their plural forms. Although the rules work sometimes, they don't work for all words. For example *–oo-* sometimes changes to *–ee-* to form the plural form, but the plural of *moose* is *moose*, not *meese*.**

   The plural of *mouse* is *mice*. The word *house* also ends with *-ouse*, but the plural of *house* isn't *hice*. It's *houses*. The poster can help decide how the irregular nouns form their plural forms, but the rules have lots of exceptions. There are lots of words that don't follow the patterns.

   Use the bottom section of Lesson F worksheet. **Write the plural form of the irregular nouns. If you're not sure how they change you can look them up in a dictionary. Think *one _______, two _________***

   Display the poster where students can refer to it daily.

3. Read *The Rabbits and the Frogs*. **Read the fable again. This time use different voices to read what the rabbits say and what the frogs say.**

   Ask the following questions:

   What do you think *persecuted* means by reading the story? Check your definition by finding the word in the dictionary.
   What was the lesson taught in this fable? (There is always someone worse off than yourself.)
   What does that mean? (Even though my situation may seem bad, there is probably someone else who is dealing with a more difficult situation.)
   How did the rabbits deal with their fear at the beginning of the fable? (They ran from everything. They felt life wasn't worth living.)
   How did the rabbits view of life change after scaring the frogs? (They saw that things weren't as bad as they thought they were. Other animals lived in fear, too.)
   Have you seen this lesson to be true in your life? (Answers vary)
   How can this be comforting to us? (Sometimes when we have a problem it seems so huge. If we understand that other people have bigger problems and yet manage to find a solution or to at least live well, we can be encouraged that we can handle our problems.)
   Tell the story of the rabbits and the frogs in your own words.

   Have students outline the story. Write the words *Beginning*, *Middle*, and *End* or use a copy of the *Fable and Folktale Outline Sheet*. Have students write details describing each part of the story.

   Read *The Lion and the Statue*. **Read the fable again. This time use different voices to read what the man says and what the lion says.**

   Ask the following questions:

   What was the lesson taught in this fable? (We can easily represent things as we wish them to be.)
   What does that mean? (We can believe something to be true based on false proof.)
   Did either character change their opinion of who was stronger at the end of the fable? (No)
   Tell the story of the lion and the statue in your own words.

Worksheet Answers

Top section

1. We will buy fireworks for Independence Day. (i → I, d → D)
2. The sailboat is on Reindeer Lake. (r → R, l → L)
3. The best brand of jelly is Grannies Jellies. (g → G, j → J)
4. A Christmas present was under the tree. (c → C)
5. The king lived in England. (e → E)
6. The book was printed by McRuffy Press. (m → M, p → P)

Bottom section

1. foot — feet
2. deer — deer
3. knife — knives
4. child — children
5. tooth — teeth
6. yourself — yourselves
7. mouse — mice
8. sheep — sheep
9. baby — babies
10. fungus — fungi

Lesson G

Lesson Objectives

1. Students will use irregular nouns in sentences. (L)
2.. Students will write irregular verbs. (L)
3. Students will read and recount fables. (R)
4. Students will research and write about jackals. (W)

Materials (Resource Pack)

Special Unit Lesson G worksheet (LAR workbook)
Irregular Verbs Poster
Folktale *Why Has Jackal a Long Stripe On His Back?* and *Cloud-eating*
Fable and Folktale Outline Sheet

Teaching

1. Use the top section of the Lesson G worksheet. **Read the sentences on the worksheet. Change the nouns to plural where needed. Write the correct words on the lines below the sentences.**

2. **Nouns are irregular when the change from the singular to plural form is done in a way other than adding s at the end. Verbs are irregular if the past tense is formed in a different way than adding –ed at the end of the word. The past tense of walk is walked. Walk is a regular verb. The past tense of win is not winned. It is won. The verb win is an irregular verb.**

   Look at the Irregular Verbs poster. It lists several common irregular verbs. Read the words frequently so you can become more familiar with how these words change. There are many more irregular verbs that are not on this list.

   Display the poster where students can refer to it daily so they become more aware of irregular verbs.

   Use the bottom section of the workbook page. **Write the past tense of these irregular verbs.**

3. Read *Why Has Jackal a Long Black Stripe on His Back?* **Read the folktale again. This time use a different voice to read what the jackal says.**

   Ask the following questions:

   This story doesn't have a lesson to be learned. What is the purpose of the story? (It is explaining how the Jackal got a stripe on its back.)
   Do you think it is true, is this why jackals have black stripes? Why do or don't you think this is true? (No, answers vary. Examples: The sun is bigger than the earth. It is too hot and would have burnt up the jackal.)

   Read *Cloud-eating.* **Read the folktale again. This time use a different voice to read what the jackal says and what the hyena says.**

3. (Continued) **What was the purpose of this story?** (It is explaining why hyena's hind feet are shorter than their front feet.)
   What details about this story let you know it couldn't be true? (The jackal and hyena ate clouds, but clouds are just water vapor. They floated into the air.)

   Have students outline the story. Write the words *Beginning*, *Middle*, and *End* or use a copy of the *Fable and Folktale Outline Sheet*. Have students write details describing each part of the story.

   Retell one of the stories in your own words.

4. Writing assignment: **Research jackals. Write an informational report telling facts about jackals. Include a concluding statement that is backed up by the facts in your writing. For example, in a story about elephants, a writer might tell about all the food an elephant eats in a day and then concludes by stating: It is very expensive to feed an elephant.**

Worksheet Answers

1. There are three loaf of bread on the two shelf.

   loaves — shelves

2. The calf were taken by a band of cattle thief.

   calves — thieves

3. The woman are taking care of six child.

   women — children

4. The flock of goose had webbed foot.

   geese — feet

Write the past tense of these irregular verbs.

1. see saw	6. have had
2. eat ate	7. do did
3. give gave	8. say said
4. feed fed	9. win won
5. get got	10. keep kept

Lesson H

Lesson Objectives

1. Students will change and organize irregular nouns. (L)
2. Students will use irregular verbs in sentences. (L)
3. Students will read and recount fables. (R)

Materials (Resource Pack)

Special Unit Lesson H worksheet (LAR workbook)
Irregular Nouns Poster
Irregular Verbs Poster
Folktales *The White Man and Snake* (2 versions) and *The Woodman and the Serpent*
Fable and Folktale Outline Sheet

Teaching

1. Use the top section of the Lesson H worksheet. **A list of irregular nouns is in the box. Below the box is a list telling how the plural is formed. Write the plural forms of the words on the lines under the rules.**

2. **Use the bottom section of the Lesson H worksheet. Change the sentences to the past tense. The verbs are irregular. In some sentences a word is dropped when the past tense is formed.**

3. **Have students read the first version of** *The White Man and Snake.* **Read the folktale again. This time use a different voice for each character: white man, snake, hyena, and jackal.**

   Ask the following questions:

   This story doesn't have a lesson, but think of the roles of each character.
   Which character was just trying to be helpful? (white man)
   Which character was ungrateful? (snake)
   Which character was being greedy? (hyena)
   Which character was wise? (jackal)

   If you read several fables, you might see the same characteristics in the animals. For example, the jackal is usually the wise or tricky animal. In the English fables, the fox is often shown as being tricky, too. Both are dog-like animals.

   Have students read the second version of *The White Man and Snake.* **Read the folktale again. This time use a different voice for each character: Dutchman, snake, hare, and jackal.**

   How is this version different from the first version? (The hare takes the place of the hyena. There are fewer details.)

   Why do you think there would be two different versions of the same story? (Different people may have heard the same story and retold it differently.) **These stories were not written down for many years. They would have been told from person to person.**

3. (Continued) Outline the story. Write the words *Beginning*, *Middle*, and *End*. Have students write details describing each part of the story.

Retell the story in your own words. You can even choose other animals if you would like.

Have students read *The Woodman and the Serpent.*

How is this like *The White Man and the Snake*? (A snake is rescued in both stories.)
What lesson was learned in this fable? (No gratitude from the wicked.)
Could this same lesson be applied to *The White Man and the Snake*? (Yes)
Why? (The snake wasn't grateful to the man for lifting the rock. It wanted to bite the man.)
How could this be applied to people? (Bad people are not thankful when they are helped.)
The jackal in the other stories was presented as wise or tricky. How is the snake shown in both the English and the African fables? (ungrateful, mean, deadly)

Worksheet Answers

self fish hoof foot city moose tooth puppy

1. Change y to i and add es.

puppies　　cities

2. Change f or fe to v and es.

hooves　　selves

3. Don't change it at all.

fish　　moose

4. Change oo to ee.

teeth　　feet

Change these sentences to past tense and write them on the lines.

1. We can find the coins.

We found the coins.

2. He makes us lunch.

He made us lunch.

3. You can shake the bottle.

You shook the bottle.

Lesson I

Lesson Objectives

1. Students will capitalize proper nouns and use irregular verbs. (L)
2. Students will find and change irregular nouns in a paragraph. (L)
3. Students will find and change irregular verbs in sentences. (L)
4. Students will read and recount fables. (R)

Materials (Resource Pack)

Special Unit Lesson I worksheets (2) (LAR workbook)
Irregular Nouns Poster
Irregular Verbs Poster
Folktale *King Tasio*
Fable and Folktale Outline Sheet

Teaching

1. Use the first Lesson I worksheet. **Read the questions. Write answers to the questions. Start with the word *I* to answer that you did what the question asked. There are also some proper nouns in the questions that need to be capitalized. Write the words correctly capitalized in your answer.**

   Capitalize all the words in a product name. For example, Zippy Candy Bar would capitalize the first letter in each word Zippy, Candy, and Bar.

   Capitalize all words in a place. For example, Waldo Road both Waldo and Road would be capitalized.

   Capitalize all words in holidays as well.

   In the second section of the worksheet write the proper noun that fits each description from the questions. Remember to capitalize them correctly.

2. **Use the top part of the second Lesson I worksheet. Read the paragraph. There are errors in the paragraph with some of the nouns. Some irregular nouns need to be changed to their plural forms. Circle those words. Write the plural forms on the lines below the paragraph.**

3. **Use the bottom part to the second Lesson I worksheet. Read the sentences. Each sentence has two irregular verbs that need to be changed. Find the two verbs and write them correctly on the lines at the end of the sentence.**

4. Have students read King Tasio. **Use different voices for the king and Juan.This story is from the Philippines. Find the Philippines on a map.**

   Ask the following questions:

   Why did the King test Juan so many times? (Because Juan said he knew more than anyone else.)

4. (Continued) **Do you think Juan was the smartest person in the kingdom? Why or why not?**
What was your favorite test that Juan passed?
The word *consent* is in dark print. What do you think the word *consent* means? (permission)
Juan rode around in a cart with dirt from his own orchard. The king felt uncomfortable. Why? (The people he was in charge of were watching. It made him look bad or less intelligent than Juan.)
How did Juan get the squash in the jar? (Instead of putting the large squash in the jar, he let a small one grow in it until it became large.)
What do you think happened to Juan after the end of the story?

Have students outline the story. Write the words *Beginning*, *Middle*, and *End* or use a copy of the *Fable and Folktale Outline Sheet*. Have students write details describing each part of the story.

Retell the story in your own words.

LAR Answers

Worksheet 1

1. Did you find the house on main street?

I found the house on Main Street.

2. Did you feed people on new years day?

I fed people on New Years Day.

3. Did you freeze the tub of chilly's ice cream?

I froze the tub of Chilly's Ice Cream.

From the sentences above write:

the name of a holiday

New Years Day

the name of a product

Chilly's Ice Cream

the name of a place

Main Street

Worksheet 2

Two (man) were driving a cart on the dusty road. The cart was pulled by a team of (ox). It was loaded with a box and a cage with two (goose). Suddenly they were stopped by an band of (thief). The thieves had sharp (knife). "Please don't take our (life)," cried the men in the cart.

"Give us your money," said the theives.

"We only have a handful of (penny)," said the men.

"Then we shall take this box," said the thieves.

The thieves took the box. Later they opened it up. The box was full of pet (mouse). The men in the cart had been taking them to their five (child).

men	oxen	geese
thieves	knives	lives
pennies	mice	children

Find the two irregular verbs in each sentence. Write the past tense forms on the lines after the sentences. Read the sentences with the changed verbs.

1. The boys keep the turtle they find. kept found
2. The champ take the prize she win. took won
3. We see what make the sound. saw made
4. We eat the leftover food we keep. ate kept
5. The teacher know I sleep in class last hour. knew slept

Lesson J

Lesson Objectives

1. Students will review collective nouns. (L)
2. Students will review reflexive pronouns. (L)
3. Students will read and recount fables. (R)

Materials (Resource Pack)

Special Unit Lesson J worksheet (LAR workbook)
Irregular Nouns Poster
Irregular Verbs Poster
Folktale *How the Wicked Sons Were Duped*
Fable and Folktale Outline Sheet

Teaching

1. Use the top section of the Lesson J worksheet. **What are collective nouns?** (Nouns that refer to groups of people or things.)

   Read the sentences. Find the collective noun and write it on the lines after the sentences.

2. **Use the bottom section of the Lesson J worksheet. Remember that reflexive pronouns will match up with another noun or pronoun in a sentence. Reflexive pronouns are compound words. What words do reflexive pronouns end with?** (self or selves)

   Why do they end with two different words? (self is singular, selves is plural)

   Complete each sentence with the correct reflexive pronoun. Write the words on the lines in the sentences. A list of reflexive pronouns is in the box.

3. **This folktale comes from India. Find India on a map. Read *How the Wicked Sons Were Duped.* Use different voices for the characters: father, 4 sons, and the father's friend.**

   The word *Salaam* is in dark print toward the end of the story. It is used like we use the word *goodbye*. It means *peace*.

   Ask the following questions:

   What was the father's problem? (His sons were treating him poorly.)
   When did the father's problem begin? (After he divided his property among his sons)
   Why did the sons treat the father well in the beginning and the end of the story? (They wanted to get more of the father's wealth. They were competing with the other sons.)
   Do you think the sons loved their father? Why or why not?
   How do you think the father felt about his sons?
   What did the friend give the father? (He gave him bags of rocks.)

3. (Continued) **Why did he tell the father to keep the bags from his sons?** (He wanted the sons to think they were full of money.)
   What do you think the word *duped* means? Look it up in a dictionary if you are not sure. How were the sons duped? (They were tricked into thinking the bags were full of money, so they began to take good care of their father again.)

   Have students outline the story. Write the words *Beginning*, *Middle*, and *End* or use a copy of the *Fable and Folktale Outline Sheet*. Have students write details describing each part of the story.

   Retell the story in your own words.

Worksheet Answers

Write the collective nouns used in the sentences on the lines.

1. The batch of cookies smells so good. batch
2. The necklace was a string of pearls. string
3. A roll of quarters is in the drawer. roll
4. I was frightened by the pack of wolves. pack
5. An army of caterpillars crawled to the tree. army
6. The crew of sailors lifted the sail. crew

Complete the sentences with reflexive pronouns.

myself ourselves yourself yourselves itself herself himself themselves

1. My older sister drove the car by herself.
2. The geese built the nests for themselves.
3. You may help yourself (or yourselves) to more salad.
4. May I help myself to more cupcakes?
5. Did the cat hurt itself when it jumped from the tree?

Lesson 81

Lesson Objectives

1. Students will read long oo words spelled with ew and ou. (P)
2. Students will spell words correctly. (S)
3. Students will learn vocabulary words. (L)
4. Students will prepare to read *Chocolate Mousse Stew.* (R)
5. Students will copy sentences neatly and correctly. (H)

Materials

LAR
SAP
Chocolate Mousse Stew
Writing Skills Workbook page is available

Word List: blew, brew, chew, crew, dew, drew, few, flew, grew, hew, hewn, Jew, knew, Lewis, new, pew, screw, skew, stew, threw, yew, croup, group, Lou, mousse, soup, you, youth

Teaching

1. Write the words blue, gnu, and due. Have students read the words. **Do they all have the same vowel sound?** Ask students to say the vowel sound in these words. Next write the words dew, knew, and blew. Tell students that these are homophones for the first list of words. Have students match the homophones. (blue-blew, gnu-knew, due-dew)

   Have students identify the letters that made the vowel sound in the second set of words. (ew) Write the word *you.* Students should know the word. Ask what letters make the vowel sound in this word. (ou) **Is it the same sound found in blew and knew?** (yes)

   Write the words group and youth. Tell students that these words have the same vowel sound as *you.* Have students read the new words.

   Discuss other homophones

2. Use the SAP page. Have students read and spell the words. Spelling list: grew, blew, threw, chew, soup, youth, flew, knew, screw, stew, group, drew, jewel, view.

   Top of the SAP page: **Alphabetize the two groups of words.**

   Bottom section: **Write the spelling words that are the past tense of the words.**

3. Use LAR workbook page. Students will read the simplified definitions. Answer the questions at the bottom of the page.

4. *Chocolate Mousse Stew* focuses on words spelled with ou and ow (long oo sound). In addition to those words, the following word may be new to students and will require some instruction: **chocolate, minutes, really.** The words and pronunciation guide are on the LAR workbook page.

   The word *chocolate:* Separate into syllables. Cho- (short o) -co- (schwa e the syllable can be silent) –late (short i sound) .

   The word *minutes:* Separate into syllables: mi-nutes. The u is short.

   The word *really:* Separate the suffix from the root. Real-ly. The y has a long e sound.

   Introduce the story: Ask a student to read the title of the book. **What is the name of this story?** *Chocolate Mousse Stew* **Do you recognize the girls on the cover?** (Emily and Elaine Rose) Ask students about other Emily and Elaine Rose stories. Who always causes problems? (Elaine) Have students rcad thc story to find out what problem Elaine causes this time and how she solves it.

   Students will silently read as much of the story as they can in the time allowed.

5. Use the handwriting sheet or have the children write the following:

   The group sat on the new pew.
   The dew was still on the yew.

   Note for those using the handwriting books: The transitional handwriting program begins with this lesson. The handwriting sheet will introduce the letter a. An additional letter will be added each day. Only one of the sentences will be on the handwriting page in the transitional program. Students will continue printing sentences until the cursive alphabet has been completely introduced. The second sentence may be skipped or given as sentence dictation. Both sentences will be printed in handwriting books that continue with the printing program (traditional or modern).

LAR Answers

1. stew
2. yew
3. brew
4. hew
5. dew
6. croup
7. pew
8. mousse

SAP Answers

1. blew	5. grew
2. chew	6. group
3. drew	7. knew
4. flew	

1. jewel	5. threw
2. screw	6. view
3. soup	7. youth
4. stew	

knew grew drew
blew threw flew

Chocolate Mousse Stew

Second Grade Phonics & Reading

Book 15
Lessons 81 to 85

Chocolate Mousse Stew

Written and illustrated by
Brian Davis

"I grew these myself," said Mrs. Lewis. She chopped up some carrots. Mrs. Lewis was Emily and Elaine's new neighbor.

"I've never brewed stew before," said Emily.

Elaine chewed a carrot. "This would taste better with chocolate."

Mrs. Lewis chuckled. "We could make chocolate mousse stew."

"Really!" yipped Elaine.

"No, I'm just teasing," said Mrs. Lewis.

"How about just plain old chocolate soup?" asked Elaine.

Mrs. Lewis just smiled. She handed carrots to the girls.

"Here stew crew. Put these in the pot, please."

2

3

Chocolate Mousse Stew

Mrs. Lewis stirred the big pot.

"Will you teach me to sew now?" asked Emily.

"Sure, Emily," said Mrs. Lewis. "Maybe we could make a new doll dress!"

Emily and Mrs. Lewis started to leave. Elaine stayed in the kitchen.

"I'll watch the stew brew," said Elaine.

"You don't need to," said Mrs. Lewis.

"I've never seen stew brew," said Elaine.

Mrs. Lewis giggled, "There's not much to see. You'll want to join us after a few minutes."

Emily and Mrs. Lewis left.

4

5

Elaine was very quiet.

"Chocolate mousse stew," mumbled Elaine.

She thought it sounded great. Elaine sneaked around the kitchen. She found a few bars of chocolate. She threw the chocolate into the pot.

"Chocolate mouse stew, yum yum."

Elaine waited and waited. The chocolate began to melt.

"I can't wait," thought Elaine.

She took the spoon Mrs. Lewis had used. She dipped it into the pot. Elaine pulled out a chocolate coated carrot. She bit into it. She began to chew.

"Yuck!" yelled Elaine.

6

7

Chocolate Mousse Stew

Elaine knew she had made a mistake. She scooped out a group of chocolate carrots. Elaine opened a window. She threw the carrots out.

Elaine looked into the pot.

"It looks like new," thought Elaine. "We just lost a few carrots."

"Meow," came a sound outside the door.

Mrs. Lewis had a cat. It's name was Soupy. Elaine let Soupy in. The cat flew right past her.

"Hello Soupy," said Mrs. Lewis in the other room. "What's in your fur?"

"It's chocolate," said Emily.

"Oh no!" thought Elaine. "I threw the stew on Soupy!"

She ran to Mrs. Lewis.

"I think it's just dew," said Elaine.

8

"No, it's chocolate. Soupy needs a bath," said Mrs. Lewis.

She put him in the bathtub. Soon, Soupy was as good as new.

9

The stew brewed for hours.

"It's supper time," said Mrs. Lewis.

Mrs. Lewis dipped a spoon into the stew.

"Oh my!" said Mrs. Lewis. "My jewelry is gone!"

"I saw it on your wrist," said Emily. "You were stirring the pot."

"You're right," said Mrs. Lewis. "It must have fallen in the stew. Elaine, would you look into the stew? Do you see my jewelry?"

Elaine poked around in the stew. There was no jewelry.

"Oh my!" thought Elaine. She must have thrown it out the window.

"It's not here," said Elaine. "You look inside the house. I'll look outside."

Elaine dashed out the back door.

10

11

Chocolate Mousse Stew

Elaine looked in the yews. She knew where she threw the stew. The yews were coated with chocolate stew. She found a few chocolate carrots.

She didn't find the jewelry. She sat down on the back step. She began to think. Soupy the cat purred.

"Where is the jewelry?" sighed Elaine.

Then, Elaine began to smile. "Soupy, you were in the yews. The jewelry fell on you."

She felt his collar. There was no jewelry.

"Mrs. Lewis gave you a bath!" said Elaine.

She ran to the tool shed. Elaine found a fishing line and hook. She ran to the house.

12

13

"How did you get chocolate on your hands?" asked Mrs. Lewis.

"Uhh...it's just dirt," said Elaine. "I'll clean them."

She rushed past Mrs. Lewis. Elaine ran to the bathtub. She bent down on her knees. Elaine held the fishing line. She put it in the drain.

"I'll get the jewelry. Just a few more minutes," thought Elaine.

Just then, Emily came in. The line slid down the drain.

"Oh, no!" sighed Elaine. "I lost it."

"What are you doing?" asked Emily.

"I think the jewelry is in the drain," said Elaine. "I was fishing for it. I dropped the hook. How can I get Mrs. Lewis new jewelry?"

"You didn't lose it. Mrs. Lewis lost it," said Emily.

"Maybe I helped," answered Elaine. She knew what she had to do.

14

15

Chocolate Mousse Stew

Mrs. Lewis was chewing stew.

"This is funny tasting stew," said Mrs. Lewis to Elaine. "It has a chocolate taste."

"Oh, Mrs. Lewis," cried Elaine. "I did it!"

"Did what?" asked Mrs. Lewis.

"I put chocolate in the stew," said Elaine. "I threw it on Soupy. I lost your jewelry. I think I threw it out the window."

Mrs. Lewis giggled. She lifted a spoon full of stew.

"Mrs. Lewis," said Elaine. "Your jewelry is on your wrist."

"I left it in my sewing basket," said Mrs. Lewis. "Now how about some chocolate mousse stew?"

16

Chocolate Mousse Stew word list:

answered	Emily	minutes	some
basket	few	mistakes	Soup
bathtub	flew	mousse	Soupy
better	funny	myself	stew
brewed	grew	neighbor	tasting
carrots	group	never	teach
chew	here	new	teasing
chewed	hours	now	thought
chocolate	inside	opened	threw
chopping	jewelry	outside	thrown
crew	join	please	tool
dashed	kitchen	quiet	window
dew	knew	really	would
down	leave	scooped	wrist
Elaine	Lewis	sew	yew
			you

Lesson 82

Lesson Objectives

1. Students will use homophones. (L)
2. Students will use spelling words in sentences. (S)
3. Students will read the story *Chocolate Mousse Stew.* (R)
4. Students will copy sentences neatly and correctly. (H)

Materials

LAR
SAP
Book: *Chocolate Mousse Stew*

Teaching

1. Review homophones. **Homophones are words that sound alike, but are spelled differently.** Use the LAR workbook page. **Read the definitions for the homophones. Use them in the sentences at the bottom of the page.**

2. Use the top of the SAP workbook page. **Read the sentences. A word is underlined. Replace the word with the spelling word that changes the sentence the least.**

   Bottom section: **Find the spelling word within each of the longer words. Write the words on the lines.**

3. Review the words **chocolate, minutes, really.** Students will read pages 1 to 8 out loud. Next, ask the following questions:

   Who is Emily and Elaine's neighbor? (Mrs. Lewis)
   What were they making? (stew)
   What did Emily want to learn? (sewing)
   How did Elaine change the stew? (She added chocolate.)
   What did Elaine do with the chocolate carrots? (She threw them out a window.)
   Where did the chocolate land? (It landed on Soupy the cat.)
   What did Elaine tell Mrs. Lewis about the chocolate on Soupy? (She said it was dew.)
   Why do you think she said that? (answers vary)
   What should she have done? (answers vary)
   Why do you think this story is called *Chocolate Mousse Stew*? (answers vary)

4. Use the handwriting sheet or have the children write the following:
   Cursive: b, review a
   Lewis ate the hot soup.
   The wind blew a few leaves.

Lesson 82

LAR Answers

1. moose mousse
2. threw through
3. blew blue
4. you ewe
5. knew new
6. Do dew
7. flu flew

SAP Answers

1. screw
2. jewel
3. chew
4. stew
5. blew

youth chew blew

jewel screw view

soup drew knew

Lesson 83

Lesson Objectives

1. Students will review parts of speech. (L)
2. Students will review verb tense. (L)
3. Students will review spelling words. (S)
4. Students will read the story *Chocolate Mousse Stew.* (R)
5. Students will copy sentences neatly and correctly. (H)

Materials

LAR
SAP
Chocolate Mousse Stew

Teaching

1. Review parts of speech. Write the sentence: Did you brew the hot tea for Lewis? **What are the nouns in this sentence?** (you, tea, Lewis) **Find a verb in this sentence.** (brew, did) **Brew is a verb, it is an action a noun can do.**

   Words like did, do, is, are, be, were, and will are also verbs. They may be the only verb in a sentence. For example: Ruff is a dog. Ruff and dog are nouns. Sometimes they help other verbs by defining the tense in a sentence. Listen to these two sentences. Ruff was running. Ruff is running. Running is a verb, but it needed the help of was and is to determine the tense of the sentence. (Tense will be discussed further in the teaching section 2)

   Look at the sentence again. Can you find an adjective? (hot) **Remember, adjectives tell us more about a noun.**

   Use the top of the LAR page. **Fill in the circles to mark the words that are nouns or verbs. Fill in the n circle above nouns. Fill in the v circle below verbs. Underline the adjective in each sentence.**

2. Write the words ran and run. **How is the meaning of these two words are alike?** (They both mean to use your feet to move quickly.) **How are they are different?** (Ran means it happened in the past.)

   Write the words past tense. **We say that ran is the past tense of run. Tense means how a word is used to show when something happened. We run today. We ran yesterday. Other words have a past tense. The car stops. The car stopped. Which sentence used the past tense of stop?** (The second)

   Many verbs are made past tense by adding the suffix ed. These are called regular verbs. Sometimes other letters change to make the past tense. These are called irregular verbs. Write the words sing, do, and take. **These are all irregular verbs. What is the past tense of each of these words?** (sang, did, took)

   Use the bottom of the LAR workbook page. **Choose the word that is the past tense to complete the sentences. Which verb is not an irregular verb? Circle the number before the sentence that was completed with a regular verb.**

3. Use the SAP page. Top section: **Read the sentences. If you move one word to the beginning of each sentence, you can turn it into a question. Write the sentences as questions. Don't forget the question mark.**

   Bottom section: **Read the short words. Write the spelling words that have the letters to make those words. If there are two blanks, two spelling words can make that word. Write both words.**

4. Review the first half of the book Chocolate Mousse Stew. Next, read the second half of the book. After completing the story ask the students the following questions:

   What did Mrs. Lewis lose? (Jewelry)
   Where did she think she lost it? (in the stew)
   Why did Elaine go to the bathtub? (She thought the jewelry might be in the drain.)
   Why did Elaine feel she had to get the jewelry? (She thought it was her fault.)
   Where did Mrs. Lewis find the jewelry? (In her sewing basket)
   Do you think Mrs. Lewis knew that Elaine put chocolate in the stew? (answers vary)
   What did Elaine do that was wrong? (She put chocolate in the stew. She lied about the cat. She didn't tell Mrs. Lewis that the jewelry may have been tossed out.)
   What did Elaine do right? (She tried to find the jewelry. She finally told the truth.)
   Emily and Elaine are twins. How are Emily and Elaine different? (answers vary)

5. Use the handwriting sheet or have the children write the following:
   Cursive: c, the word cab
   Did you chew the meat in the stew? The youth loved the chocolate mousse.

LAR Answers

1. A screw fell out of my new skateboard.
2. Sue ate the stew and the chocolate mousse.
3. The youth knew who threw the old baseball.
4. We grew the carrots that were put into the hot soup.
5. The work crew blew up the large rock that was blocking the road.

○ know	● knew
● grew	○ grow
● blew	○ blow
○ fly	● flew
● screwed	○ screw

SAP Answers

Will the youth group eat the soup?
Did you view the red jewel on the ring?
Should he chew the meat from the stew?

red	drew	web	blew
out	youth	new	knew
he	threw, chew		
sew	screw, stew		
up	soup, group		

Lesson 84

Lesson Objectives

1. Students will review spelling words. (S)
2. Students will write a recipe. (CW)
3. Students will read the story *Chocolate Mousse Stew.* (R)
4. Students will copy sentences neatly and correctly. (H)

Materials

LAR
SAP
Hedgehog Fudge recipe (LAR page 52 or copy master)
Chocolate Mousse Stew

Teaching

1. Use the SAP page. **Match the spelling words to the descriptions.**

2. Students will write a recipe for chocolate mousse stew. Use the LAR page or plain paper. Students will refer back to the Hedgehog Fudge recipe as an example of a recipe. It is on page 52 of the LAR workbook. A copy master of the recipe is in the test and assessment pack in case the workbook page is no longer available or to make it easier for students to see the recipe while working on the LAR page.

   In the book *Chocolate Mousse Stew* Elaine tries to make chocolate stew with vegetables. **How would you make chocolate stew? Who would you share it with?**

   The story doesn't talk about all the ingredients in the stew, so you're going to make up your own recipe. You can make it a real recipe, something you'd actually like to eat, or a silly recipe. Be sure to list your ingredients and tell how much of each one is used. Then give directions for mixing and cooking.

   In the next lesson, you'll share your recipe. Pretend you've entered your recipe in a contest and try to convince other people that your recipe is the best. Be ready to tell why yours is the best and describe what it would taste like.

3. Read the book *Chocolate Mousse Stew* again. Next, have students look at the back of the book and answer the following questions about the word list. You may do this orally or have students write answers:

   In what words do the letters ou make the vowel sound you hear in moon?
   (group, mousse, soup, Soupy, you)
   What words have the vowel digraph ou but don't make the sound you hear in moon?
   (hours, outside, thought, would)
   What word is the opposite of loud? (quiet)
   What words begin with silent letters? (knew, wrist)
   What –ew words end with suffixes? (brewed, chewed)
   What word means moisture on the grass? (dew)
   What word is a kind of bush? (yews)
   Spell a word that is a homophone of this word (yew)**?** (y-o-u)
   What –ew word does not have the vowel sound you hear in stew? (sew)
   What –ew words begin with f? (few, flew)

4. Use the handwriting sheet or have the children write the following:

   Cursive: d, the words bad, dab
   We drew a horse for you.
   Lou fixed the door with a screw.

LAR Answers

Answers vary.

SAP Answers

drew	grew
screw	view
blew	chew
threw	stew
flew	soup
youth	knew
jewel	group

Lesson 85

Lesson Objectives

1. Students will be tested on phonics concepts. (P)
2. Students will be tested on language concepts. (L)
3. Students will take a spelling test. (S)
4. Students will identify the story sequence. (R)
5. Students will read the recipes they have written. (R)
6. Students will copy a sentence neatly and correctly. (H)

Materials

LAR
Creative writing assignment from lesson 84
Assessment 85
Chocolate Mousse Stew

Teaching

1. Use part A of the assessment as a phonics test. Have the students fill in the circles next to the words that complete the sentences.

2. Use part B of the assessment page. Students will choose the correct form of the word to complete the sentences.

3. Have students number their paper from 1 to 14. Give the following words as dictation.

   Spelling word list:

   1. **flew, 2. blew, 3. soup, 4. screw, 5. threw, 6. chew, 7. knew, 8. drew, 9. grew 10. group 11. youth, 12. stew, 13. view, 14. jewel**

4. Use the LAR page. **Number the sentences in the order they happened in the story. Number them without using your book, then use the book to check your answers and make any corrections.**

   One the bottom section, fill in the ovals to answer the questions about the story.

5. Have students take turns reading the recipes written during the creative writing section of the previous lesson. Tell why it is the best recipe. Describe how it would taste.

6. Use the handwriting sheet or have the children write the following:
   Cursive: e, the words bed, Deb
   I knew who threw the baseball.
   The crew ate all the soup.

Assessment Answers

1. brew
2. yews
3. chewing
4. mousse
5. dew

1. drew
2. chewed
3. grew
4. threw
5. flew

LAR Answers

5
7
1
9
3
6
10
2
8
4

1. 

2. 

3. 

4. 

5. 

no

Lesson 86

Lesson Objectives

1. Students will read long i words spelled with y and -ie. (P)
2. Students will spell words correctly. (S)
3. Students will learn vocabulary words. (L)
4. Students will prepare to read the story *Ruff's Spy Plane*. (R)
5. Students will copy sentences neatly and correctly. (H)

Materials

LAR
SAP
Ruff's Spy Plane
Writing Skills Workbook page is available

Word List: buy, by, cry, dye, dry, eye, fly, fry, guy, lye, my, ply, pry, rye, shy, sky, sly, spy, spry, sty, thy, try, why, brier, cried, crier, cries, die, died, dried, drier, dries, dryer, flied, flier, flies, fries, fried, lie, lied, pie, spied, tie, tied, tried, tries, vie

Teaching

1. Some of the words from this list are review words from lessons 31 to 35.

   Write the words niece, field, Connie. **What two vowel digraphs do each of these words have in common?** (-ie) **What sound does the digraph make?** (Long e) Write the words pie and cries. Ask: **Do these words have the –ie digraph?** (Yes) **The words are pie and cries. What sound does the digraph make in these words?** (Long i) Write the words dried, tried, and flier. **The i-e digraph makes the long i sound. Read the words.**

   Students should be familiar with the long i, y sound as in by and my. Write by and my. **Read these words.** Next introduce the long i sound of uy. Write buy and guy. **The letters u-y make the long i sound in these words. Read them.** Finally introduce the words that end with silent e. Write the words eye, lye, and rye. **The letters y-e make the long i sound in these words. Read the words.**

2. Use the SAP workbook page. Have students read and spell each word. Spelling list: why, dryer, spied, fry, cried, eye, buy, spy, tied, fried, flies, pie, diet, goodbye, try.

   Top section: **In some of the words the long i is spelled with a y. In other words, the long i sound is spelled with i-e. Sort the words into the two boxes by the way the long i sound is spelled.**

   Bottom section: **Remember the spelling rules for adding suffixes to words that end with y as you add the letter s to the word on the first line. On the bottom row, you'll write the root words of the three spelling words to match the future tense of the sentence.**

3. Use the LAR workbook page. **Read the definitions at the top of the page. Use them to help decide which word completes each sentence.**

4. *Ruff's Spy Plane* focuses on words spelled with y and ie (long i sound). In addition to those words, the following word may be new to students and will require some instruction: **parachute, reward, gone, motor.** The words and pronunciation guides are printed on the LAR workbook page.

   The word *parachute:* Ch has the sh sound. The u makes the long oo sound.

   The word *reward:* Re- the e is long. The letters ar make the or sound.

   The word *gone:* The o is short.

   The word *motor:* The first o is long.

   Introduce the story: Ask a student to read the title of the book. **What is the name of this story?** *(Ruff's Spy Plane).* **Do you recognize the picture on the cover?** (It's the workbook cover picture.) **Just by looking at the picture, what might one of Ruff's problems be? He's learning to fly as he reads the book. What do you think the story is about?**

   Students will read the words on the back of the book out loud.
   Students will silently read as much of the story as they can in the time allowed.

5. Use the handwriting sheet or have the children write the following:
   Cursive: f, Write the words fed, fee
   We can buy two apple pies.
   The shy girl cried.

LAR Answers

1. pry
2. rye
3. lye
4. sty
5. dye
6. vie
7. plywood
8. crier

SAP Answers

Top section

Spelled with y (any order)

why dryer fry eye buy spy goodbye try

Spelled with i (any order)

spied cried tied fried flies pie diet

Bottom section

tries fries pies

spy fry cry

Ruff's Spy Plane

Second Grade Phonics & Reading

Book 16
Lessons 86 to 90

Ruff's Spy Plane

Written and illustrated by
Brian Davis

Ruff McRuffy was a nice dog. He belonged to a guy named Tom.

Ruff wanted to fly. He saved his money. He wanted to buy a spy plane. One day, a truck pulled up.

"My spy plane is here!" cried Ruff.

Ruff pried open the box. The plane was in pieces.

That didn't bother Ruff. He liked to make things.

2

"I will soon be a flier," thought Ruff.

Ruff worked on the plane. He tied things. He glued things.

Ruff waited for the glue to dry. He waited for the paint to dry. Ruff lifted his eyes to the sky.

"I think I'll try to fly now," said Ruff.

3

Ruff's Spy Plane

He tried to start the plane. It wouldn't run. Ruff tried and tried. It still wouldn't start.

"Why won't my spy plane fly?" asked Ruff.

Violet was a flower. She was Ruff's friend. Violet pried open the hood.

"Oh," said Ruff, "I forgot the motor."

The spy plane didn't come with a motor.

"Where can I find a motor?" asked Ruff.

Then Ruff had an idea.

4

5

Soon, the spy plane was running. "Let's fly, Violet," said Ruff.

Violet ran away.

"Are you afraid to fly?" asked Ruff.

Violet nodded yes.

"OK.," said Ruff. "I'll try to fly alone."

Ruff didn't know how to fly. He did have a book. Ruff began to read the book.

"It says to push this button," Ruff pushed a button.

The plane began to fly.

"Pull back on the handle," Ruff kept reading.

The plane shot up. Ruff flew right by Tom's window.

6

7

Ruff's Spy Plane

Tom woke up. He rubbed his eyes.

"What is that sound?" asked Tom.

Ruff zipped by Tom's window.

"My dog is flying!" cried Tom. "Ruff! Sit Boy! I mean stay! I mean land, boy!"

Tom ran down the stairs. Ruff was flying away. Tom ran to his car. It wouldn't start.

"Why won't my car start?" asked Tom.

Violet pointed to the hood. Tom pried open the hood.

"My motor is gone! Why is my motor gone?" thought Tom.

Just then, Ruff buzzed over. He was still reading the book.

"Oh no!" cried Tom. "Ruff is flying with my motor.

Tom sighed, "Why does my dog want to fly?"

8

9

Ruff was having a great time. Then, the motor began to sputter. The motor died. Ruff tried and tried to start it.

The plane began to sink. Ruff skipped to the end of the book. It didn't say why the plane quit running.

Then, Ruff spied a red button. He pushed the button. Ruff shot out of the plane. He flew up into the sky. The plane glided to the highway.

"Its going to crash!" cried Tom. "I'll need to buy a new motor."

The plane landed on a car. The car ran off the road. It stopped in a ditch. Police cars stopped all around the wrecked car.

"Oh no!" cried Tom. "Ruff and I are going to jail."

10

11

Ruff's Spy Plane

The police car drove up to Tom.

"Was that your flying dog?" asked the policeman.

"Yes," answered Tom.

He put out his hands. He waited for handcuffs. The policeman looked at Tom's hands.

"I don't have the reward," said the policeman. "You'll have to go to the bank."

"What reward?" asked Tom. "Aren't you taking me to jail?

"No," said the policeman. "That dog's spy plane stopped the bank robbers. He's great at flying. He could use some work on landing."

12

13

The police car drove away.

"Ruff is a great dog," thought Tom. "Oh no!" cried Tom. "What happened to Ruff?"

Just then, a truck came zooming down the street.

It was loaded with pies. Its horn was honking.

"Get out of the way!" cried the driver. "My brakes don't work."

Violet pointed up to the sky. Tom lifted his eyes to the sky. Ruff floated down on a parachute. He landed on the back of the pie truck. The parachute made the truck stop.

"What a brave dog!" said the pie truck driver. "You saved my life and my pies."

14

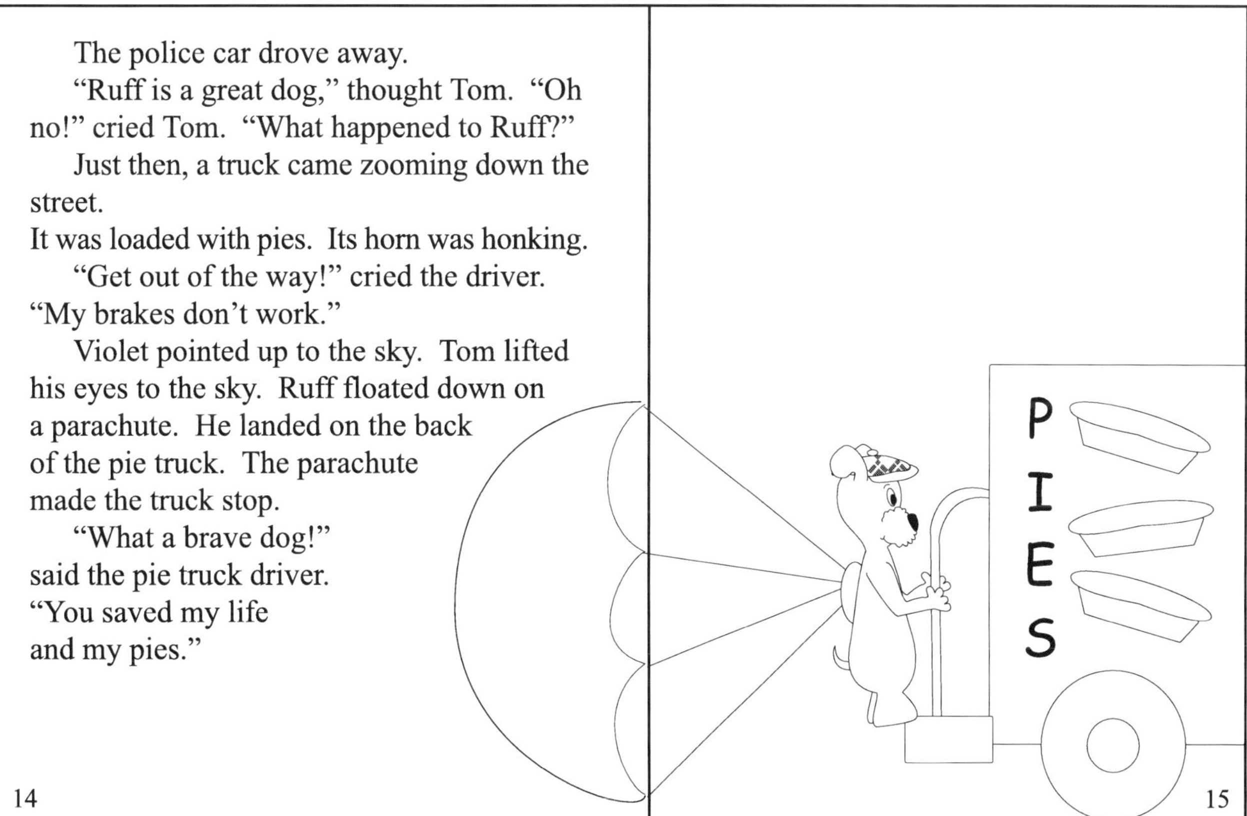

15

Ruff's Spy Plane

Ruff got a big reward at the bank. Tom was able to buy a new motor. Each day, the pie man gave them fresh pies. Tom was glad Ruff was safe.

"No more spy planes, Ruff," said Tom. "You could have died."

Ruff agreed. He raised his eyes to the sky. He did like flying.

"I don't need a spy plane," thought Ruff. "I should try to make a spy rocket.

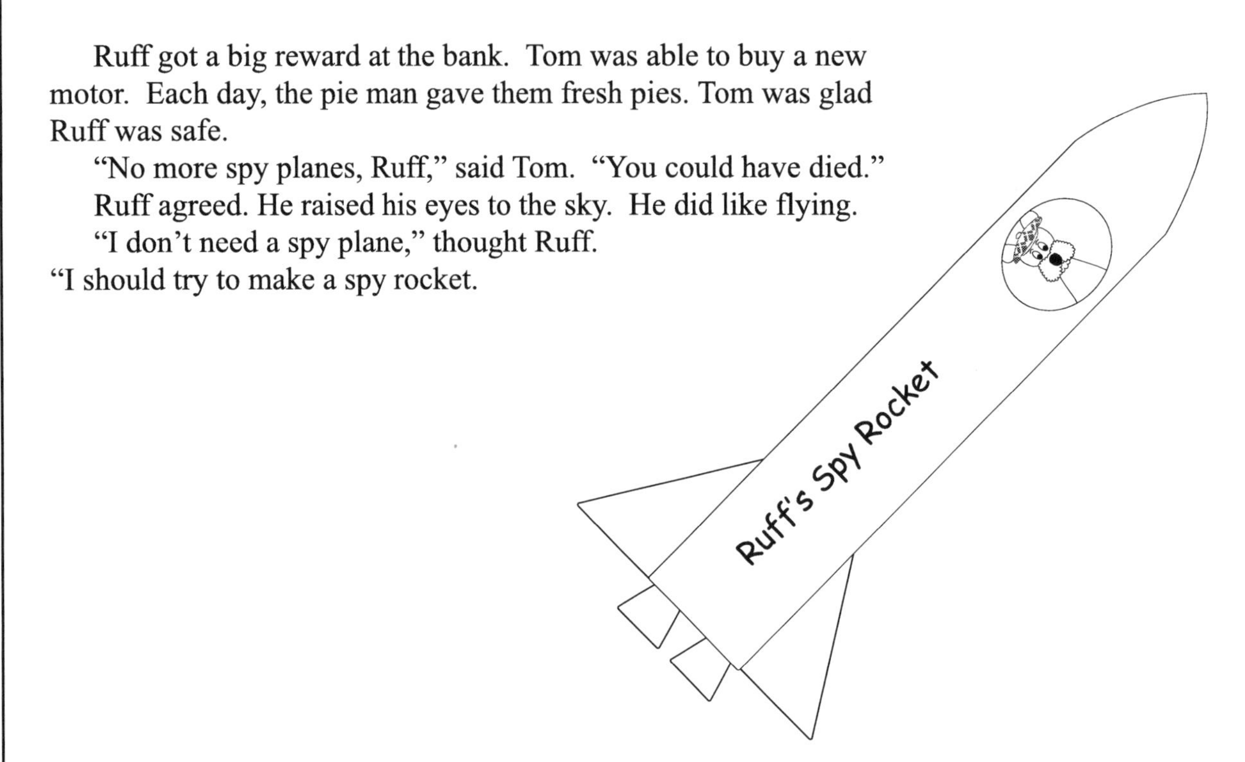

16

Ruff's Spy Plane word list:

away
began
belonged
bother
button
buy
by
cried
died
ditch
driver
dry
eyes
flew
flier
fly
flying
glued
gone
great
guy
handcuffs
handle
happened
highway
money
motor
my
new
now
open
parachute
pieces
pies
pointed
police
policeman
pried
push
reading
reward
right
rocket
rubbed
sink
sky
spied
sputter
spy
thought
tied
tried
try
Violet
wanted
why
window
won't
wouldn't
wrecked
zooming

Lesson 87

Lesson Objectives

1. Students will combine sentences. (L)
2. Students will identify complete and incomplete sentences. (L)
3. Students will review spelling words. (S)
4. Students will use spelling words in sentences. (S)
5. Students will read the story *Ruff's Spy Plane*. (R)
6. Students will copy sentences neatly and correctly. (H)

Materials

LAR
SAP
Ruff's Spy Plane

Teaching

1. Use the top of the LAR workbook page. **Combine the two sentences. Use the words that are underlined in both sentences. Keep the meaning of the sentences the same.**

2. **Sentences must have a noun or pronoun and a verb. Sometimes you can have a noun and verb and still not have a sentence. There are actually two parts to a sentence. A subject part and a part called the predicate. It's the part that includes the verb.**

   Write the words: Walked to the store. **This looks like a sentence, but does it really sound like a sentence? All we know is that someone or something walked to the store. The sentence is incomplete because it doesn't tell us the subject - what or who was walking. It has a verb, walking. It has a noun, store, but the word store didn't walk. We need to know who or what walked. Add a subject part to the beginning of this sentence to make it complete.** (Answers vary. Sample answer: We walked to the store.)

   Here is another incomplete sentence: The fluffy bunny. What's missing in this sentence? We know it's about a fluffy bunny, but we don't know what the fluffy bunny is doing. It's missing the predicate - the part that tells the action. Add a predicate part to tell what the bunny does. (Sample answer: The fluffy bunny hopped to the fence.)

   Use the bottom of the LAR workbook page. **Are the sentences complete or incomplete? Answer yes or no. Make up another part of a sentence to complete the incomplete sentences.**

3. Use the top of the SAP workbook page. **In each box are sets of three spelling words. Look at the word list below the spelling words. What words can be made using any of the letters from the three spelling words? Fill in yes if the word can be made with the letters from the spelling list. Answer no if the word cannot be made.**

4. Use the bottom of the SAP page. **Complete the pairs of sentences from the spelling word choices in each box.**

5. Review the words **parachute, reward, gone, motor.** Students will read pages 1 to 8 out loud. Next, ask the following questions:

   What was the plane like when Ruff got it? (It was in pieces.)
   How did Ruff put it together? (He tied it and glued it.)
   Describe Violet. (Violet is a flower and a friend of Ruff's. Other answers may vary.)
   Why wouldn't the spy plane start? (It didn't have a motor.)
   How did Ruff learn to fly? (He read a book.)
   We can learn a lot by reading books. Do you think it is a good idea to learn to fly while reading a book? (Answers vary. Ask why or why not.)
   Why did Tom wake up? (Ruff flew by his window.)
   Why wouldn't his car start? (Ruff took the car motor.)
   How do you think this made Tom feel? (answers vary)

6. Use the handwriting sheet or have the children write the following:

   Cursive: g, Write the words beg, Gab
   Can I try to make French fries?
   Why was the dog tied to the tree?

LAR Answers

Top part
Exact wording may vary

The dust in my eye is making me cry.
The clothes dried on the line.
We will try the apple pie.

Complete sentences:

1. no
2. yes
3. yes
4. no

Completing the sentences:
Answers vary

SAP Answers

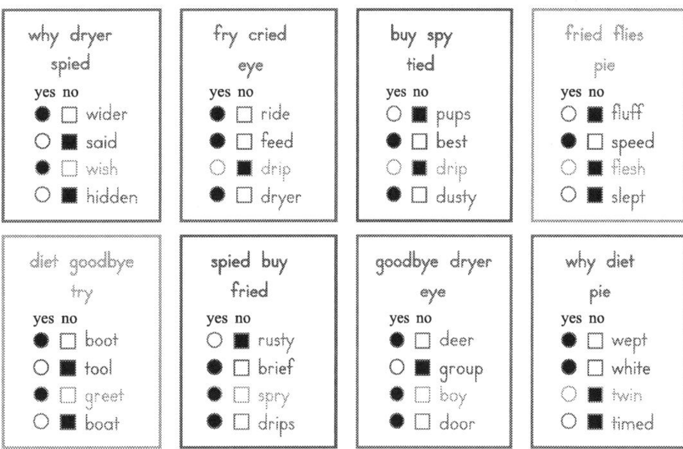

1. They cried as they waved goodbye.
2. Why did the boys try to spy on us?

3. Did she buy a new dryer?
4. I must go on a diet after eating the fried pie.

Lesson 88

Lesson Objectives

1. Students will choose the review homophones. (L)
2. Students will review sentence tense. (L)
3. Students will review spelling words. (S)
4. Students will read the story *Ruff's Spy Plane.* (R)
5. Students will copy sentences neatly and correctly. (H)

Materials

LAR
SAP
Ruff's Spy Plane

Teaching

1. Write the words buy, by, eye, I, die, dye, lie, lye, pried, pride. Have the students read the homophones. Discuss the meaning of each word.The brief definitions are given at the top of the LAR workbook page. Buy: spend money, by: next to something, eye: part of the body that sees, I: speaking about myself, die: quit living, dye: change the color, lie: be untruthful, lye: used to make soap, pried: wedged open, pride:a feeling

   Use the top of the LAR workbook page. **Choose the correct homophones to complete the sentences. Fill in the circles.**

2. Say the sentences: **The horses ran to the fence. The horses are running to the fence. What is the difference in the meaning of these two sentences?** (One tell about the horses running in the past. The other tells about horses running now.) **We call this difference the tense of a sentence. The first sentence is written in the past tense. The second sentence is written in the present tense.**

   Use the bottom of the LAR workbook page. **Is the tense of each sentence present or past? If the sentence reads like it is happening now, it is the present tense. If it sounds like it already happened, it is the past tense. Fill in the now circle if it is present tense. Fill in the past circle if the sentence happened in the past.**

3. Use the SAP workbook page. **Fill in the missing vowels or the letter y in the words at the top of the page. Remember that y acts like a vowel in some of the spelling words.**

   On the bottom section, look at the words. Part of each word is a spelling word. Look for the spelling words in the longer words and write them on the lines.

4. Review the first half of the book *Ruff's Spy Plane.* Next, read the second half of the book. After completing the story ask the students the following questions:

Why did the plane begin to sink? (The motor stopped running.)
What happened when Ruff pushed the red button? (He flew out of the plane.)
What happened to the plane? (It landed on a car.)
Who was in the car that the plane hit? (Bank robbers were in the car.)
What did Tom think the policeman was going to do to him? (Arrest him)
Who gave Ruff a reward? (The bank)
How did Ruff stop the pie truck? (His parachute stopped it.)
What did Ruff do with the reward money? (He bought Tom a new motor.)
Why do you think Ruff liked to fly? (answers vary)

5. Use the handwriting sheet or have the children write the following:

Cursive: h, the words had, He
Those guys pried open the door.
Did the spray make the flies die?

LAR Answers

1. ○ lye ● lie
2. ● buy ○ by
3. ● eye ○ I
4. ○ pride ● pried
5. ○ died ● dyed

1. ○ now ● past
2. ● now ○ past
3. ○ now ● past
4. ○ now ● past
5. ● now ○ past

SAP Answers

Top
why dryer spied fry cried
eye buy spy tied fried
flies pie diet goodbye try

Bottom
fry eye
diet buy pie
tied spy fried
flies cried try

Lesson 89

Lesson Objectives

1. Students will complete a graphic organizer. (L)
2. Students will review spelling words. (S)
3. Students will write a story. (CW)
4. Students will read the story *Ruff's Spy Plane*. (R)
5. Students will copy sentences neatly and correctly. (H)

Materials

LAR
SAP
Ruff's Spy Plane
Writing Skills Workbook page is available

Teaching

1. Use the LAR page. **Look at the workbook page. The story, *Ruff's Plane,* is broken down into three parts: Ruff builds the plane, Ruff flies the plane, and Ruff leaves the plane. Twelve numbered details happen in these three parts of the story. Write the numbers in the boxes that match each part of the story. As long as you fit the details in the right part of the story, it doesn't matter what order you put them in.**

2. Use the SAP page: **Match the spelling words to the descriptions. Write the words on the lines.**

3. Students will write a Ruff McRuffy story. Say: **What does Ruff plan to make on the last page of the book Ruff's Spy Plane?** (A spy rocket.) **What do you think might happen if he builds a rocket? Will he build it from a kit or things around the house? Where will he go? What might happen? Write your own story about Ruff's Spy Rocket.**

4. Read the book *Ruff's Spy Plane* again. Next, have students look at the back of the book and answer the following questions about the word list. You may do this orally or have students write answers:

   What words are homophones? (buy, by)
   In what word does the letters ie make the long e sound? (pieces)
   What –ie words are past tense? (cried, died, pried, spied, tied, tried)
   What words are compound words? (handcuffs, highway, policeman)
   What word is also a color? (Violet)
   What word has a long a sound spelled ea? (great)
   What word is the opposite of wet? (dry)
   What word are things on your face? (eyes)
   What word has the vowel sound you hear in moose? (zooming)
   What words are contractions? (won't, wouldn't)

5. Use the handwriting sheet or have the children write the following:

   Cursive: i, the words If, big
   The hurt bird tried to fly.
   The sly fox lied to the hen.

LAR Answers

Ruff builds the plane
Any order: 1, 4, 8, 11

Ruff flies the plane
Any order: 2, 5, 7, 9

Ruff leaves the plane
Any order: 3, 6, 10, 12

SAP Answers

try	
fry	buy
goodbye	dryer
why	eye
pie	tied
flies	spied
fried	cried
spy	diet

Lesson 90

Lesson Objectives

1. Students will be tested on phonics concepts. (P)
2. Students will be tested on language concepts. (L)
3. Students will take a spelling test. (S)
4. Students will recognize story sequence. (R)
5. Students will read the story they have written. (R)
6. Students will copy a sentence neatly and correctly. (H)

Materials

LAR
Creative writing assignment from lesson 89
Assessment 90

Teaching

1. Use part A of the assessment as a phonics test. Have the students fill in the circles next to the words that complete the sentences.

2. Use part B of the assessment page. Students will choose the correct form of the word to complete the sentences.

3. Have students number their papers from 1 to 15. Give the following words as dictation.

   Spelling word list:

   1. spied, 2. buy, 3. why, 4. pie, 5. fry, 6. tied, 7. spy, 8. dryer, 9. eye 10. fried 11. flies, 12. cried, 13. goodbye, 14. diet, 15. try

4. Use the top of the LAR workbook page. **Number the sentences in the order they happened in the story *Ruff's Spy Plane.*** One the bottom section: **Answer the questions about *Ruff's Spy Plane.***

5. Have students take turns reading the books or stories that were written during the creative writing section of the previous lesson.

6. Use the handwriting sheet or have the children write the following:

   Cursive: j, the words Jed, jab
   The spry old man had brown eyes.
   The sun dried the plywood.

Assessment Answers

1. buy
2. vie
3. dryer
4. sty
5. pry

1. dried
2. try
3. fried
4. tie
5. lie

LAR Answers

9
2
5
10
1
7
4
8
6
3

1. yes **no**
2. yes **no**
3. **yes** no
4. yes **no**
5. yes **no**

Lesson 91

Lesson Objectives

1. Students will read words spelled with wa. (P)
2. Students will spell words correctly. (S)
3. Students will learn vocabulary words. (L)
4. Students will prepare to read the story *Walter's Warning*. (R)
5. Students will copy sentences neatly and correctly. (H)

Materials

LAR
SAP
Walter's Warning
Optional: Encyclopedia entry about walruses
Writing Skills Workbook page is available

Word List: wad, waddle, waffle, wahoo, walk, wall, wallaby, wallet, wallop, wallow, walnut, walrus, Walter, waltz, wand, Wanda, wander, want, war, warble, ward, warden, wardrobe, warfare, warm, warmth, warn, warning, warp, warpath, warrant, warship, wart, warthog, was, wash, washtub, washy, wasp, watch, water, watt, what

Teaching

1. Write the words wag, wait, and wave. Have students read the words. Ask what are the first two letters in each word. (w and a). Ask what sound the letter *a* makes in each word. (Short a in wag, long a in wait and wave.) The list from this week features words where the letter *a* takes on an *o* sound when following the letter w.

   Write the words walk and war. Say: **The a in these words makes an *o* sound, the short o sound.** Have students try to read the words. **The a in walk makes the short o sound. The a in war combines with r to make the *–or* sound.**

   Help students divide some of the two-syllable words into syllables: waffle, wallet, walnut, wardrobe. Divide some of the compound words into two words: warpath, warship, warthog, washtub.

2. Use the SAP workbook page. Have students read and spell each word. Spelling list: what, walnut, wander, watch, washtub, waffle, warn, wallaby, warm, wallet, waltz, walrus, want, water.

   Review syllables. **Sort the spelling list by syllables. Remember every syllable must have a vowel sound. A syllable is like a beat you can clap.** Demonstrate by saying and clapping the syllables in these words: **goodbye, fly, family.**

   Bottom section: **Read the six words at the bottom of the page.**
   Write the spelling word that rhymes with each word.

3. Use the LAR workbook page. **Read the definitions. Use them to help you choose the words to complete the sentences.**

4. *Walter's Warning* focuses on words spelled with w-a. In addition to those words, the following words may be new to students and will require some instruction: **captain, lowered.** The words and pronunciation guide are printed at the bottom of the LAR page.

   The word *captain:* Break down into syllables: cap-tain. The a in t-a-i-n is silent.

   The word *lowered:* Break into syllables: low-er-ed.

   Introduce the story: Ask a student to read the title of the book. **What is the name of this story?** *(Walter's Warning)* **What kind of animal is Walter?** (a walrus – you may want to read an encyclopedia entry about walruses or students can read about them on workbook page 81.) **What's a warning?** (telling someone that something dangerous is about to happen.) **Read the story to find out what was Walter's warning.**

   Students will read the words on the back of the book out loud.
   Students will silently read as much of the story as they can in the time allowed.

5. Use the handwriting sheet or have the children write the following:

   Cursive: k, Write the words Kid, back
   A wallaby wandered into camp.
   The waffles were very warm.

LAR Answers

1. warble
2. wahoo
3. watt
4. warden
5. warn
6. wasp
7. wallet
8. waddle

SAP Answers

Any order within each box

One syllable: what watch warn warm waltz want

Two syllables: walnut wander washtub waffle wallet walrus water

Three syllables: wallaby

Rhymes

notch, watch	corn, warn
hot, what	yonder, wander
font, want	hotter, water

Walter's Warning

Second Grade Phonics & Reading

Book 17
Lessons 91 to 95

Walter's Warning

Written and illustrated by
Brian Davis

Walter the walrus was on an iceberg. He was asleep. His wife, Wanda rolled over. She bumped Walter into the water. Walter the walrus floated on the water. Walter was still asleep.

2

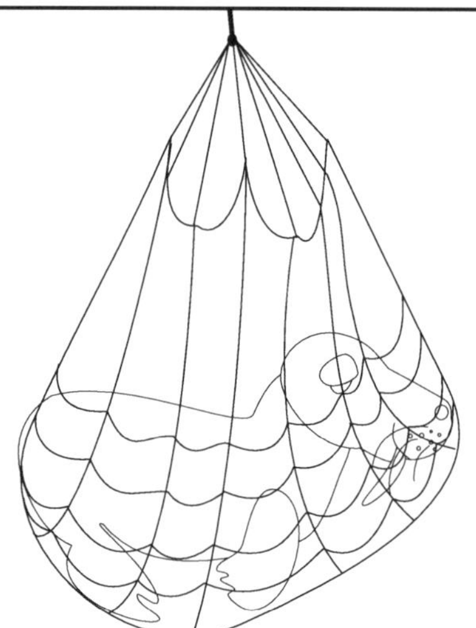

Walter's fins wrapped around a net. The net lifted the walrus out of the water. The net was lowered into a boat.

3

Walter's Warning

Hours later, Walter woke up. Walter was surrounded by walls.

"Wanda! Where are you?" barked Walter. "Where am I?" thought Walter.

It was dark and warm in the boat.

"I must be in a big washtub," said Walter.

Then Walter smelled shrimp. Walter loved shrimp. He did not like the warmth. Walter was used to icebergs.

"I've got to get back to the water," said Walter.

The shrimp smelled good to Walter. "I think I'll eat first."

He was about to have a shrimp snack. That's when Walter smelled something new. He liked the smell.

4

5

Walter waddled up some steps. He wandered into the kitchen. There was a stack of waffles. They were topped with walnuts.

"What are these?" thought Walter. "There's one way to find out," said Walter as he gobbled a waffle.

Walter wanted more. He ate all the waffles and walnuts. The kitchen was very hot. Walter waddled to a door. He opened up the icebox.

"Ahh," sighed Walter.

He waddled into the icebox.

6

7

Walter's Wawrning

The cook came back to the kitchen.

"Where are my waffles?" asked the cook.

He looked around.

"Where are my walnuts?"

The cook followed a trail of pots and pans. Walter had made a mess as he waddled. The cook followed the trail to the icebox.

The cook opened the door. There was Walter. He smiled and waved his fin.

"Help! There's a walrus in the icebox!" shouted the cook.

The cook ran off. All the shouting scared Walter.

8

9

Walter waddled up to the deck of the boat. The boat was in a dense fog. Men were wandering around. They were looking for Walter. The fog made it hard to see.

"That cook is on the warpath," thought Walter.

Walter was used to fog. Then, Walter saw something in the water.

"What is that?" thought Walter.

10

11

Walter's Warning

The captain was also looking for Walter. No one was watching the steering wheel. Walter waddled into the cabin.

That's when Walter saw the warship. The boat had wandered into its path. The warship was going to crash into the boat.

"I've got to warn the ship," thought Walter.

Walter flipped a switch. That turned on a loud speaker. Walter barked as loud as he could.

The warship blew a whistle back. The warship's captain could hear Walter's warning. The warship turned just in time.

The men raced to the cabin. "The walrus saved us," said the cook.

"Wahoo!" yelled all the men.

12

13

The men found a big washtub. They filled it with ice. Walter wallowed in the ice. It was kind of like home.

The cook made waffles and walnuts. The captain fed Walter plates of shrimp. Walter liked it at first.

Then, he began to miss Wanda. He missed waltzing in the water with her. Walter wanted to go home. The captain watched Walter grow sad. The captain knew what to do.

14

15

Walter's Warning

One day, a sound woke up Walter. He had been dreaming of waltzing with Wanda. Walter wallowed in sorrow.

Walter waddled to the deck of the boat. The captain was there to greet him.

"What is this?" thought Walter.

"You're home, Walter!" said the cook.

Walter waddled to the rail of the ship. He looked into the water. Wanda was floating on a chunk of ice.

"Wahoo! It's Wanda!" Walter let out a loud bark.
The men lowered him in a net.

"I've missed you, Wanda," barked Walter.

"I've missed you, too," barked Wanda.

Walter jumped from the net. Walter and Wanda waltzed in the water. The men on the boat waved good-bye. They tossed waffles and walnuts to Walter and Wanda.

16

Walter's Warning word list:

around	something	warmth
cabin	sorrow	warpath
captain	surrounded	warship
chunk	waddled	was
dense	waffles	washtub
dreaming	wahoo	watched
floating	wallowed	watching
gobbled	walls	water
hours	walnuts	what
iceberg	walrus	wheel
icebox	Walter	when
kitchen	waltzing	where
loved	Wanda	whistle
lowered	wandered	wife
new	wandering	woke
scared	wanted	wrapped
shrimp	warm	you're

Lesson 92

Lesson Objectives

1. Students will alphabetize words to the third letter. (L)
2. Students will use spelling words in sentences. (S)
3. Students will puntuate sentences with quotation marks. (L)
4. Students will read the story *Walter's Warning*. (R)
5. Students will copy sentences neatly and correctly. (H)

Materials

LAR
SAP
Walter's Warning

Teaching

1. Review nouns, verbs, and adjectives. Write the sentence: The walnut fell off the large tree. **What are the nouns in this sentence?** (walnut, tree) **What is the verb?** (fell) **What is the adjective?** (large)

   Use the top of the LAR workbook page. **One of the words in each sentence is in black print. Is it a noun or verb? Fill in the circles to mark your answers. Underline the adjectives.**

2. Write the sentence without quotation marks. Where did Walter go? asked Wanda. **This sentence is missing some punctuation. Do you know what is missing? When characters are speaking in a story, the words they say are surrounded by quotation marks. Quotation marks are made at the top of letters, like apostrophes. They come before the first words the character speaks and after the last word the character speaks. The first set looks like the number 66 with the circles filled in. The last set looks like the number 99 with the circles filled in.**

   There is a punctuation mark that comes before the second quotation mark. It is a comma if there are words after it that explain who was talking. If the character asked a question, there will be a question mark. If the character is excited you might see an exclamation mark. If it is the end of the sentence and there are no words after it there will be a period, question mark, or exclamation mark.

   Show students where to draw the exclamation marks in the sample sentence: "Look out Walter!" yelled Wanda.

   Use the bottom of the LAR workbook page. **Read the sentences. Draw in the quotation marks where they belong.**

3. Use the SAP page. **Choose a spelling word that can take the place of the underlined word and change it the least.**

4. Review the words **captain,** and **lowered.** Students will read pages 1 to 8 out loud. Next, ask the following questions:

   What was Walter sleeping on? (an iceberg)
   How did he fall off? (Wanda bumped him.)
   How did Walter get into the boat? (A net lifted him.)
   What animal was Walter going to eat? (shrimp)
   What did Walter eat in the kitchen? (waffles with walnuts)
   Where did Walter find a cool place? (in the icebox)
   Who found Walter? (the cook)
   What did Walter do when he saw the cook? (He waved and smiled)
   What scared Walter? (the cook's shouting)

5. Use the handwriting sheet or have the children write the following:

   Cursive: l, Write the words Lad, hill
   Walter washed the puppy in a washtub.
   Wanda wanted a new wardrobe.

LAR Answers

1. Walter will walk to the new store.	○ noun	● verb
2. The wallaby nibbled the tall grass.	● noun	○ verb
3. My new watch is on my left wrist.	● noun	○ verb
4. We can watch the funny cartoon.	○ noun	● verb
5. Wanda washed her dirty hands.	○ noun	● verb

1. "Wahoo I did it!" yelled Wanda when she won the race.
2. "I must warn the captain," said Walter.
3. The squirrel said, "That walnut is mine."
4. "Is it warm out?" asked Connie.
5. "Don't wander off," warned Mom.

SAP Answers

1. watch
2. warm
3. walrus
4. washtub
5. wallet
6. waffles
7. warn
8. What
9. waltz
10. walnut
11. water
12. want

Lesson 93

Lesson Objectives

1. Students will practice comprehension skill (non-fiction). (L)
2. Students will review spelling words. (S)
3. Students will read the story *Walter's Warning*. (R)
4. Students will copy sentences neatly and correctly. (H)

Materials

LAR
SAP
Question Words Poster
Walter's Warning

Teaching

1. Use the LAR page. **Look at the workbook page. How can you quickly tell what the article is about?** (Look at the pictures and the bold print words.) **Just by looking at the pictures what is a way walruses and warthogs are alike?** (tusks)

   Students will read the descriptions of the animals. **Read the sentences at the bottom of the page. Fill in the circles next to the animals that match the statements. The choices are walrus, warthog, or both.** Students may need help reading the words walruses, and Africa.

   Why did the author compare walruses to seals?

   Use the Question Poster. **Write four questions about walruses or warthogs. Use the question words to begin the questions.**

   Have students do further research on either walruses or warthogs and compare the information to the information on the workbook page.

2. Use the SAP workbook page. Top section: **Fit all the spelling words into the grid. Start with the three clue spaces.**

   Bottom section: **Find the letters that make spelling words in each row of boxes. Fill in the boxes for the letters that do not belong. A spelling word is in each set of boxes.**

3. Review the first half of the book *Walter's Warning*. Next, read the second half of the book. After completing the story ask the students the following questions:

   Why was it hard for people to see on the boat? (There was a dense fog.)
   What was going to hit the boat? (a warship)
   How did Walter warn the ship? (He barked into a loud speaker.)
   What did the men on the boat give Walter? (a tub of ice, waffles, walnuts, and shrimp)
   What kind of dance did Walter do with Wanda? (waltz)
   How do you think the captain knew Walter was sad? (answers vary)
   Why was this book called Walter's Warning? (answers vary)
   How do you think Walter felt when he saw Wanda? (answers vary)

4. Use the handwriting sheet or have the children write the following:
   Cursive: m, the words Mack, Kim
   Walnuts fell on the sidewalk.
   The walrus waddled on the shore.

LAR Answers

● walrus	❍ warthog	❍ both
❍ walrus	● warthog	❍ both
● walrus	❍ warthog	❍ both
❍ walrus	❍ warthog	● both
● walrus	❍ warthog	❍ both
● walrus	❍ warthog	❍ both
❍ walrus	● warthog	❍ both
❍ walrus	● warthog	❍ both
● walrus	❍ warthog	❍ both

SAP Answers

waltz
waffle
warm
washtub
walrus
wallaby
wallet
warn
walnut
wander
want
what
watch
water

w a ■ s ■ ■ h t u ■ b ■
w ■ a l ■ l ■ a b ■ ■ y
w a ■ ■ f f ■ ■ l e
w a l ■ n ■ u ■ t ■
w a ■ l r u s ■ ■ ■
w a ■ n ■ d ■ e r ■
w a l l ■ ■ e ■ t ■

w a ■ t ■ ■ e r ■
w a ■ ■ ■ t c ■ h
w ■ h a ■ ■ t ■
w ■ a ■ ■ r n ■
w a ■ ■ r ■ m ■
w ■ a l ■ t ■ z
w a ■ ■ n ■ t ■

Lesson 94

Lesson Objectives

1. Students will review spelling words. (S)
2. Students will write a story. (CW)
3. Students will read the story *Walter's Warning*. (R)
4. Students will copy sentences neatly and correctly. (H)

Materials

LAR
SAP
Walter's Warning

Teaching

1. Use the SAP page. **Match the spelling words to the descriptions.**

2. Students will write a story. Say: **What came on the boat in the story Walter's Warning?** (A walrus.) **The boat next went to Australia. Write a story about a wallaby on a boat.**

   Use the LAR workbook page. **To write about a wallaby, you may need more information. The workbook page gives you some information about wallabies.**

   The content from the workbook page is reprinted on the next page.

3. Read the book *Walter's Warning* again. Next, have students look at the back of the book and answer the following questions about the word list. You may do this orally or have students write answers:

   What words end with the suffix -ing? (dreaming, floating, waltzing, wandering, watching)
   What word means someone who is in charge of a boat? (captain)
   What word begins with a silent letter? (wrapped)
   What words are foods? (shrimp, waffles, walnuts)
   What words are names? (Walter, Wanda)
   What word doesn't mean anything, it's just a word you shout? (wahoo)
   What word is the opposite of old? (new)
   What word describes the way a walrus walks? (waddled)
   What word is the opposite of cool? (warm)
   What word is a contraction? (you're)
   What words are compound words? (iceberg, icebox, something, warpath, warship)

4. Use the handwriting sheet or have the children write the following:

   Cursive: n, the words Nap, men
   The warthog chased the warden.
   The warship warned the little boat.

LAR Page

A walrus came aboard the boat in the story *Walter's Warning*. The boat next went to Australia. This time they accidentally picked up a wallaby. Write a story about a wallaby on a boat.

Preparing to write.

Background Information: When you write a story you may have to get more information. Below is information about wallabies that can help you write a story about a wallaby on a boat. If there's not enough information here, where else might you look to find out about wallabies?

Over thirty animals are called wallabies. Some look more like rabbits, but many look like small kangaroos. They can have a mixture of colors of fur. They can have gray, brown, and red fur with some white parts. They have strong back legs and long tails that help them hop.

Female wallabies are called **fliers**. They have pouches for carrying their children. The babies are called **joeys**. They are very tiny when they are born. They may weigh only a tenth of an ounce. They live in the pouch for several months. Male wallabies have a name, too. They are called **boomers**.

Most wallabies live in **Australia**. They eat leaves, grass, and roots. Sometimes they damage crops. Farmers think they are pests. Other people keep them as pets. They feed them fruits and vegetables.

Brainstorming: Think of different ideas for your story. Don't start writing at this point. Just make notes of your ideas. You may or may not use these ideas in your story. Below are questions that may help you brainstorm. Maybe you can even think of your own questions. Use a piece of paper to take notes. Write answers to the questions you think will help you write your story. Write any other ideas you may have to write the story.

How did it get on the boat?

Did the sailors know it was there? If so, what did they do when the found it? How did they find it?

Was it a good or bad animal to have it on the boat? What good did it do or what harm did it do?

Did it get home? If so, how? If not, what did it do instead?

Imagine having a pet wallaby. What would you do with it? How might it be fun?

SAP Answers

walnut	warn
waltz	warm
walrus	wallet
watch	waffles
wallaby	water
washtub	wander
what	want

Lesson 95

Lesson Objectives

1. Students will be tested on phonics concepts. (P)
2. Students will be tested on language concepts. (L)
3. Students will take a spelling test. (S)
4. Students will review story sequence. (R)
5. Students will read the story they have written. (R)
6. Students will copy a sentence neatly and correctly. (H)

Materials

LAR
Creative writing assignment from lesson 94
Assessment 95

Teaching

1. Use part A of the assessment as a phonics test. Have the students fill in the circles next to the words that complete the sentences.

2. Use part B of the assessment page. Students will read the sentences. A word is underlined. Tell if it is a noun or a verb. Fill in the correct circle.

3. Have students number their papers from 1 to 14. Give the following words as dictation.

   Spelling word list:

   1. warm, 2. water, 3. walnut, 4. walrus, 5. wander, 6. wallaby, 7. waltz,

   8. washtub, 9. wallet 10. what 11. waffle, 12. watch, 13. want, 14. warn

4. Use the LAR workbook page. Top section: **Number the sentences from 1 to 10 in the order they are taken.**

   Bottom section: **Answer the questions about the story, *Walter's Warning*. Fill in the ovals to mark your answers.**

5. Have students take turns reading the books or stories that were written during the creative writing section of the previous lesson.

6. Use the handwriting sheet or have the children write the following:
   Cursive: o, the words Off, knob
   A wad of cash was in the wallet.
   I walloped the wasp with the wand.

Assessment Answers

1. water
2. wasp
3. warthog
4. waffles
5. waltz

1. noun
2. verb
3. noun
4. noun
5. verb

LAR Answers

5
9
1
6
8
4
10
3
7
2

yes no

Lesson 96

Lesson Objectives

1. Students will read words spelled with au, augh, and ought (broad o sound). (P)
2. Students will spell words correctly. (S)
3. Students will proofread sentences. (L)
4. Students will prepare to read the story *A Jewel For Paula.* (R)
5. Students will copy sentences neatly and correctly. (H)

Materials

LAR
SAP
A Jewel For Paula
Writing Skills Workbook page is available

Word List: August, auto, autumn, author, because, caught, caulk, cause, daughter, daunt, fault, flaunt, fraud, fraught, gaunt, gauze, haul, haunch, haunt, haughty, jaunt, launch, laundry, Maud, maul, naught, naughty, Paul, paunch, pause, sausage, Saul, slaughter, staunch, taught, taunt, taut, vault, bought, brought, fought, ought, sought, thought, thoughtful, thoughtless

Teaching

1. Many words in this may not be in the child's speaking vocabulary. Even the unfamiliar words will help students practice the phonics concepts. Introduce the following words to the students. Tell the students that the vowels make the same sound that the letter a makes in the word talk.

   Introduce any of the following: caulk, cause, fault, flaunt, fraud, gauze, haul, haunch, haunt, launch, Maud, maul, Paul, paunch, pause, Saul, staunch, taunt, taut, vault. Ask what letters make the vowel sound. (au)

   Introduce the following words. Tell the students that the words have the same vowel sound. The letters augh make the vowel sound. Caught, fraught, taught, naught. Some words are two syllable: daughter, haughty, naughty, slaughter.

   Introduce the following words. Tell the students that the words have the same vowel sound. The letters ough make the vowel sound: bought, brought, fought, ought,
   sought, thought.

2. Use the SAP workbook page. Have students read and spell each word. Spelling list: auto, thought, cause, launch, author, autumn, sausage, laundry, haul, brought, pause, sauce, applause, fault.

   Top section: **Alphabetize the words in each box.**

   Bottom section: **Read the sentences. Circle the spelling words.**

3. Use the LAR workbook page. **Read the words and definitions. Use the definitions to help choose the correct word to complete the eight sentences.**

4. *A Jewel For Paula* focuses on words spelled with au, augh, and ough (broad o sound). In addition to those words, the following words may be new to students and will require some instruction: **allowed, armor, beautiful, finally, kingdom, search, whoever.** The words and pronunciation guide are printed at the bottom of the LAR workbook page.

   The word *allowed:* The ow makes the vowel sound heard in cow.
   The word *armor:* Break into syllables: ar-mor
   The word *beautiful:* eau make a long u sound.
   The word *finally:* The i is long. The y makes the long e sound.
   The word *kingdom:* Break into syllables: king-dom
   The word *search:* ear makes the -er sound.
   The word *whoever:* Break into syllables: who (the w is silent), ev-er

   Introduce the story: Ask a student to read the title of the book. **What is the name of this story?** *A Jewel For Paula* **What is a jewel?** (a pretty rock that is very valuable, such as a diamond, ruby, etc.) **Read the story to find out who is Paula and why she is getting a jewel.**

   Students will read the words on the back of the book out loud.
   Students will silently read as much of the story as they can in the time allowed.

5. Use the handwriting sheet or have the children write the following:
   Cursive: p, Write the words Pam, hop
   The naughty puppy mauled the shoe.
   Dad bought a tube of white caulk.

LAR Answers

1. gaunt
2. jaunt
3. naught
4. maul
5. flaunt
6. gauze
7. staunch
8. fraught

SAP Answers

1. applause	5. brought
2. author	6. cause
3. auto	7. fault
4. autumn	

1. haul	5. sauce
2. launch	6. sausage
3. laundry	7. thought
4. pause	

The cook brought in the sausage and the sauce.

We can haul the laundry in the auto.

The cause of the pause is my fault.

The rocket will launch this autumn.

A Jewel For Paula

Second Grade Phonics & Reading

Book 18
Lessons 96 to 100

A Jewel For Paula

Written and illustrated by
Brian Davis

There once was a king named Saul. He was a very rich king. He had a beautiful daughter. Her name was Princess Paula.

The king thought his daughter should get married. King Saul loved his daughter. He wanted her to have the best husband.

"My daughter is like a jewel," said the king. "Whoever brings her the biggest jewel will be her husband."

So, he launched a search for a husband. He sent his knights to all the other kingdoms.

2

3

A Jewel For Paula

One day, the knights were camping in some woods. They were very hungry. The knights saw a cow in a field.

"We ought to ask the farmer for that cow," said a knight.

The knight went to the poor farmer. The farmer's name was Paul.

"We are very hungry," said the knight to Paul. "We want to slaughter your cow."

Paul said no. "I need my cow. She gives me milk. She gives me cream."

This made the knights angry. A knight tossed the farmer a coin.

"Now we have bought the cow."

The knights slaughtered the cow. This made Paul very angry. He didn't want the coin. He wanted his cow.

"I should have fought them," thought Paul. But, there were three knights.

4

5

That night, the farmer's barn caught on fire. The knight's campfire had caused his barn to burn. The barn caught Paul's house on fire.

Paul fought the fire. All he saved was a bag of flour.

The farmer called his big, red dog. "Come, Ruby. Those knights need to be caught. I have lost my farm. It's all their fault."

Paul and Ruby sought the naughty knights. Ruby sniffed the trail for days.

6

7

A Jewel For Paula

Paul and his dog caught up with the knights. The knights made a camp in a dark wood. They were swimming.

"It is time to launch my plan," thought Paul.

Paul found a hollow log. He had Ruby stand by the log. Paul covered himself with flour. Ruby started howling into the hollow log.

The howl sounded spooky. Paul started walking to the knights. This caught the knights by surprise.

"It's the farmer!" cried a knight.

"He's a ghost," cried another knight. "He must have died in the fire. He's come back to haunt us!"

The three knights ran out of the water. They hopped on their horses. The three knights rode away.

8

9

"We taught those naughty knights a lesson," said Paul. "Now we need to see their king."

The knights had left their armor. Paul took his coin. He bought an old cart. Ruby and Paul hauled the armor. They walked for days.

Paul and Ruby came to a town. On a hill was a huge castle.

"Is that King Saul's castle?" Paul asked a woman.

"Yes," answered the woman. The woman looked at the cart.

"What are you hauling?" asked the woman.

"Just some armor," said Paul.

"I buy and sell armor," said the woman. "I know three knights who are looking for armor."

The woman bought Paul's armor.

10

11

A Jewel For Paula

"Now I shall see King Saul," said Paul.

"Dressed like that?" asked the woman.

Paul looked at his old torn clothes.

"I have just what you need," said the woman.

She brought out some fine clothes. "You'll look just like a prince."

Paul smiled. He bought the clothes. Paul and Ruby walked to the castle gate.

"No dogs allowed," said the knight at the gate.

Paul did not want to leave Ruby. Paul went back to the woman. He bought a large bag. Ruby climbed into the bag.

12

13

This time the knight let him in the gate. Paul waited in line to see the king. Princes had come from other kingdoms. They brought jewels for Princess Paula.

Paula didn't like the jewels. Finally, it was Paul's turn to see the king. Paul was going to tell about the naughty knights.

Then, he saw the king's daughter. Paul thought she was very beautiful.

"Do you have a jewel for the princess?" asked King Saul.

Ruby was getting hot in the bag. The dog began to wiggle. Paul dropped the bag. Ruby ran to Princess Paula.

14

15

A Jewel For Paula

"Come back, Ruby," called Paul.

Princess Paula giggled. She had always wanted a dog. She hugged Ruby.

"You are a jewel, Ruby," said Princess Paula.

The king saw how happy his daughter was. He looked at Paul.

"You shall marry my daughter," said King Saul. "You brought your dog. Ruby is the biggest jewel. You are the best husband for my daughter. You know how to make Paula happy."

Paul and Paula got married. They were very happy. The naughty knights were not so happy. Their new job was to haul dog food for Ruby.

Dog
Food

16

A Jewel For Paula word list:

allowed	dressed	large	slaughter
angry	fault	launch	sniffed
another	field	launched	sought
answered	finally	leave	sounded
armor	flour	loved	spooky
away	fought	married	surprise
beautiful	ghost	naughty	swimming
bought	haul	new	taught
brings	hauled	night	thought
brought	hauling	once	three
buy	haunt	other	town
camping	himself	ought	very
castle	hollow	Paul	walking
caught	howling	Paula	wanted
climbed	husband	Princess	water
clothes	jewel	Ruby	what
coin	king	Saul	whoever
cried	kingdoms	search	wiggle
daughter	knights	should	woman

Lesson 97

Lesson Objectives

1. Students will practice comprehension skills. (L)
2. Students will review spelling words.
3. Students will use spelling words in sentences. (S)
4. Students will read the story *A Jewel For Paula.* (R)
5. Students will copy sentences neatly and correctly. (H)

Materials

LAR
SAP
A Jewel For Paula

Teaching

1. Use the LAR workbook page. **Solve the crossword puzzle.**

2. Use the top of the SAP workbook page. **Inside each box are two spelling words. Can the words in the list below them be made with the letters from the two spelling words? Answer yes or no.**

3. Write the sentence: Did he <u>teach</u> you the song? (underline teach) **We've changed questions into statements in other lessons by moving a word. This time we'll change the question into a statement. First we'll get rid of the first word. Then we'll change the tense of the underlined word, *teach*. We'll make it past tense.** Change the sentence to read: He taught you the song. **Notice that the question mark was changed to a period.**

   Use the bottom of SAP workbook page 78. **Read the two questions. Take off the first word. Change the underlined word to the spelling word that is the past tense.**

4. Review the words: **allowed, armor, beautiful, finally, kingdom, search,** and **whoever.**
   Students will read pages 1 to 8 out loud. Next, ask the following questions:

   What did King Saul ask men to bring Paula? (jewels)
   Why did the knights want the cow? (They were hungry.)
   Why didn't the farmer give them his cow? (He was poor and needed it.)
   What should the knights have done? (answers vary)
   What happened to the farmer's barn? (It caught on fire.)
   What were the knights doing when Paul found them? (swimming)
   How did Ruby help scare the knights? (She howled in a hollow log.)
   What did the knights think Paul was? (a ghost)
   What did the knights do? (They rode away on their horses.)

5. Use the handwriting sheet or have the children write the following:

   Cursive: q, Write the words Quick, queen
   Paul's daughter is an author.
   I thought autumn began in August.

LAR Answers

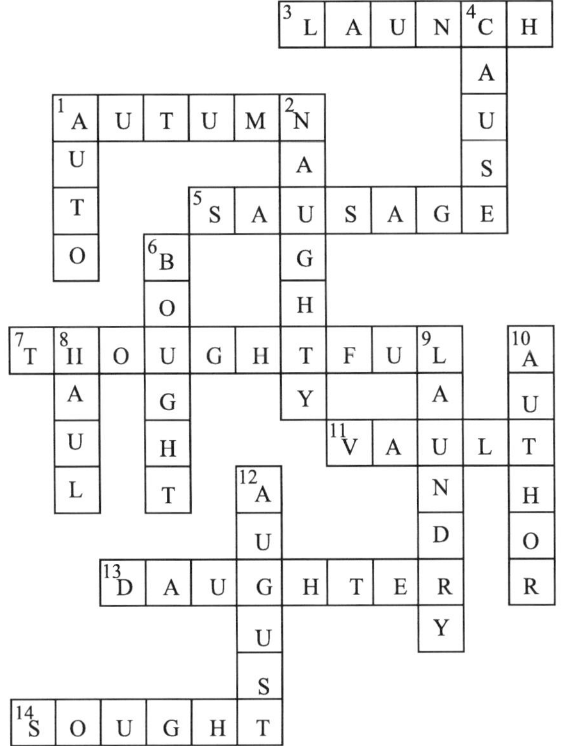

SAP Answers

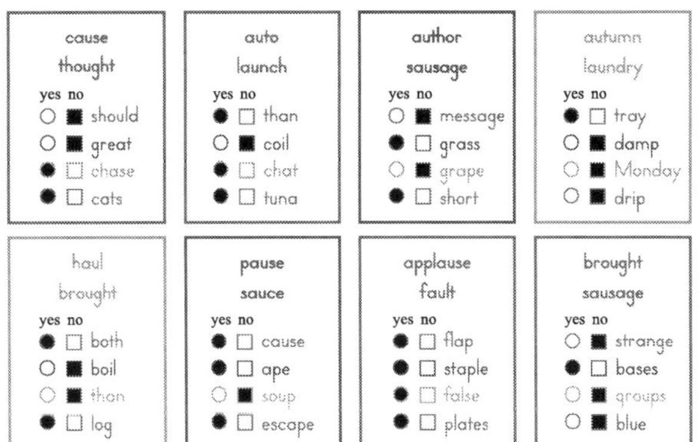

1. They thought the sausage was spicy.
2. The author brought a stack of books.

Lesson 98

Lesson Objectives

1. Students will recognize homophones. (P)
2. Students will choose the correct tense to complete sentences. (L)
3. Students will add quotation marks to sentences. (L)
4. Students will review spelling words. (S)
5. Students will read the story *A Jewel For Paula.* (R)
6. Students will copy sentences neatly and correctly. (H)

Materials

LAR
SAP
A Jewel For Paula
Writing Skills Workbook page is available

Teaching

1. Have students find homophones spelled with au, augh, for the following words:

   paws (pause), hall (haul), not (naught), caws (cause), Otto (auto), knotty (naughty), cot (caught).

   Find a homophone for taut. (taught)

2. Make a matching exercise. Write the words: catch, teach, buy, bring, seek, fight, and think in one column. Write the words: brought, thought, caught, sought, bought, fought, and taught. Have students match the present tense words to the past tense words.

   Use the top of the workbook page. **Complete the sentences by filling in a circle. Choose the word with the correct tense.**

3. Use the bottom of the LAR workbook page. **Remember quotation marks? When do we use them?** (Around the words people say.) **Put in the quotation marks for the five sentences at the bottom of the page.**

4. Use the top of the SAP page. **Fit all the spelling words into the boxes of the grid. The letter r is your first clue.**

   Bottom section: **Fill in the missing vowels to complete the spelling words.**

5. Review the first half of the book *A Jewel For Paula.* Next, read the second half of the book. After completing the story ask the students the following questions:

   What did the knights forget? (Their armor)
   What did Paul do with the armor? (He sold it.)
   What did the woman sell Paul? (clothes and a bag)
   Why couldn't Paul get in the gate the first time? (No dogs were allowed.)
   What did Paula do when she saw Ruby? (She giggled and hugged Ruby.)
   Why did the King say Ruby was a jewel? (There is a jewel called a Ruby.)
   What happened to Paul? (He married the princess.)
   What happened to the naughty knights? (They had to haul dog food.)

6. Use the handwriting sheet or have the children write the following:
   Cursive: r, the words Red, car
   The auto paused at the yellow light.
   We ought to watch the rocket launch.

LAR Answers

1. ● think ○ thought
2. ○ bring ● brought
3. ○ fight ● fought
4. ● teach ○ taught
5. ○ buy ● bought

1. " I caught the dog before it got hit," said the daughter.
2. "The pup caused the driver to stop," said Paul
3. "Naughty dog!" shouted its owner.
4. He said, "I was fraught with fear."
5. "The pup must be taught a lesson," said the father.

SAP Answers

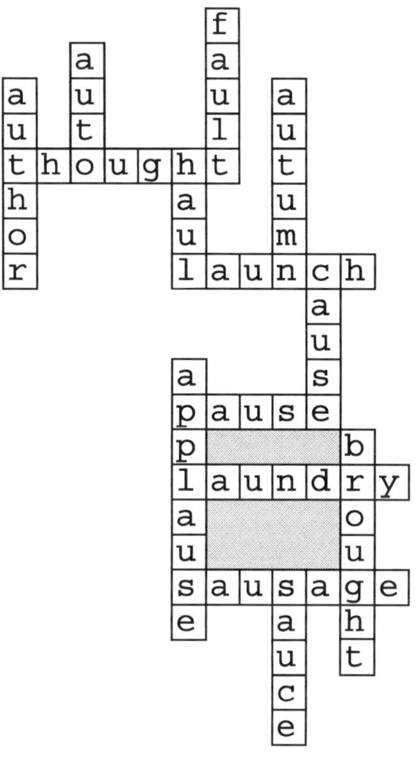

auto	thought	laundry	
author	autumn	suasage	
haul	brought	pause	sauce
applause	fault	launch	cause

Lesson 99

Lesson Objectives

1. Students will match cause and effect. (L)
2. Students will review spelling words. (S)
3. Students will write a story. (CW)
4. Students will read the story *A Jewel For Paula.* (R)
5. Students will copy sentences neatly and correctly. (H)

Materials

LAR
SAP
A Jewel For Paula

Teaching

1. Write the sentences: The tree fell over. It put a hole in the roof of the house.

   The first sentence is a cause. The second sentence is the effect. The tree falling caused damage to the roof.

   Use the LAR page. **Look at the wheel on the page. It lists eight causes in the story *A Jewel for Ruby.* Write the number for the missing effect on the bottom of the page. For two of the causes you'll write the effect on the lines.**

   Look at the cause with the red answer circle at the top of the wheel. The king launches a search. What was the effect for that? (3. The knights went to other kingdoms.) **Write a 3 in the small red circle at the top of the wheel.**

2. Use the SAP page. **Match the spelling words to the descriptions. Write the answers on the lines.**

3. Students will write a story. Say: **What happened to the knights at the end of the story A Jewel For *Paula?*** (They had to haul dog food.) **One day, the naughty knights got tired of taking care of Ruby. What do you think happened next?**

4. Read the book *A Jewel For Paula* again. Next, have students look at the back of the book and answer the following questions about the word list. You may do this orally or have students write answers:

   What word is the past tense of catch? (caught)
   What word is a synonym for pretty? (beautiful)
   What word means a girl child? (daughter)
   What word is something knights wear? (armor)
   What words are names? (Paul, Paula, Ruby, Saul)
   What words are spelled with ough? (bought, brought, fought, ought, sought, thought)
   What word is the opposite of running? (walking)
   What word is a number? (three)
   What word is the opposite of nice? (naughty)
   What words have a long i sound? (buy, climbed, cried, finally, knights, night, surprise)
   What word is a compound word? (whoever)

5. Use the handwriting sheet or have the children write the following:

   Cursive: s, the words Sip, pass
   Maude brought the sausage pizza.
   It was thoughtful of you to do the laundry.

LAR Answers

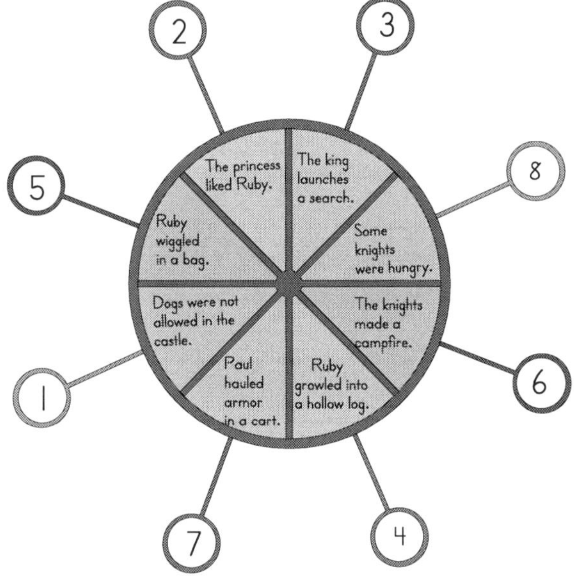

Answers may vary. Sample answers:
4. The knights were afraid
8. They killed Paul's cow.

SAP Answers

thought	sauce
applause	author
haul	auto
autumn	laundry
cause	brought
sausage	fault
pause	launch

Lesson 100

Lesson Objectives

1. Students will be tested on phonics concepts. (P)
2. Students will be tested on language concepts. (L)
3. Students will take a spelling test. (S)
4. Students will put the story in correct sequence. (L)
5. Students will read the story they have written. (R)
6. Students will copy a sentence neatly and correctly. (H)

Materials

LAR
Creative writing assignment from lesson 99
Assessment 100

Teaching

1. Use part A of the assessment as a phonics test. Have the students fill in the circles next to the words that complete the sentences.

2. Use part B of the assessment page. Students will read the sentences. Fill in the circle with the word that has the correct tense to complete the sentence.

3. Have students number their papers from 1 to 14. Give the following words as dictation.

   Spelling word list:

   1. autumn, 2. auto, 3. fault, 4. thought, 5. sauce, 6. sausage, 7. haul,

   8. launch, 9. brought 10. pause 11. applause, 12. author, 13. laundry, 14. cause

4. Use the LAR workbook page. **Read the sentences on the workbook page. Number them in the order they happened in the story.** Have students do the exercise without looking at the book. After finishing the assignment students may use their books to check or correct their answers.

   Bottom of the page: **Read the statements about the story *A Jewel for Paula.* Are they true or false? Fill in the ovals to mark your answers.**

5. Have students take turns reading the books or stories that were written during the creative writing section of the previous lesson.

6. Use the handwriting sheet or have the children write the following:
   Cursive: t, the words Tap, sat
   It is thoughtless to taunt people.
   The dogs fought because of the bone.

Assessment Answers

1. laundry	1. caught
2. thoughtful	2. paused
3. author	3. taught
4. brought	4. seek
5. caused	5. buy

LAR Answers

7
3
4
10
8
1
6
2
9
5

1. true **false**

2. **true** false

3. true **false**

4. **true** false

5. true **false**

Lesson 101

Lesson Objectives

1. Students will read words that begin with the prefix un. (P)
2. Students will change sentences into opposites. (L)
3. Students will spell words correctly. (S)
4. Students will prepare to read the story *Jonathan's Unday*. (R)
5. Students will copy sentences neatly and correctly. (H)

Materials

LAR
SAP
Jonathan's Unday
Writing Skills Workbook page is available

Word List: unaware, unbolt, unbutton, unbuckle, unchain, unclean, uncoil, uncover, uncut, under, underfoot, undergo, underground, underline, undermine, undershirt, understand, understood, undertake, undo, undress, unfair, unfold, unforgiving, unfriendly, unglued, unhappy, unhitch, unjust, unkind, unknown, unlatch, unless, unlike, unload, unlock, unpack, unplug, unquiet, unreal, unrest, unroll, unscrew, unselfish, unskilled, unsnap, unsound, unstop, unstring, unstuck, untidy, untie, until, unto, untold, untrue, untwist, unwilling, unwind, unwise, unwrap, unzip

Teaching

1. Write the words cross and come. Have students read the words. Add the letter a to cross. (across). Add the letters b-e to come. (become) Say: **Letters added at the end of words are called suffixes. What are some suffixes we have added to words?** (ed, ing, er, est) **Letters added to the beginning of words are called prefixes. What are the prefixes in the words across and become?** (a, be)

   Today we will begin using a new prefix. Introduce the prefix *un*. Write the prefix and have students read it. **The prefix *un* changes the meaning of words a few different ways. In many words it means the reverse of the action: button, unbutton, lock, unlock.**

   Sometimes it means not: snapped, unsnapped, fair, unfair.

   Also in the list are compound words beginning with under. Under, of course, means below in many of these words. An undershirt is a shirt worn under another shirt. To underline means to draw a line below something. Underground means below ground.

   Use the top of the LAR workbook page. **Build words by adding parts. Write the new words on the lines.**

2. Use the bottom of the LAR workbook page. Add the prefix un- to the word with lines before it. Have students read the sentences with and without the prefix. Have students discuss how the sentence changed. (It made the sentence mean the opposite.)

3. Use the SAP workbook page. Have students read and spell each word. Spelling list: unsnap, understand, unknown, unplug, unwrap, unkind, unload, until, undershirt, unzip, unselfish, untwist, underline, unhappy.

Review syllables by having students read the spelling list once more and clap the syllables. Have students sort the words by the number of syllables in the top two box of the SAP page.

Bottom section: **Read the words. Change the words over to under to make different words.**

4. *Jonathan's Unday* focuses on words beginning with the prefix un.

Introduce the story: Ask a student to read the title of the book. **What is the name of this story?** *(Jonathan's Unday)* **One of these words is not a real word. Which one is it?** (Unday) **What do you think an unday might be? Read the story to find out.**

Students will read the words on the back of the book out loud.
Students will silently read as much of the story as they can in the time allowed.

5. Use the handwriting sheet or have the children write the following:
Cursive: u, Write the words uncut, untrue
My uncle unpacked the boxes.
I need to unbutton my shirt to undress.

LAR Answers

unbolted
unfriendly
unaware
uncovering
understanding

1. unload
2. unwrap
3. unkind
4. unfold
5. unfriendly
6. unzipped
7. unlock

SAP Answers

Two sylalbles (any order)

unsnap unknown unplug unwrap

unkind unload until unzip untwist

Three syllables (any order)

understand undershirt unselfish

underline unhappy

Bottom section

underpay

undercook underdress

underhand undertake

Jonathan's Unday

Second Grade Phonics & Reading

Book 19
Lessons 101 to 105

Jonathan's Unday

Written and illustrated by
Brian Davis

My name is Jonathan. Do you know what an unday is? This is a story about my unday.

My unday happened on a Saturday. As the day unfolded, I became more unhappy. It was unlike most days.

2

I almost didn't get out of my room. I couldn't get the door unlocked. Then, the doorknob came unscrewed.

I couldn't find a screwdriver. Finally, I uncovered one on the floor. I fixed the doorknob. I unlocked the door. The door still didn't open.

I couldn't get it unstuck. I pounded until my dad came. He pushed it open.

"There's too much stuff underfoot," said my dad.

"Your room is untidy. No playing until it is uncluttered."

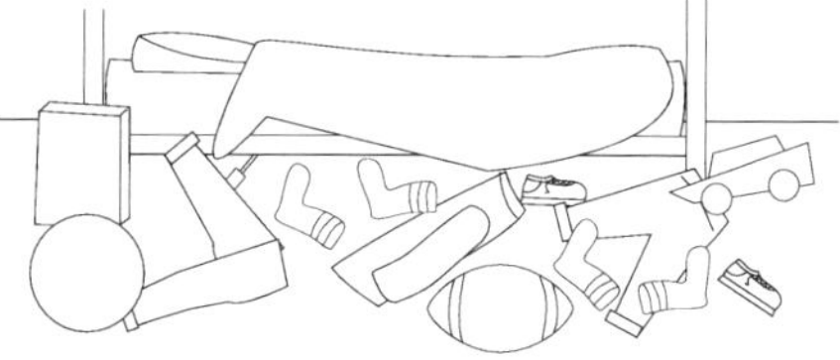

3

Jonathan's Unday

It seemed unfair. My dad was undermining my day.

I said, "Please understand. I need to unwind. Playing helps me do that."

Dad was unmoved. "Unless the room is clean, you will not play."

So, I undertook cleaning my room. I put my unclean clothes in a laundry basket. I picked up my toys. That uncovered most of the floor.

It took me until ten o'clock. Soon, my play time was under way.

4

5

I found some uncut boards. I took them to my tree house. I tied a rope around them. I pulled them up into the tree.

The rope came untied. The boards made a loud noise. My sister Rosie ran to the tree house.

"Can I help?" asked Rosie.

"No," I said. "You are unskilled at tree house making."

"You're being unkind, Jonathan," said Rosie. "I'm going to tell."

Soon, Rosie came back with my mom.

"You should understand what Rosie is feeling," said Mom. "Don't be so unkind."

So Rosie came up into the tree house.

6

7

Jonathan's Unday

Rosie began unwinding the rope. I was unaware of it until it was too late.

"Don't do that," I yelled. "That's my burglar trap."

Rosie had already unleashed my burglar trap. It couldn't be undone. A bucket of water fell on me. I was very unhappy.

I went back to my room. I had to get undressed. I couldn't get my coat unzipped. Then, I couldn't find an undershirt.

"You're all wet," said my mom. "Don't go outside until your hair is dry. It's unwise to play outside with wet hair. It's too cool today."

She unwrapped a new undershirt. "Please keep this one dry," said my mom.

8

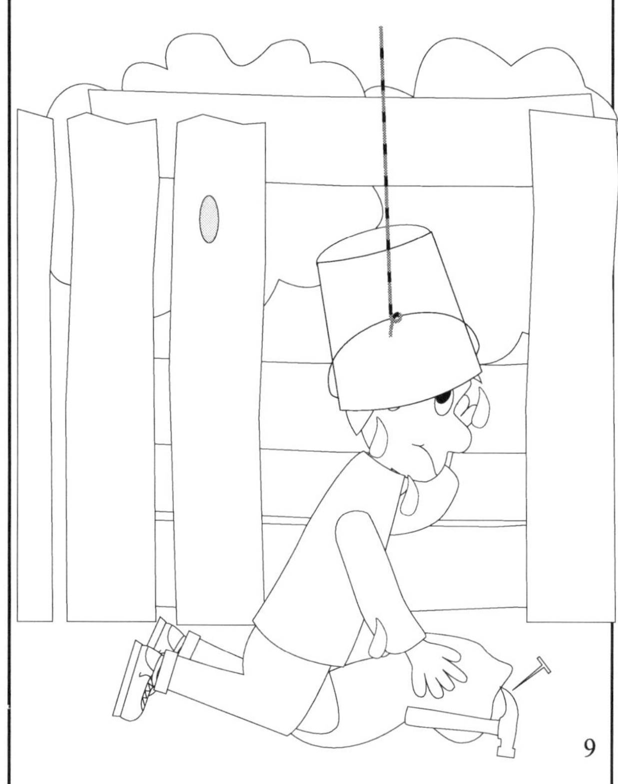

9

I didn't go outside until after lunch. Rosie played in my tree house. I thought it was so unfair.

Mom called me for lunch. I couldn't get my door unlocked again. The doorknob came unscrewed again. It was unreal.

I finally got my door open again. Oil got on my hands.

"Your hands are unclean," said my mom. "Go wash them. Don't eat until they're clean."

10

11

Jonathan's Unday

I went into the bathroom. I went to the faucet. I turned the handle. It came unbolted.

The handle fell off. Water filled up the sink. I couldn't get the sink unstopped.

I wrapped a rag around the faucet. That was unwise. Water sprayed all over.

I unwrapped the rag. My dad came in. He turned off the water.

"No lunch until this is cleaned up," said Dad.

It was so unfair. I unfolded some towels. I wiped up the water.

12

13

After lunch I went back outside. My neighbor's dog barked at me. That dog is so unfriendly.

I was unaware that the dog was unchained. I was unaware that the gate was unlatched.

I was unaware that my neighbor wasn't home. The dog chased me. I ran to my house. I couldn't get the door unlocked.

I ran to my tree house. The dog nipped my undershirt. The undershirt ripped.

I climbed until the dog couldn't reach me. An hour later, my neighbors came home. They called their dog. The dog left.

14

15

Jonathan's Unday

I rang the doorbell. Mom answered the door.

"I'm, sorry," said my mom. "I didn't know it wasn't unlocked."

Dad was in the bathroom. He was fixing the sink.

"I'm sorry," said my dad. "I didn't know it was unbolted. I'll fix your doorknob next."

My neighbor called. "I'm sorry," said my neighbor. "I didn't know my dog was unchained. I'll buy you a new undershirt."

Rosie made me a card. She had scribbled on it.

"It says I'm sorry for unwinding the rope," said Rosie.

"I understand," I said to everyone. "I don't want to be unforgiving."

Dad brought me a package.

"It's from your uncle. It's just for you."

I unwrapped the gift. It was an unglued model airplane.

"I thought I wasn't getting this until my birthday," I said. "It's just the thing to undo my unday."

16

Jonathan's Unday word list:

almost	playtime	underfoot	unlike
basket	pounded	undermining	unlocked
birthday	Saturday	undershirt	unmoved
boards	screwdriver	understand	unreal
burglar	scribbled	undertook	unscrewed
clean	sprayed	undo	unskilled
couldn't	thought	undone	unstopped
didn't	today	undressed	unstuck
doorbell	towels	unfair	untidy
doorknob	unaware	unfolded	untied
faucet	unbolted	unforgiving	until
finally	unchained	unfriendly	unwind
happened	uncle	unglued	unwinding
laundry	unclean	unhappy	unwise
neighbor	uncluttered	unkind	unwrapped
open	uncovered	unlatched	unzipped
outside	uncut	unleashed	water
package	under	unless	wrapped

Lesson 102

Lesson Objectives

1. Students will review adjectives. (L)
2. Students will add suffixes to spelling words. (S)
3. Students will unscramble spelling words. (S)
4. Students will read the story *Jonathan's Unday*. (R)
5. Students will copy sentences neatly and correctly. (H)

Materials

LAR
SAP
Jonathan's Unday
Writing Skills Workbook page is available

Teaching

1. Review the term adjective. **Adjectives describe nouns. Wecan say that adjectives modify nouns. That means to tell more about them.** Use the following sentence as an example: **The mouse squeaked. What is the noun in the sentence?** Write the sentence putting in a blank to write an adjective before the word mouse. The ______ mouse squeaked. Have students think of adjectives to put in the blank. Some examples might be: gray, little, happy, scared, silly.

   Write or say the following sentences and have students find the adjectives:
   The happy girl smiled. (happy) **The funny painting made us giggle.** (funny) **A big bee buzzed.** (big)

   Many times an adjective is the word between the words *a* or *the* and the noun. Point this out in the previous sentences. **Sometimes the position of the word can make it an adjective. Consider the word brick. The brick is a part of a house. We live in the brick house. Brick is a noun in the first sentence. Brick is an adjective in the second sentence.**

   Use the LAR page. **Adjectives add details. Look at the workbook page. Adjectives can add details that answer questions such as: How many? What kind? and Which one? Look at the three lists of adjectives that can answer the different questions. Add one more word to each list. The words *a, an,* and *the* are special adjectives called *articles.***

   Use the middle of the workbook page. **Read the sentences. Fill in the circle next to the words that are used as adjectives in the sentences. Underline the nouns they describe.**

   Use the bottom section: **Add adjectives to the three sentences. Don't use the same adjective twice.**

2. Use the SAP page. **Add suffixes to the different spelling words. Remember spelling rules for adding suffixes. Look at the first two rows of spelling words. They end with short vowel syllables and a single consonant. Double the last consonant before adding the suffixes ed and ing. Doubling the last consonant keeps words from being confused with long vowel words where the silent e is dropped.**

   The next row is words that end with two consonants. Does that last consonant need to be doubled? (no)

   Look at the next row. These words end with long vowel syllables. What will you need to do to add ing to these words? Think about the spelling rules for silent e. Does the rule apply to both words? Add ing to the words.

3. **On the bottom section, unscramble the six spelling words.**

4. Students will read pages 1 to 8 out loud. Next, ask the following questions:

   What tool did Jonathan need to fix the doorknob?
   (a screwdriver)
   What did Jonathan's father tell him to do before playing?
   (clean his room)
   What sound did Rosie hear that made her run to the tree house? (the boards landing)
   Why didn't Jonathan want Rosie to help? (She was unskilled at tree house making.)
   What did Rosie unwind? (a rope)
   How did Jonathan get wet? (The burglar trap fell on him.)
   Why did Jonathan's mother tell him to stay inside? (His hair was wet.)

5. Use the handwriting sheet or have the children write the following:
   Cursive: v, Write the words Violet, van
   I waited until the door was unlocked.
   We had to unplug the cord to untwist it.

LAR Answers

Answers vary on top and bottom

Middle section:

1. The unhappy boy untied his shoe.	● unhappy	○ boy	○ untied
2. Mom unwrapped the large box.	○ Mom	● large	○ box
3. We couldn't get the rusted bolt unstuck.	○ bolt	● rusted	○ unstuck
4. The unfriendly cat tried to bight me.	● unfriendly	○ tried	○ bight
5. I had to wear the unclean undershirt.	○ wear	○ undershirt	● unclean

SAP Answers

unsnapping	unplugging
unwrapped	unzipped
understanding	untwisting
underlining	unloading

until	unkind
undershirt	unselfish
unknown	unhappy

Lesson 103

Lesson Objectives

1. Students will combine sentences using a conjunction. (L)
2. Students will recognize incomplete sentences. (L)
3. Students will review spelling words. (S)
4. Students will read the story *Jonathan's Unday.* (R)
5. Students will copy sentences neatly and correctly. (H)

Materials

LAR
SAP
Jonathan's Unday

Teaching

1. Write the sentences: She won second prize. She was unhappy. **We've combined sentences before by choosing words from both sentences to add details. Today we're going to add a word to combine sentences. Words like *and, but,* and *or* are called conjunctions. Today, we'll use the conjunction *but.* Change the period on the first sentence to a comma. Next, add the word *but* and the second sentence. Change the first letter of the second sentence to lower case unless it is a proper noun (a name).** Demonstrate with the sample sentence: She won second prize, but she was unhappy.

   Use the top of the LAR workbook page. **Read the sample on the page. Bear cubs look cute. Don't try to pet them. What's the new sentence with the conjunction *but.*** (Bear cubs look cute, but don't try to pet them.)

   Combine the next two sets of sentences using the conjunction *but.*

2. Use the bottom of the LAR workbook. **Read each of the five sentences. Some of them are not complete sentences. Fill in the yes oval if the sentence is complete. Fill in the no oval if part of the sentence is missing, if it doesn't say a complete thought. That would make it an incomplete sentence.**

   Use the lines to turn the incomplete sentences into complete sentences.

3. Use the SAP workbook page. **The short words can be made from letters from the spelling words. Write the numbers for the spelling words that have the letters to make the smaller word. Write a number for each space.**

   On the bottom section, write the spelling words that can take the place of the underlined words in each sentence. Choose the words that change the sentences the least.

4. Review the first half of the book Jonathan's Unday. Next, read the second half of the book. After completing the story ask the students the following questions:

   What happened to the doorknob at lunch time? (It fell off again.)
   How did Jonathan get oil on his hands? (from fixing the doorknob)
   What happened to the faucet? (The handle came off.)
   What chased Jonathan? (the neighbor's dog)
   Where did Jonathan hide? (in his tree house)
   What did Jonathan's uncle give him? (an unglued model airplane)
   What do you think an unday is? (answers vary)

5. Use the handwriting sheet or have the children write the following:
   Cursive: w, the words Write, unwrap
   That undershirt is unclean. The unselfish people understood.

LAR Answers

The tailor was hooked to the truck,
but it came unhitched

The cub wanted to keep all the honey,
but its mother was unselfish.

1. The mole dug underground. (yes filled in) no
2. Unpacked the bags. yes (no filled in)
3. The undershirt on the bed. yes (no filled in)
4. Your shoe is untied. (yes filled in) no
5. It's unfair. (yes filled in) no

SAP Answers

sun 1,2,4,7,11
pan 6,9,11 won 5
in 1,3,4,7,12,13,14 pup 6
old 10 twin 7 dunk 12 fish 4 lint 13
red 1,2,3 pun 6,8,9,11,14
strand 2 loud 10 gulp 8 sit 1,7

1. unhappy
2. unwrap
3. unselfish
4. untwist
5. understand
6. unload
7. unkind

Lesson 104

Lesson Objectives

1. Students will review spelling words. (S)
2. Students will review adjectives. (L)
3. Students will read a poem. (R)
4. Students will write a story. (CW)
5. Students will read the story *Jonathan's Unday.* (R)
6. Students will copy sentences neatly and correctly. (H)

Materials

LAR
SAP
Jonathan's Unday

Teaching

1. Use the SAP page. **Match the spelling words to the descriptions. Write the answers on the lines.**

2. Review adjectives. **Remember adjectives modify nouns. Modify means to change or add details. An adjective might add details about how something looks, a person's feelings, or the number of things, or many other kinds of details.**

   Write the sentence: The _____ car stopped. Have students think of adjectives that can fill in the blank. Repeat with the sentence: The ______ puppy crossed the road.

3. **You've been reading a story about an unday. An unday is a made-up word for the story. Today you'll read a poem with a made-up word in the title. Look at the workbook page. What is the title of the poem?** (Travel Tips for Northeastern Unland) **What is the made-up word?** (Unland)

   What do you think Northeastern Unland would be like?

   Read the poem to find out. See how many words you can find with the un prefix. Find another word in the poem that's made up, like Unland. The poem is reprinted on the following page.

   Have students read the poem. Afterward, you may ask them to underline all the un words. Ask students to identify the other made-up word. (unmeal)

   Why do you think it is called an unmeal? (You don't eat it, because it is still alive.)

4. Students will write a story. Say: In the story *Jonathan's Unday* nothing seemed to go right. His unday had a lot of words that began with the prefix un in it. Have you ever had a day when lots of things didn't go right? Write a story about your own unday.

5. Read the book *Jonathan's Unday* again. Next, have students look at the back of the book and answer the following questions about the word list. You may do this orally or have students write answers:

   What word is the opposite of chained? (unchained)
   What day is a time to celebrate? (birthday)
   What is something that sprays water? (faucet)
   What word is something you wear? (undershirt)
   What word is someone who lives near you? (neighbor)
   What word is a tool? (screwdriver)
   What words have silent w's? (unwrapped, wrapped)
   What word is the opposite of uncluttered? (untidy)
   What word means the brother of your mother or father? (uncle)
   What words are compound words that begin with door? (doorbell, doorknob)
   What compound words begin with under? (underfoot, undermining, undershirt, understand, undertook)

6. Use the handwriting sheet or have the children write the following:

   Cursive: x,y, the words wax, Yes, my
   I was unaware that I had been unfair.
   Don't unlock the door until Mom is home.

Travel Tips for Northeastern Unland

If you ever travel to Northeastern Unland
There are a few things that you must first understand
Don't be too quick to decide to unpack
Soon it may be too late for you to turn back

The people there are unfriendly at best
Until they find out that you are an unguest
Then there is nothing they won't undertake
They'll stand watch at your door when you're unawake

Which is a good thing because the doors are unlocked
It seems quite unsafe with the creatures unblocked
Everything there may seem quite unreal
Especially when you don't eat an unmeal

It's so under prepared with the food all uncooked
It crawls to the table when its chain is unhooked
But don't you dare leave with your check unpaid
Give your dinner the cash and act unafraid

SAP Answers

unkind	until
unsnap	unselfish
undershirt	unwrap
underline	unzip
unhappy	understand
unknown	untwist
unload	unplug

Lesson 105

Lesson Objectives

1. Students will be tested on phonics concepts. (P)
2. Students will be tested on language concepts. (L)
3. Students will take a spelling test. (S)
4. Students will put sentences in sequential order. (R)
5. Students will read the story they have written. (R)
6. Students will copy a sentence neatly and correctly. (H)

Materials

LAR
Creative writing assignment from lesson 104
Assessment 105

Teaching

1. Use part A of the assessment as a phonics test. Have the students fill in the circles next to the words that complete the sentences.

2. Use part B of the assessment page. Students will read the sentences. Fill in the circle next to the word that was used as an adjective in the sentence.

3. Have students number their papers from 1 to 14. Give the following words as dictation.

   Spelling word list:

   1. understand, 2. unkind, 3. untwist, 4. unsnap, 5. unplug, 6. unload, 7. unzip,

   8. until, 9. unselfish 10. undershirt 11. unknown, 12. unwrap, 13. unhappy, 14. underline

4. Read the sentences on the LAR workbook page. Number them in the order that they happened in the story. Have students do the exercise without looking at the book. After finishing the assignment students may use their books to check or correct their answers.

   Bottom section: **Read the statements. Decide if they are true or false statements about the story, *Jonathan's Unday.***

5. Have students take turns reading the books or stories that were written during the creative writing section of the previous lesson.

6. Use the handwriting sheet or have the children write the following:
   Cursive: z, the words Zebra, unzip
   It is unwise to unhitch the trailer.
   If you are unforgiving you will be unhappy.

Lesson 105

Assessment Answers

1. unhappy
2. unbutton
3. underground
4. until
5. untied

1. unplugged
2. unselfish
3. blue
4. old
5. steel

LAR Answers

9
4
1
8
5
10
3
6
2
7

1. 

2. 

3. 

4. 

5. 

false

Lesson 106

Lesson Objectives

1. Students will read words that have the f sound spelled with gh or ph. (P)
2. Students will learn the meanings of parts of words. (L)
3. Students will spell words correctly. (S)
4. Students will prepare to read the story *The Elephant and the Alphabet.* (R)
5. Students will copy sentences neatly and correctly. (H)

Materials

LAR
SAP
The Elephant and the Alphabet
Writing Skills Workbook page is available

Word List: cough, enough, laugh, rough, tough, trough
alphabet, elephant, gopher, graph, orphan, pamphlet, phantom, phase,
Phillip, phone, phonebook, phonics, photocopy, phonograph,
photograph, phrase, physical, physics, telegraph, telephone

Teaching

1. Write the words taught and thought. Have students read the words. Ask**: What sound do the letters gh make in these words?** (They are silent) **Today you will learn more words that have gh. The letters gh are not silent in these words. The letters gh make the f sound.**

   Write the words cough and trough. Tell the students that these words have the short o vowel sound. Have students try to read the words. Write the words rough and tough. These words have the short u vowel sound. Have students read the words. Write the word enough. It also has the short u sound. It begins with the long e sound.

   Finally, write the word laugh. It has the short a sound. Have students read the word.

   Say: **Another consonant digraph also makes the f sound. The letters ph make the f sound.** Have the students read the words graph, phase, phrase and phone. Help students read the words alphabet, elephant, and gopher.

   Use the top of the LAR workbook page. Have students circle the letters that make the f sound.

2. Use the middle of the LAR workbook page. Students will build words using the roots. Introduce the four roots and their meanings: tele – from far away, phone - to use sound, graph – to write, and photo – to use light. Have students write the word from the list that matches the meanings of the roots.

3. Use the SAP page. Have students read and spell each word. Spelling list:rough, photograph, alphabet, tough, orphan, cough, phrase, gopher, elephant, laugh, enough, telephone, dolphin, pamphlet.

   Top section: **Sort the spelling words by syllables.**

   Bottom section: **Write the spelling words that rhyme with the three words. Three words rhyme with fluff.**

4. *The Elephant and the Alphabet* focuses on words beginning with the f sound spelled with ph or gh. In addition to those words, the following words may be new to students and will require some instruction: **finished, learned, school, tonight, village.** The vocabulary words and punctuation guide is on the bottom of the LAR page.

   The word *finished:* Break into syllables, fin-ished.
   The word *learned:* The letters e-a-r make the –er sound.
   The word *school:* The letters ch make the k sound.
   The word *tonight:* Break into syllables, to-night.
   The word *village:* Break into syllables, vil-lage (pronounced vil-aje).

   You may also review the following words: everyday, finally, library, taught, young, unkind.

   Introduce the story: Ask a student to read the title of the book. **What is the name of this story?** *(The Elephant and the Alphabet)* **What words have the f sound spelled with ph? (elephant, alphabet). In this story, an elephant wants to learn the alphabet. Why would an elephant want to learn the alphabet? Read the story to find out.**

   Students will read the words on the back of the book out loud.
   Students will silently read as much of the story as they can in the time allowed.

5. Use the handwriting sheet or have the children write the following:
   Note for students using the transitional handwriting program: Now that all the cursive letters have been introduced, students will begin writing sentences in cursive.

   We photographed the elephant.
   I cough when I have a cold.

LAR Answers

go(ph)er   lau(gh)   (ph)one

cou(gh)   pam(ph)let   (ph)otogra(ph)

telephone
phonograph
photocopy
telegraph
photograph

SAP Answers

One syllable (any order)
rough tough cough phrase laugh

Two syllables (any order)
orphan gopher enough dolphin pamphlet

Three syllables (any order)
photograph alphabet elephant telephone

Rhyming words
fluff: rough, tough, enough *(in any order)*
off: cough
graze: phrase

The Elephant and the Alphabet

Second Grade Phonics & Reading

Book 20
Lessons 106 to 110

The Elephant and the Alphabet

Written and illustrated by
Brian Davis

There was once an elephant who wanted to read. The elephant's name was Phillip. All the other elephants laughed at him.

"Elephants don't need to read. You're so silly, Phil," they teased.

But, Phillip did not give up. He knew of a school in the village. One day, Phillip sneaked into the school.

2

3

The Elephant and the Alphabet

He hid in the back row. Phillip sat on a bench. The boy next to him started screaming.

The teacher turned around. She gave Phillip an unkind look. Phillip pointed to the boy.

"The teacher must have thought I screamed," thought Phillip.

The whole class laughed.

"What is your name, young elephant?" asked the teacher.

"Phillip," mumbled Phillip.

"This is a school for orphans, Phillip. This is not a school for elephants. You must leave. Don't make me phone the game warden."

Phillip sighed, "I am an orphan. I've had a rough life. I can't read. Please teach me the alphabet."

4

5

"It must be tough being an orphan elephant," said the teacher. "Still, there is not enough room for you here. You may sit outside the window and watch."

Phillip was very pleased. The teacher taught him to make an a. Phillip then learned to make a b. Finally, Phillip made a c. The elephant learned their sounds.

"You are good at phonics," said the teacher. "I think you've learned enough for today."

Phillip was so happy. He rushed back to the other elephants.

"I'm learning the alphabet. I'm learning phonics. Soon, I'll know how to read."

The other elephants still laughed at him.

6

7

The Elephant and the Alphabet

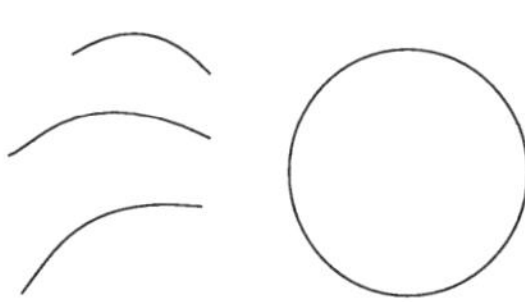

The next day, Phillip showed the teacher the letters a, b, and c.

"The phrase is true," said the teacher. "Elephants never forget."

Phillip learned more about phonics everyday. Soon, he had learned enough to read. Phillip knew the alphabet, too.

He was one of the best students in class. Phillip was even good at basketball. Of course, he was the basket. The other orphans loved him.

8

9

Phillip got a library card. He was reading stacks of books a day. The other elephants still laughed at him.

"I can teach you to read, too," Phillip told them. "It's not too tough. You know the phrase. An elephant never forgets. I can check out enough books for us all to read."

"Why do elephants need to know the alphabet?" asked the other elephants. "It's a waste of time. You could be eating leaves."

10

11

The Elephant and the Alphabet

Phillip marched off. He went to his reading spot. It was at the edge of the jungle. Phillip held a book in his trunk. He began to read.

That's when the trucks came. It was a group of poachers. Phillip watched the men from the edge of the jungle. The poachers trapped Phillip's herd of elephants.

The men put the elephants in cages. They covered the cages with tree branches. "The game warden can't see them from his airplane," said the men. "We'll come back tonight. We'll haul the elephants away."

12

13

"I've got to get to a telephone," thought Phillip.

He ran back to the village. Phillip found a telephone. He found a telephone book. He read the game warden's number. Phillip called the game warden.

"How can I find the elephants?" asked the game warden.

"Just fly over," said Phillip.

The game warden hopped in his airplane. Phillip had finished just as the airplane flew over. The game warden saw the logs. Phillip had made a sign.

"That elephant knows phonics," laughed the game warden.

14

15

The Elephant and the Alphabet

The game warden landed the airplane. He opened the cages.

"It's a good thing Phillip knows the alphabet," said the game warden. "I would have never found you."

The elephants hugged Phillip with their trunks.

"Thank you, Phillip. We shouldn't have laughed at you. It is good to know the alphabet," said the elephants.

Phillip smiled.

The next day, the elephants started school. Phillip taught them the alphabet. He taught them phonics. All the elephants loved Phillip. He had saved their lives. That was something the elephants never forgot.

16

The Elephant and the Alphabet word list:

airplane	haul	Phil	taught
alphabet	hugged	Phillip	telephone
basketball	jungle	phone	thought
don't	laughed	phonics	tonight
edge	learned	phrase	tough
elephant	library	poachers	unkind
enough	loved	rough	village
everyday	mumbled	school	wanted
finally	never	screaming	warden
finished	once	sign	watch
forget	opened	sneaked	window
forgot	orphans	something	you're
happy	outside	students	young

Lesson 107

Lesson Objectives

1. Students will learn the review the term adjective. (L)
2. Students will proofread sentences. (S)
3. Students will use spelling words in sentences. (S)
4. Students will read the story *The Elephant and the Alphabet.* (R)
5. Students will copy sentences neatly and correctly. (H)

Materials

LAR
SAP
The Elephant and the Alphabet

Teaching

1. Review the term adjective. **Adjectives describe nouns.** Use the following sentence as an example: **The cute gopher dug a hole. What word is an adjective?** (cute) **What word is a verb?** (dug) **What words are nouns?** (gopher, hole)

   Use the top of the LAR workbook page. **Read the sentences. A word is black print. Fill in the circle next to the word that tells how the black word was used.**

   Bottom section: **Add an adjective to each sentence on the lines. Don't use the same adjective twice.**

2. Use the SAP page. Top section: **Read the two sentences. Circle the mistakes. Write the sentences correctly on the lines.**

3. Bottom section: **Write the spelling word that can take the place of the underlined words and change the spelling the least.**

4. Students will read pages 1 to 8 out loud. Next, ask the following questions:

   What was the elephant's name? (Phillip)
   Where was the school? (It was in the village.)
   Why did a boy start screaming? (Phillip was sitting next to him.)
   Why did the class laugh? (Phillip was pointing at the boy.)
   What were the first letters Phillip learned? (a, b, and c)
   What game was Phillip good at? (basketball)
   What phrase did the teacher say was true? (Elephants never forget.)

5. Use the handwriting sheet or have the children write the following:

   The sandpaper was rough.
   We made a pie graph.

LAR Answers

1. noun
2. adjective
3. verb
4. adjective
5. noun

Bottom section answers vary.

SAP Answers

The elephant called on the telephone.

Was a dolphin on the pamphlet?

1. gopher
2. tough
3. laugh
4. cough
5. enough

Lesson 108

Lesson Objectives

1. Students will use comprehension skills and practice answering multiple choice questions. (L)
2. Students will write spelling words. (S)
3. Students will read the story *The Elephant and the Alphabet.* (R)
4. Students will copy sentences neatly and correctly. (H)

Materials

LAR
SAP
Questions Word Poster
The Elephant and the Alphabet
Writing Skills Workbook page is available

Teaching

1. Use LAR workbook page. The text from the article is reprinted on the next page. **Look at the workbook page. What is the title of the article?** (Two Kinds of Elephants) **Just by quickly glancing at the words can you tell me the names of the two kinds of elephants?** (African elephants and Asian elephants) **What helped you find the answers quickly?** (The words in bold print.)

   Read about elephants. Answer the questions. They are multiple choice. Fill in the circle next to the best answer.

   How are the trunks of the two kinds of elephants alike? (they have lips at the end.) **How are they different?** (The African elephant has 2 lips. The Asian elephant has 1 lip.)

   Use the Question Poster. **Write four questions about walruses or warthogs. Use the question words to begin the questions.**

   Have students do further research about either African or Asian elephants compare the information to the information on the workbook page.

2. Use the SAP workbook page. Top section: **Fit the spelling words into the grid. The letter e is your first clue. The blue column marks the longest word.**

   Bottom section: **Fill in the missing vowels to spell the spelling words.**

3. Review the first half of the book *The Elephant and the Alphabet*. Next, read the second half of the book. After completing the story ask the students the following questions:

   Where did Phillip get his books? (At the library)
   Phillip liked to read. What would the other elephants rather do? (eat leaves)
   Who was in the trucks? (poachers)
   Why did the poachers hide the cages? (so the game warden couldn't find them.)
   How did knowing how to read help Phillip use a phonebook? (He could read the warden's name)
   How did Phillip make a sign? (He moved logs)
   What did Phillip's sign say? (Elephants need help)
   Why did the elephant decide they wanted to read? (They saw how important it was.)

4. Use the handwriting sheet or have the children write the following:
   A gopher made a hole. The monkeys made us laugh.

Two Kinds of Elephants

There are two kinds of elephants. There are **African elephants** and there are **Asian elephants**. They are unlike in many ways. The African elephants are bigger. They grow to 13 feet tall. Asian elephants grow up to nine feet tall.

Their ears are also unlike. African elephants have larger ears. They are five feet long. They are four feet wide. An Asian elephant's ears are three feet long. Their ears are only two feet wide. An elephant's ears help keep them cool. African elephants live in hotter places. That's why they need bigger ears.

Both kinds of elephants have trunks. The trunks have lips at the end. The lips help them grab things. African elephants have two lips. Asian elephants just have one.

Even their toenails are unlike. Both have five toenails on their front feet. The Asian elephant has four toenails on its back feet. African elephants have three toenails on their back feet.

LAR Answers

1. B 2. C
3. C 4. A
5. B 6. C

SAP Answers

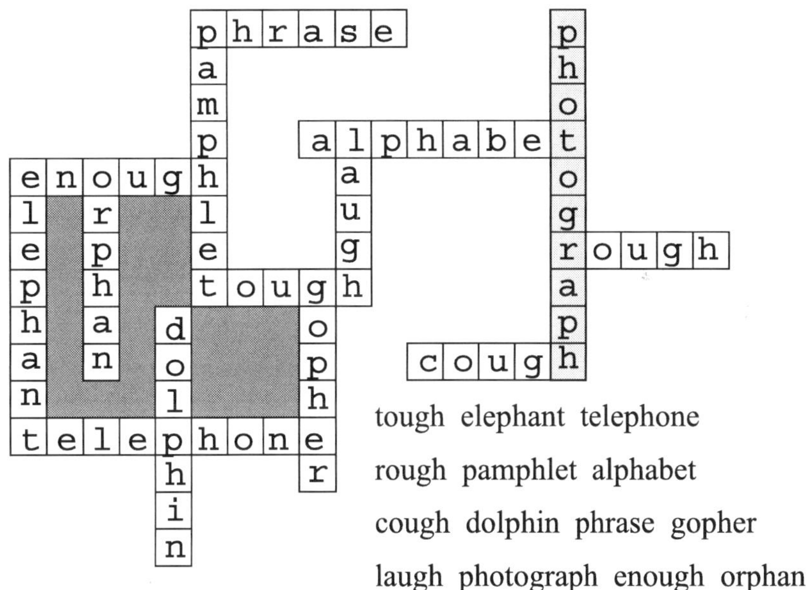

Lesson 109

Lesson Objectives

1. Students will compare characters. (L)
2. Studetnts will match spelling words to descriptions. (S & L)
3. Students will write a story. (CW)
4. Students will read the story *The Elephant and the Alphabet.* (R)
5. Students will copy sentences neatly and correctly. (H)

Materials

LAR
SAP
The Elephant and the Alphabet

Teaching

1. Use the LAR page. This activity can be completed independently by the student, but it is suggested that it be completely teacher directed. Teacher directed: Read each characteristic at the bottom of the page. Ask students which where to place that characteristic on the circle diagrams. The overlapping circles show where a characteristic would apply to more than one character. Have students tell specific details from the story that support the choice. Students will write the characteristic in the circles.

   Answers may vary, but suggested answers are in the answer section of the next page. Word list:

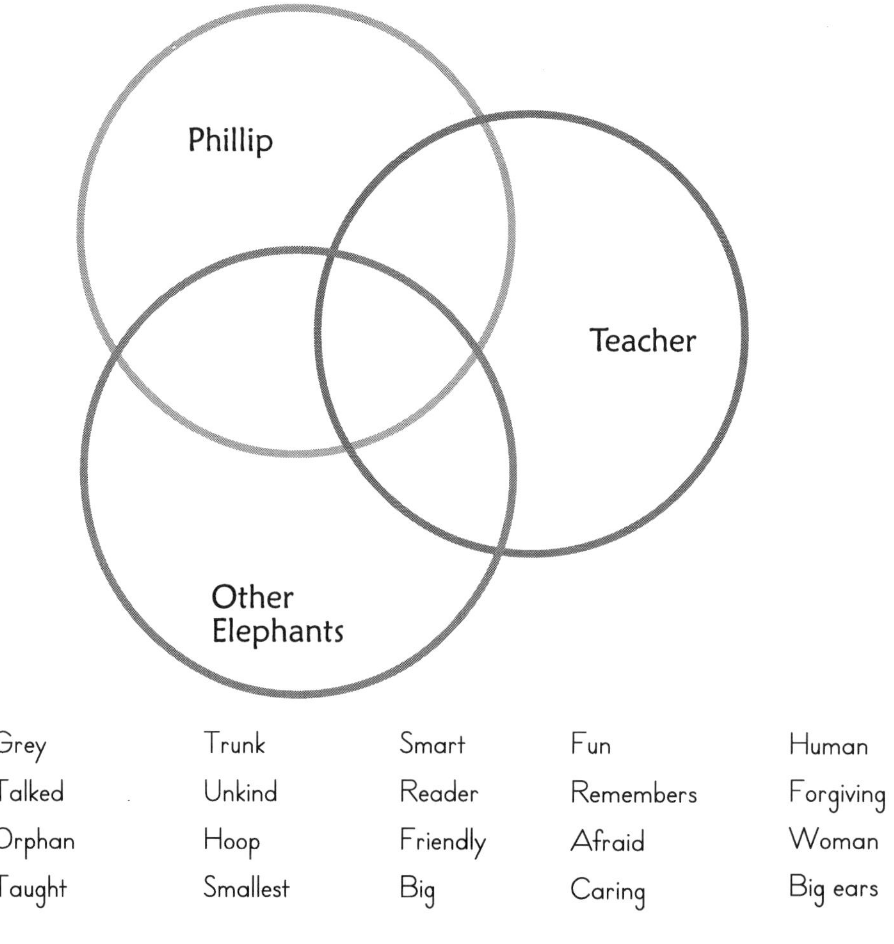

Grey	Trunk	Smart	Fun	Human
Talked	Unkind	Reader	Remembers	Forgiving
Orphan	Hoop	Friendly	Afraid	Woman
Taught	Smallest	Big	Caring	Big ears

2. Use the SAP page. **Match the spelling words to the descriptions. Write your answers on the lines.**

3. Students will write a story. Say: In the story, ***The Elephant and the Alphabet***, the elephants learned to read. One day, Phillip decided he wanted to learn math, too. Write a story about Phillip learning math. Why would he want to learn math? What are things he would do? Would he count, add, subtract, divide, or multiply? How would he learn math?

4. Read the book The Elephant and the Alphabet again. Next, have students look at the back of the book and answer the following questions about the word list. You may do this orally or have students write answers:

   What word is the opposite of kind? (unkind)
   What words are places to learn things? (library, school)
   What word is the past tense of forget? (forgot)
   What word is the opposite of smooth? (rough)
   What words have ph in the middle? (elephant, orphans, telephone)
   What word begins with a vowel and ends with the f sound? (enough)
   What word means people who hunt illegally? (poachers)
   What word is a synonym for town? (village)
   Who is like a park policeman? (warden)
   What words are compound words? (airplane, basketball, everyday, outside, something, tonight)
   What words are contractions? (don't, you're)

5. Use the handwriting sheet or have the children write the following:

   The telephone kept ringing.
   Phillip is learning phonics.

LAR Answers

Suggested answers- categorizing other ways is acceptable if students can give a reasonable explanation

Phillip: forgiving, orphan, hoop, fun
Teacher: smallest, human, woman, taught
All: remembers, talked
Phillip and elephants: gray, big ears, big, trunk
Phillip and teacher: smart, reader, friendly, caring
Other elephants: unkind, afraid

SAP Answers

laugh	elephant
photograph	cough
alphabet	tough
orphan	phrase
telephone	pamphlet
dolphin	enough
rough	gopher

Lesson 110

Lesson Objectives

1. Students will be tested on phonics concepts. (P)
2. Students will be tested on language concepts. (L)
3. Students will take a spelling test. (S)
4. Students will sequence sentences. (R)
5. Students will read the story they have written. (R)
6. Students will copy a sentence neatly and correctly. (H)

Materials

LAR
Creative writing assignment from lesson 109
Assessment 110
The Elephant and the Alphabet

Teaching

1. Use part A of the assessment as a phonics test. Have the students fill in the circles next to the words that complete the sentences.

2. Use part B of the assessment page. Students will read the sentences. A word is underlined. Fill in the circle next to the word that tells how the word was used (noun, verb, adjective).

3. Have students number their papers from 1 to 14. Give the following words as dictation.

   Spelling word list:

   1. alphabet, 2. tough, 3. phrase, 4. rough, 5. telephone, 6. cough, 7. photograph,

   8. laugh, 9. gopher 10. enough 11. elephant, 12. orphan, 13. pamphlet, 14. dolphin

4. Use the LAR page. **Read the sentences on the workbook page. Number them in the order that they happened in the story.** Have students do the exercise without looking at the book. After finishing the assignment students may use their books to check or correct their answers.

   Bottom section: **Read the statements about the story. Are they true or false? Fill in ovals to mark your answers.**

5. Have students take turns reading the books or stories that were written during the creative writing section of the previous lesson.

6. Use the handwriting sheet or have the children write the following:

   Do you have enough money?
   The cow drank from a trough.

Assessment Answers

1. rough
2. trough
3. elephant's
4. phonebook
5. Phonics

1. adjective
2. noun
3. adjective
4. verb
5. noun

LAR Answers

10
2
7
4
9
3
8
5
1
6

1. true (filled in) false
2. true false (filled in)
3. true false (filled in)
4. true (filled in) false
5. true (filled in) false

Lesson 111

Lesson Objectives

1. Students will read words that have the short e sound spelled with ea. (P)
2. Students will spell words correctly. (S)
3. Students will use comprehension skills. (L)
4. Students will prepare to read the story *Long John Featherhead.* (R)
5. Students will copy sentences neatly and correctly. (H)

Materials

LAR
SAP
Long John Featherhead
Writing Skills Workbook page is available

Word List: ahead, bread, breakfast, breast, breath, breathless, cleanse, dead, deaf, death, dread, feather, head, headache, health, heavy, instead, lead, meadow, measure, peasant, pheasant, pleasant, read, ready, realm, spread, stead, steady, stealth, sweat, thread, threat, threaten, tread, treasure, unhealthy, unpleasant, unread, unsteady, wealth, wealthy, weapon, weather

Teaching

1. Write the words team and great. Have students read the words. Ask**: What sound do the letters ea make in the word team?** (Long e) **What sound do they make in the word great?** (Long a) **The letters ea make another sound.** Write the word head. **This word is something that sits on your neck. What is it?** (head) **What sound do the letters ea make in the word head?** (short e)

   Have students read the words: bread, dead, sweat, threat, and wealth.

   Next, introduce some to the two-syllable words: feather, meadow, measure, pheasant, ready, treasure, weather.

   Introduce the compound words: breakfast, headache (the ch makes the k sound), instead.

   Introduce the words with prefixes: ahead, unpleasant, unhealthy, unsteady, unread.

2. Use the SAP page. Have students read and spell each word. Spelling list: ready, feather, bread, healthy, spread,weather, measure, head, treasure, pleasant, heavy, pheasant, sweat, thread

   Top section: **Sort the spelling words by syllables.**

   Bottom section: **Add suffixes or prefixes to the spelling words at the bottom of the page. What spelling rule will apply to adding ing to treasure?** (Drop the e, add ing) **Look at the word measure. You'll add the suffix *ment.* Will you drop the silent e? It might look like you should, but the suffix begins with a consonant, m. If the suffix begins with a consonant, silent e's are not dropped. If you dropped the e it would look like the r formed a consonant blend with the m like in the word *arm.* So, the e stays to show that the m begins a new syllable.**

   Look at heavy. What will happen to the *y*? (changes to i)

3. Use the top of the LAR page. **Read the words and definitions. Complete the sentences using the words.**

4. *Long John Featherhead* focuses on words beginning with the f sound spelled with ph or gh. In addition to those words, the following words may be new to students and will require some instruction: **moving, forehead, John.** The words and pronunciation guide are printed on the bottom of the LAR page.

 The word *moving:* Sounds like moo-ving
 The word *forehead:* Break into two words, fore head
 The name *John:* The h is silent.

 You may also review the following words: daughter, pretty, underneath, salesman, without

 Introduce the story: Ask a student to read the title of the book.
 What is the name of this story? *(Long John Featherhead)*
 What do you think Long John Featherhead is? (a pirate)
 Long John Featherhead wants to be a pirate, but he has a problem. He's missing a few things. Read the story to find out if he can solve his problem.

 Students will read the words on the back of the book out loud.
 Students will silently read as much of the story as they can in the time allowed.

5. Use the handwriting sheet or have the children write the following:

 Father toasted the bread.
 We ate it for breakfast.

LAR Answers

1 pleasant
2. steady
3. dread
4. tread
5. pheasant
6. realm
7. instead
8. stealth

SAP Answers

One syllable (any order):
bread spread head sweat thread

Two syllables (any order)
ready feather healthy weather
measure treasure pleasant heavy pheasant

Suffixes

treasuring unhealthy
measurement threading
unpleasant forehead heaviness

Long John Featherhead

A long time ago, pirates roamed the seas. They threatened people on ships. Everyone dreaded them. Long John Featherhead wanted to be a pirate. He tried to be the most dreaded of all.

Every dreaded pirate had a parrot. Long John Featherhead went to the Pirate Pet Shop. Parrots were not cheap. Long John Featherhead was not wealthy.

So, he bought a pheasant instead. "I bought you instead of a parrot," Long John Featherhead told the pheasant. "So, I will call you Instead. Now we need a pirate ship."

2

3

Long John Featherhead

Long John Featherhead went to a store. It was Pleasant Pete's Pirate Ship Store.

"May I please have a pirate ship?" Long John Featherhead asked Pleasant Pete.

"Pretty please," squawked Instead.

"That's a funny looking parrot," said Pleasant Pete.

"He's a pheasant," said Long John Featherhead.

"I'm a pleasant pheasant," squawked Instead.

"He is rather pleasant for a pheasant," agreed Pleasant Pete. "I'll trade you a ship for the pheasant."

Long John Featherhead dreaded trading his pheasant. He needed a ship. Every dreaded pirate had a ship.

"OK," said Long John Featherhead.

He named his ship Instead. He had a ship instead of a pheasant.

"Now I need a crew," said Long John
4 Featherhead.

5

Long John Featherhead went to the Unpleasant Help Store.

"What do you want?" growled the salesman.

"I need a pirate ship crew," answered Long John Featherhead.

"I've got just the crew. They love to threaten people," said the salesman.

"Are they unpleasant?" asked Long John Featherhead.

"They are very dreaded," smiled the salesman.

"What will it cost me?" asked Long John Featherhead.

"Your ship," answered the salesman.

A ship was no good without a crew.

"OK," said Long John Featherhead.

The salesman threw in T-shirts for the crew. The shirts read, "Crew Instead."

"Because, you have a crew instead of a ship," laughed the salesman.

"Great," said Long John Featherhead. "Now I need a cannon."

6

7

Long John Featherhead

Every dreaded pirate had a cannon. It was a pirate's best weapon. Long John Featherhead went to the cannon store. A pleasant salesman was ready to help.

"Our latest cannon will make you dreaded. It's called the Instead model. It fires feathers instead of cannon balls.

The boom gives people headaches. The feathers make them laugh. Have you ever laughed with a headache? It really hurts. You can threaten all kinds of ships," said the salesman.

"I've read about this cannon," said Long John Featherhead. "What will it cost me?"

"We've had a boom in cannon sales. We need help. One unpleasant pirate crew will do," said the salesman.

"That's what I thought," said Long John Featherhead. "OK. I'll take the Instead Cannon."

The cannon was very heavy.

"I'll need a wagon," said Long John Featherhead.

8

9

The wagon maker was Fred Instead. He measured the cannon.

"It looks heavy. You'll need my heavy load model." said Fred Instead. "That wagon costs a lot."

"How much?" asked Long John Featherhead.

"I need a good cannon. It threatens burglars. I'll trade you a wagon for the cannon," said Fred Instead.

Long John Featherhead thought about it. Moving a heavy cannon is unpleasant. He dreaded it.

"OK," said Long John Featherhead.

Fred Instead had a wagon ready. "You'll treasure your new Instead wagon. Now all you need is a mule," said Fred Instead.

"I forgot," said Long John Featherhead. "I'd be out of breath pulling that wagon. No one dreads a breathless pirate."

"It's not good for your health," said Fred Instead.

10

11

Long John Featherhead

Long John Featherhead went to the stable.

"I have a new Fred Instead wagon. I need a mule."

The man in the stable scratched his head. "I have a mule for sale. I thought he was a horse. He was a mule instead. I call him Instead."

"I'm not surprised. What will it cost me?" asked Long John Featherhead.

"How about that Fred Instead wagon?" asked the man in the stable.

Long John Featherhead was ready for that. Pulling a wagon made him breathless.

"I'll take Instead the mule, instead of the wagon," said Long John Featherhead.

He could at least ride it.

"Mules need a steady supply of grass," said the man at the stable.

"I'll need a meadow," said Long John Featherhead.

12

13

Long John Featherhead went to the farmer.

"I need a meadow for my mule," said Long John Featherhead.

The farmer rubbed his head. "I have a patch of meadow. I call it Instead Meadow. I just let the grass grow instead of farming it."

"What will it cost me?" asked Long John Featherhead.

"My old mule is almost dead," said the farmer. "I'd like your mule, Instead."

"OK," said Long John Featherhead.

So, he took a pleasant walk in his meadow. He came upon a rock. An X was on the rock. Long John Featherhead lifted the rock. Underneath was a treasure chest.

"I'm wealthy," thought Long John Featherhead.

14

15

Long John Featherhead

Long John Featherhead no longer needed to be a pirate. He was wealthy. He farmed his meadow, Instead.

Long John Featherhead met Fred Instead's daughter. Her name was Beth. She was a pleasant peasant. They fell in love. He married Beth Instead.

Long John Featherhead bought back his pheasant, Instead.

"Long John Featherhead, breakfast is ready," called Beth one day.

"Please call me John, instead," said Long John Featherhead.

"That is more pleasant," said Instead the pheasant.

John never became a dreaded pirate. He was the pleasant farmer of the meadow, instead.

16

Long John Featherhead word list:

about	feathers	measured	stable
afford	forehead	moving	steady
almost	forgot	mule	supply
Beth	great	new	surprised
bought	head	parrot	thought
breakfast	headaches	patch	threaten
breath	health	peasant	threatened
breathless	heavy	people	threatens
burglars	help	pheasant	threw
cannon	instead	pirate	trading
crew	John	pleasant	treasure
daughter	latest	please	T-shirts
dead	laughed	pretty	underneath
didn't	least	rather	unpleasant
dreaded	lived	read	wagon
every	looking	ready	wanted
everyone	love	salesman	wealthy
farmer	married	scratched	weapon
Featherhead	meadow	seas	without
		squawked	you'll

Lesson 112

Lesson Objectives

1. Students will group words according to sounds. (P)
2. Students will categorize words based on meanings. (L)
3. Students will review spelling words. (S)
4. Students will read the story *Long John Featherhead.* (R)
5. Students will copy sentences neatly and correctly. (H)

Materials

LAR
SAP
Long John Featherhead
Writing Skills Workbook page is available

Teaching

1. Use the top of the LAR workbook page. **Group the words based on sounds the letters ea make. The words make long e, long a, or short e. Write the words from the list on the correct lines.**

2. Use the bottom of the LAR workbook page. **Group the words based on the category. Write the words from the second list on the lines.**

3. Use the SAP page. Top section: **Read the words. Part of each word is a spelling word. Write the spelling word on the lines.**

   Bottom section: **Look at the short words. Find the spelling words that have the letters to make the short words. Write the numbers on the lines.**

4. Students will read pages 1 to 8 out loud. Next, ask the following questions:

   What kind of bird did Long John buy? (a pheasant)
   What did Long John get for the pheasant? (a ship)
   What did the crew's T-shirts say? (Crew Instead)
   Why? (Because Long John had a crew instead of a ship.)
   What was a pirate's best weapon? (a cannon)
   How was the Instead Cannon different? (It shot feathers.)
   How did the cannon threaten people? (It gave them headaches and made them laugh.)
   Why did the cannon salesman want the pirate crew? (Sales were booming.)

5. Use the handwriting sheet or have the children write the following:

   Flowers are in the meadow.
   Heavy work makes me sweat.

LAR Answers

Long e	Long a	Short e
seal	great	head
reason	steak	steady
teacher	break	measure

Kinds of Birds	Parts of a body	Places plants grow
pheasant	head	yard
chicken	arm	meadow
parrot	foot	field

SAP Answers

feather thread

spread measure head

bread heavy sweat

wet 6,13 tree 2,6,9
red 1,3,5,14 had 8,14
hay 4,11 dear 3,14 ray 1 west 13
ram 7 bed 3 slept 10 spare 5
he 2,4,6,8,11,12,14 see 7,9
sea 5,7,9,10,12,13 heart 2
tea 2,4,6,9,10,12,13,14

Lesson 113

Lesson Objectives

1. Students will use vocabulary skills. (L)
2. Students will use spelling words in sentences. (S)
3. Students will use proofread sentences. (S & L)
4. Students will read the story *Long John Featherhead.* (R)
5. Students will copy sentences neatly and correctly. (H)

Materials

LAR
SAP
Long John Featherhead

Teaching

1. Use the LAR page. **Read the clues and write words in the grid to complete the crossword puzzle. Choose the words from the word list.**

2. Use the top of the SAP workbook page. **Read the sentences. A word is underlined. Choose the spelling word that can take the place of the underlined word. Choose the word that changes the meaning of the sentence the least.**

3. Use the bottom of the SAP workbook page. **Proofread each sentence. Look for spelling and punctuation errors. Write the sentences correctly on the lines.**

4. Review the first half of the book *Long John Featherhead.* Next, read the second half of the book. After completing the story ask the students the following questions:

   Why did the wagon cost so much? (It was the heavy load model.)
   Who made the wagon? (Fred Instead)
   Why did Long John trade the wagon? (It was too hard to pull.)
   What did the mule need? (A steady supply of grass.)
   Why was the mule named Instead? (The owner thought it was a horse instead of a mule.)
   What did the farmer give Long John for the mule? (The Instead Meadow)
   How did Long John get wealthy? (He found a treasure chest in the meadow.)
   Who did Long John Featherhead marry? (Beth Instead, Fred's daughter.)
   Why do you think Long John didn't dread not being a pirate? (answers vary)
   What do you think would have been bad for John if he had become a pirate? (answers vary)

5. Use the handwriting sheet or have the children write the following:

   The dog smelled a pheasant.
   You need thread to sew.

LAR Answers

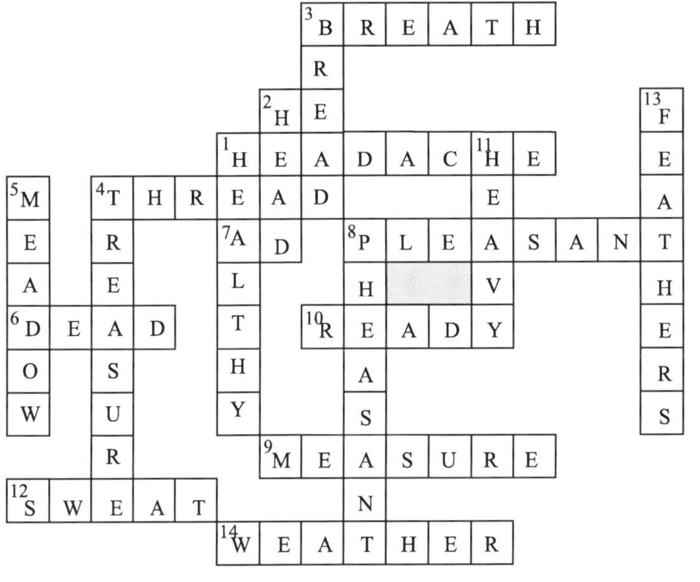

SAP Answers

1. bread
2. measure
3. treasure
4. pleasant
5. healthy
6. head
7. ready

The pheasant lost a brown feather.

The weather forecast called for heavy snow.

Lesson 114

Lesson Objectives

1. Students will combine sentences. (L)
2. Students will recognize complete and incomplete sentences. (L)
3. Students will write spelling words. (S)
4. Students will write a story. (CW)
5. Students will read the story *Long John Featherhead.* (R)
6. Students will copy sentences neatly and correctly. (H)

Materials

LAR
SAP
Long John Featherhead

Teaching

1. Use the top of the LAR page. Students will combine two sentences by adding details. This is like previous lessons, only this time the word choices are not underlined. Work through the example on the top of the workbook page.

   The eagle has white feathers. They are in its head.
   Combined: **The eagle has white feathers on its head.**

   Combine the other two sentences. Write the new sentences on the lines.

2. Use the bottom of the LAR page. **Read the sentences. Two of them are missing parts. Are the sentences complete or incomplete? Fill in yes if the sentence is complete. Fill in no if the sentence is not complete.**

   Complete the incomplete sentences on the lines.

3. Use the SAP page. **Match the spelling words to the descriptions. Write your answer on the lines.**

4. Students will write a story. Say: **In the story *Long John Featherhead*, Long John Featherhead tried to be a pirate. Later, his younger brother Short Jim Featherhead did become a pirate. He wasn't very good at it. Write a story about Short Jim Featherhead.**

5. Read the book *Long John Featherhead* again. Next, have students look at the back of the book and answer the following questions about the word list. You may do this orally or have students write answers:

   What words are opposites of pleasant? (unpleasant, dreaded)
   What words have the long e sound of the letters ea? (least, please, seas, underneath)
   What word has the long a sound of the letters ea? (great)
   What word is the opposite of light? (heavy)
   What word is a weapon? (cannon)
   What word is a synonym for field? (meadow)
   What word is a meal? (breakfast)
   What word is the opposite of poor? (wealthy)
   What three words all have the same root word? (threaten, threatened, threatens)
   What is the root word? (threat)
   What words are kinds of birds? (parrot, pheasant)

6. Use the handwriting sheet or have the children write the following:

   The treasure is underground.
   I will measure the board.

LAR Answers

Answers may vary. Likely answers:

We saw a pheasant in a meadow.

We ate a pleasant breakfast.

1. yes ⬬
2. yes ⬬
3. ⬬ no
4. ⬬ no
5. ⬬ no

SAP Answers

heavy	pleasant
feather	treasure
pheasant	bread
weather	healthy
measure	thread
sweat	ready
head	spread

Lesson 115

Lesson Objectives

1. Students will be tested on phonics concepts. (P)
2. Students will be tested on language concepts. (L)
3. Students will take a spelling test. (S)
5. Students will read the story they have written. (R)
6. Students will copy a sentence neatly and correctly. (H)

Materials

LAR
Creative writing assignment from lesson 109
Assessment 110

Teaching

1. Use part A of the assessment as a phonics test. Have the students fill in the circles next to the words that complete the sentences.

2. Use part B of the assessment page. Students will complete the sentence that tells how the words in the list are alike.

3. Have students number their papers from 1 to 14. Give the following words as dictation.

   Spelling word list:

   1. feather, 2. head, 3. bread, 4. unpleasant, 5. measure, 6. weather,

   7. healthy, 8. heavy, 9. breakfast 10. ready 11. pheasant, 12. spread

4. Read the sentences on the LAR workbook page. Number them in the order that they happened in the story. Have students do the exercise without looking at the book. After finishing the assignment students may use their books to check or correct their answers.

   Bottom section: **Read the statements about the story. Are they true or false? Fill in ovals to mark your answers.**

5. Have students take turns reading the books or stories that were written during the creative writing section of the previous lesson.

6. Use the handwriting sheet or have the children write the following:

   The weather is pleasant.
   Do not play with weapons.

Assessment Answers

Phonics:

1. measure
2. sweat
3. wealthy
4. breakfast
5. treasure

Language:

1. pheasant
2. weather
3. weapons
4. head
5. bread

LAR Answers

4
8
6
2
7
10
3
5
1
9

1.  

2.  

3.  

4.  

5.  false

Lesson 116

Lesson Objectives

1. Students will review words spelled with –ew, -ou, uy, and –ie. (P)
2. Students will review using the correct tense. (L)
3. Students will review spelling words. (S)
4. Students will copy sentences neatly and correctly. (H)

Materials

LAR
SAP

Lessons 116 to 118 will review phonics and language concepts taught in lessons 81 to 115. There will be no reading book or creative writing assignment given. Students may read books from previous weeks or have students try reading library books. **Lessons 119 and 120** will be set aside for the third unit test.

Teaching

1. Choose words from the two lists. Write the words. Ask students what letters made the vowel sounds.

   Use the top of the LAR workbook page. Read the sentences. Letters are missing in the words. Fill in the missing vowels.

2. Ask what it means when we talk about the past tense of a verb. Have students change the following words to the past tense: cry, fly, grow, try, tie. (cried, flew, grew, tried, tied)

   Bottom of the LAR workbook page: Fill in the circle next to the word that has the correct tense to complete the sentence.

3. Use the SAP page. Have the students read and spell each spelling word. These are review words from previous lessons. Spelling list: grew, soup, walrus, warm, taught, bought, understand, unwrap, elephant, laugh, rough, feather, pheasant, eye, pie.

   Top section: **Alphabetize the spelling words.**

   Bottom section: **Add suffixes to the spelling words. The spelling only changes on the root of one word. Which word is it?** (unwrap)

4. Use the handwriting sheet or have the children write the following sentences:

   Did you buy soup and pie?
   A screw was in the plywood.

LAR Answers

1. The wind blew dust in my eyes.
2. I ate the soup and pie.
3. We grew the carrots in the stew.
4. That guy tried to tighten the screw.
5. The cat spied a group of mice.

1. fry
2. cried
3. flying
4. buys
5. dried

SAP Answers

1. brought
2. elephant
3. eye
4. feather
5. grew
6. laugh

1. pheasant
2. pie
3. soup
4. tough
5. understand
6. unwrap
7. walrus
8. warm

understanding unwrapped

warmed

toughest laughter

Lesson 117

Lesson Objectives

1. Students will review words with spelled with wa, au, and ought. (P)
2. Students will review words with the un prefix. (P)
3. Students will review spelling words. (S)
4. Students will copy sentences neatly and correctly. (H)

Materials

LAR
SAP

Teaching

1. Use the top of the LAR workbook page. **Complete the sentences using words from the lists.**

2. Use the bottom of the LAR workbook page. **Fill in the words that matches the descriptions.**

3. Use the SAP page. Top section: **Fit the spelling words into the grid. The only clue is the blue column. It marks the longest word.**

   Bottom section: **Move a word in each sentence to make it into a question. Write the question on the lines.**

4. Use the handwriting sheet or have the children write the following sentences:

   I thought I saw a wallaby.
   Her daughter bought a waffle.

LAR Answers

1. bought
2. washtub
3. caught
4. watched
5. launch

1. unwrap
2. unkind
3. untrue
4. unhappy
5. unselfish
6. unbutton
7. unstop

SAP Answers

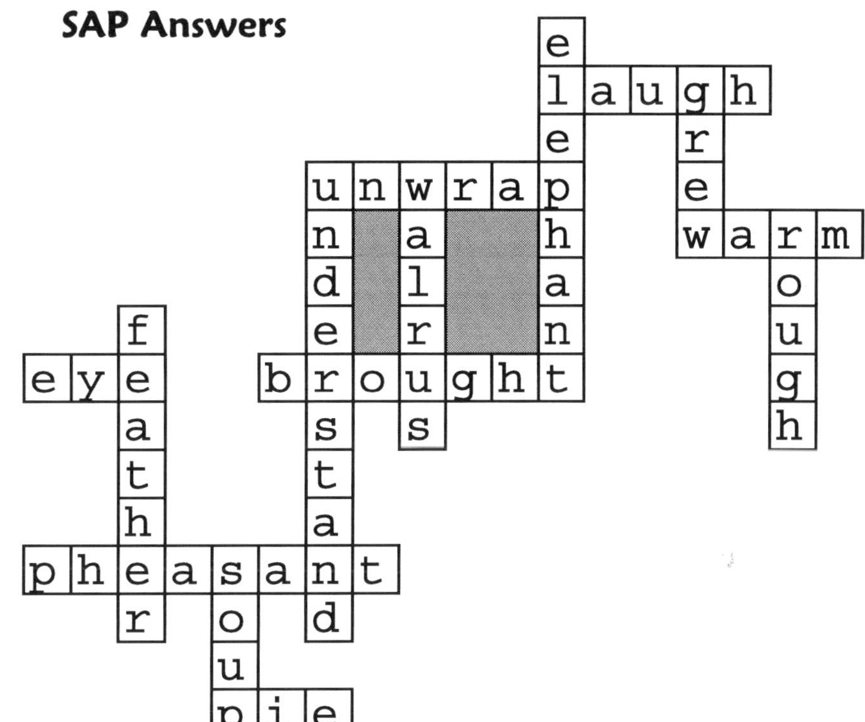

Can the walrus make us laugh?

Will you unwrap the warm apple pie?

Lesson 118

Lesson Objectives

1. Students will review the short e sound of ea. (P)
2. Students will review adjectives. (L)
3. Students will review spelling words. (S)
4. Students will proofread sentences. (S)
5. Students will copy sentences neatly and correctly. (H)

Materials

LAR
SAP

Teaching

1. Use the top of the LAR workbook page to review the short e sound of ea. **Read the list of words. Find the six words that have the short e sound for ea. Write the words on the lines.**

2. Use the bottom of the LAR workbook page. **Fill in the circle next to the word that was used as an adjective.**

3. Use the top of the SAP page. **Decode the spelling words. Write the letters in the boxes.**

4. Use the bottom of the SAP page. **Proofread the sentences. Look for spelling and punctuation mistakes. Write the sentences correctly on the lines.**

5. Use the handwriting sheet or have the children write the following sentences:

   Coughing makes me unhappy.
   The elephant has a large head.

LAR Answers

Any order:

heavy
breath
instead
pheasant
thread
health

1. rough
2. untied
3. phonics
4. dead
5. unpleasant
6. small
7. hot

SAP Answers

feather unwrap grew

laugh soup elephant warm

rough walrus brought eye

pie understand pheasant

Do elephants have rough skin?

I grew the carrots used in the warm soup.

Lesson 119
Test 3

Lesson Objectives

1. Students will review spelling words. (S)
2. Students will be tested over phonics concepts.
3. Students will copy sentences neatly and correctly. (H)

Materials

Test 3, pages 1 and 2

1. **Spelling: Match the spelling words to the descriptions. Write you answers on the lines.**
2. **Test Directions:**

   Part 1: Students will write the words that answer the questions.

   Part 2: Students will fill in the oval next to the word that completes the sentences.
3. Use the handwriting sheet or have the children write the following sentences:

   We grew vegetables to make soup.
   The pheasant had long feathers.

Lesson 120

Lesson Objectives

1. Students will be tested over language concepts.
2. Students will take a spelling dictation test.
3. Students will copy sentences neatly and correctly. (H)

Materials

Test 3, pages 3 and 4

Test Directions:

1. **Language Test:**

   Part 3: Students will read the sentences. Which word was used as an adjective? Fill in the circle next to the correct word.

   Part 4: Students will read the sentences. A word is missing. Choose the word that completes the sentence with the correct tense. Fill in the circle next to the correct word.

   Part 5: Students will number the two sets of words in alphabetical order from 1 to 5.

   Part 6: Read the three words. Fill in the word that tells how the three words are alike.
2. **Spelling Dictation Test:** Have students number their paper from 1 to 14.

   1. warm, 2. pie, 3. feather, 4. grew, 5. pheasant, 6. unwrap, 7. eye, 8. elephant, 9. rough 10. understand, 11. walrus, 12. laugh, 13. brought, 14. soup
3. Use the handwriting sheet or have the children write the following sentences:

   Do you understand how to sand rough wood?
   She taught the elephant to sit.

SAP Answers

rough
warm
unwrap
pheasant
feather
soup
elephant

eye
walrus
laugh
grew
brought
understand
pie

Test Answers

Test 3 Page 1

Part 1

1. elephant
2. unwise
3. laugh
4. meadow
5. few
6. underground
7. feathers
8. alphabet
9. telephone
10. stew

Test 3 Page 2

Part 2

1. pheasant
2. trough
3. undershirt
4. mousse
5. walrus
6. bought
7. warm
8. unlock
9. weather
10. Gophers

Test 3 Page 3

Part 3

1. unkind
2. brown
3. baby
4. fried
5. beef

Part 4

1. drying
2. flew
3. knew
4. bought
5. blew

Test 3 Page 4

Part 5

3, 5, 2, 4, 1
4, 5, 1, 3, 2

Part 6

1. chewed
2. tusks
3. names
4. move
5. fly

Lesson 121

Lesson Objectives

1. Students will read words with alternative sounds of the letter o. (P)
2. Students will spell words correctly. (S)
3. Students will practice vocabulary skills. (L)
4. Students will prepare to read the story *Lovey Dove and the Falcon.* (R)
5. Students will copy sentences neatly and correctly. (H)

Materials

LAR
SAP
Lovey Dove and the Falcon
Writing Skills Workbook page is available

Word List: above, another, become, beloved, blood, collide, color, come, comfort, comfortable, commend, community, company, compass, compare, compete, complain, complete, computer, conclude, confuse, connect, consider, control, cover, done, dove, falcon, flood, from, front, glove, love, lovely, mammoth, Monday, money, monkey, month, mother, none, nothing, of, onion, other, oven, shove, shovel, some, somewhat, somewhere, someone, sometime, something, son, talons, ton, uncover, undone, welcome

Teaching

1. Most of the shorter words in the list have been introduced as additional reading vocabulary or parts of other lists. They have never been considered as a group. The list features words where the letter o makes a short u sound or the schwa e sound. The two sounds are close in these words. For example the word come has the short u sound. In the word complete the letter o has the schwa sound. You do not have to ask students to make the distinction. They will be considered to be the same sound in these lessons.

   Write the words love, mother, and come. Have students read the words. They should already know the words. Ask what sound the o makes in each of these words. (short u)

2. Use the SAP page. Have students read and spell each word. Spelling list: welcome, cover, company, above, month, another, shovel, falcon, color, nothing, confuse, onion, love, mother.

   Top section: **Sort the words by the number or syllables.**

   Bottom section: **Write a spelling word for each picture.**

3. Use the top of the LAR page. **Read the words and definitions. Complete the sentences using the words.**

4. *Lovey Dove and the Falcon* focuses on words with the short u sound spelled with o. In addition to those words, the following words may be new to students and will require some instruction: **bury, blood.** The words and pronunciation guide is on the bottom of the LAR page.

   The word *bury:* Sounds like berry
   The word *blood:* The letters oo make the short u sound.

   You may also review the following words: daughter, pretty, underneath, salesman, without

   Introduce the story: Ask a student to read the title of the book.
   What is the name of this story? *(Lovey Dove and the Falcon)*
   What do you know about doves and falcons? (answers vary)
   In this story, Lovey Dove meets a falcon named Burton. Lovey Dove teaches the falcon something. Read the story to find out what Burton learned from Lovey Dove.

   Students will read the words on the back of the book out loud.
   Students will silently read as much of the story as they can in the time allowed.

5. Use the handwriting sheet or have the children write the following:

   Her mother has two sons.
   The rain flooded the community.

LAR Answers

1. conclude
2. comfort
3. connect
4. compare
5. confuse
6. commend
7. complain
8. collide

SAP Answers

One syllable
month love

Two syllables
welcome cover above shovel falcon color
nothing confuse onion mother

Three syllables
company another

Pictures:
shovel onion falcon

Lovey Dove and the Falcon

Second Grade Phonics & Reading

Book 22
Lessons 121 to 125

Lovey Dove and the Falcon

Written and illustrated by
Brian Davis

Burton the falcon was hungry. He wanted something good to eat. Burton wanted a fresh dove. Falcons love doves. They find them very yummy.

The falcon flew above a dove's home. It was the home of a kind dove. Her name was Lovey Dove. She was a wise old dove.

The falcon landed at her front door. He pecked the door with his sharp beak.

"I have company," thought Lovey Dove.

"Welcome! Come in," said Lovey Dove.

2

3

Lovey Dove and the Falcon

Burton the falcon opened the door.

"I have come for lunch," said Burton.

"It's always good to have company," said Lovey Dove. "I've never seen you before. Are you new to the community?" asked Lovey Dove.

Burton was confused. Most doves were afraid of him.

"I'm Burton. I'm a falcon."

"Oh," said Lovey Dove. "I thought you were big for a dove. I must fix something falcons like."

4

5

Burton was getting hungrier. Burton was getting angrier.

"Don't fix something. I'll just eat you," said the falcon.

He opened his beak. He started to bite Lovey Dove. She slapped his beak with a spoon.

"You can't eat me," said Lovey Dove. "I'm not done. Eating raw doves can make you sick. I don't want you complaining about a tummy ache. Besides, you'll get blood on my new rug."

"I've never cooked a dove," said the falcon.

"Then I'll teach you how," said Lovey Dove.

6

7

Lovey Dove and the Falcon

She pulled out her largest pan. She turned on the oven.

"First we need some onions," said Lovey Dove. "I think I have a few somewhere."

Lovey Dove looked all around her kitchen.

"There are none here," she finally said. "Would you consider getting some?"

Burton sighed. He was getting very hungry.

"OK, I'll dig up some onions. Do you have a shovel?"

"In my tool shed, dear falcon," said Lovey Dove. "Wear gloves. I don't want you complaining of sore talons."

8

9

Another dove was eating bugs in the onion patch. Her name was Wendy. She saw the falcon leave Lovey Dove's house. Burton was flying with a shovel.

"Oh no!" thought the dove. "The falcon is going to eat Lovey Dove. He will then bury her feathers. He's even wearing gloves. He doesn't want to leave his talon prints."

The dove knew just what to do. Sonny the bear loved Lovey Dove. She was like a mother to him. He would help her. Wendy the dove flew as fast as she could. She had to find Sonny the bear.

10

11

Lovey Dove and the Falcon

Burton pecked on Lovey Dove's door.

"I have the onions," said Burton.

"Come in," said Lovey Dove. "Put the shovel in the closet. Put the gloves in there, too."

The falcon did as she said.

"I'm glad I'm going to be eaten by a considerate falcon. I wouldn't want it any other way," said Lovey Dove.

She took the onions and sliced them up.

"Now it's time for the oven," said Lovey Dove. She paused, "It seems to be missing something. I know," she laughed, "A dove. That would be none other than me."

12

13

Lovey Dove hopped into the pan.

"Can you get the cover, dear?" asked Lovey Dove.

Burton the falcon grabbed the cover.

"Oh dear," said Lovey Dove. "What am I doing? How will you know when I'm done?"

"I hadn't considered that," said Burton. He was getting very confused.

Lovey Dove hopped out of the pan.

"Someone has to be in the pan. Would you consider being the dove? I'll tell you when you're done. Then you'll know how to cook doves."

Burton hopped into the pan.

"Are you comfortable?" asked Lovey Dove.

Burton nodded yes. Lovey Dove put on the cover. She shoved the pan into the oven.

14

15

Lovey Dove and the Falcon

Wendy had found Sonny.

"Come quick," panted Wendy. "A falcon is going to eat Lovey Dove!"

The bear raced to Lovey Dove's house.

"My beloved Lovey Dove are you OK?"

"I'm a little tired. But, I can't complain," answered Lovey Dove.

Lovey Dove opened the door.

"My beloved Sonny, I'm so glad you're here. I made dinner for you. Roast falcon!"

"With onions?" asked Sonny.

"With onions," smiled Lovey Dove. "Just the way you love it!"

Lovey Dove opened the oven. She uncovered the pan. Burton flew out of the oven.

"I'll never eat another dove," cried the falcon.

"I don't think you're done," sighed Lovey Dove.

"He's done eating doves," laughed Sonny.

Lovey Dove, Sonny, and Burton had a nice meal of roasted onions. Burton never considered eating another dove.

16

Lovey Dove and the Falcon word list:

above	complain	hungry	sighed
ache	complaining	I’m	slapped
afraid	confused	kind	some
always	consider	kitchen	someone
angrier	considerate	largest	something
another	cook	laughed	somewhere
answered	cover	love	Sonny
around	cried	Lovey	spoon
beak	dear	mother	talons
bear	don’t	never	teach
before	dove	new	thought
beloved	eating	none	tummy
blood	falcon	onion	uncovered
Burton	first	opened	very
bury	flew	other	wanted
can’t	fresh	oven	wearing
closet	front	quick	welcome
come	gloves	raw	Wendy
comfortable	home	roast	what
community	how	shoved	you’re
company	hungry	shovel	yummy

Lesson 122

Lesson Objectives

1. Students will group words according to sounds. (P)
2. Students will complete sentences using opposites. (L)
3. Students will use spelling words in sentences. (S)
4. Students will read the story *Lovey Dove and the Falcon.* (R)
5. Students will copy sentences neatly and correctly. (H)

Materials

LAR
SAP
Lovey Dove and the Falcon

Teaching

1. Use the top of the LAR workbook page. **Group the words based on sounds the letter o makes. The words make the long o, short o, or short u sounds. Write the words from the top list on the correct lines.**

2. Use the bottom of the LAR workbook page. **Read the sentences. Fill in the missing word with a word that is the opposite of the word under the line. Choose words from the second list.**

3. Use the SAP page. Top section: **Read each sentence. A word is underlined. Find the spelling word that can take its place and change the meaning of the sentence the least.**

4. Students will read pages 1 to 8 out loud. Next, ask the following questions:

   Why did the falcon go to Lovey Dove's house? (He was hungry.)
   Do you think Lovey Dove was really afraid of the falcon? Why? (answers vary)
   Why did Lovey Dove tell Burton not to eat her? (She wasn't done yet. He might get blood on the rug.)
   What did Lovey Dove need to cook doves? (onions)
   Why was Burton supposed to use gloves? (to keep from getting sore talons)
   Should Lovey Dove have let in a stranger? (no)
   Why not? (answers vary- She could have gotten hurt.)
   Do you think Lovey Dove will really cook herself? (answers vary)

5. Use the handwriting sheet or have the children write the following:

   A mammoth was in the iceberg.
   That company makes gloves.

LAR Answers

Top

cone	clock	come
froze	frog	front
stove	block	oven

Bottom

1. Something
2. above
3. another
4. front
5. oven

SAP Answers

Top

1. another
2. falcon
3. cover
4. month
5. welcome
6. nothing

Bottom

confuse	company
onion	above
love	shovel
mother	color

Lesson 123

Lesson Objectives

1. Students will use review nouns and adjectives. (L)
2. Students will review spelling words. (S)
3. Students will complete analogies with spelling words. (S)
4. Students will read the story *Lovey Dove and the Falcon.* (R)
5. Students will copy sentences neatly and correctly. (H)

Materials

LAR
SAP
Lovey Dove and the Falcon

Teaching

1. Ask students to define nouns. (People, places, things) Have students read this sentence: The brown dog chewed the big bone. **Which word is a noun: brown, dog or chewed?** (dog) **Are any other nouns in the sentence?** (yes, bone) **What words are adjectives?** (brown, big)

   Say the sentence: The cat played with the mouse. **Add an adjective to the sentence. Describe the cat. Add another adjective to the sentence. Describe the mouse.**

   Use the top of the LAR workbook page. **Read the sentences. Fill in the circles above the nouns.**

   Use the bottom of the LAR workbook page. **Read the sentences. Add an adjective in each blank to describe the noun. Think of your own adjectives. Don't use the same word twice.**

2. Use the SAP workbook page. Top section: **Read the short words. Which spelling word has the letters to spell the word? Write the spelling word on the lines.**

3. Use the SAP bottom section: **Read the analogies. Complete them with spelling words.**

4. Review the first half of the book *Lovey Dove and the Falcon*. Next, read the second half of the book. After completing the story ask the students the following questions:

   Who saw Burton leave Lovey Dove's house? (A dove named Wendy.)
   Who did Wendy tell about the falcon? (Sonny the bear)
   Why would Sonny help Lovey Dove? (She was like a mother to him.)
   How did Lovey Dove get Burton into the pan? (She had him pretend to be the dove.)
   Why didn't Burton say no? (He was very confused.)
   What did Lovey Dove do with the pan? (She shoved it in the oven.)
   Who was Lovey Dove cooking the falcon for? (Sonny the bear.)
   Do you think it was her plan to cook the falcon? (answers vary) **Why?**
   What did Lovey Dove teach the falcon? (not to eat doves)
   What did Burton eat instead of Lovey Dove? (roasted onions)

5. Use the handwriting sheet or have the children write the following:

   Use a shovel to cover the hole.
   The old chair was comfortable.

LAR Answers

1. Mother bought me the red gloves.
2. The onions are cooking in the oven.
3. The shovel scooped the dirt.
4. The blue cover is for the computer.
5. A falcon flew above the house.

Bottom section answers vary

SAP Answers

shovel	nothing
above	onion
cover	color
another	falcon
mother	company
confuse	welcome

Bottom

falcon	month
above	nothing
welcome	love

Lesson 124

Lesson Objectives

1. Students will find story elements. (R)
2. Students will review spelling words. (S)
3. Students will write a story. (CW)
4. Students will read the story *Lovey Dove and the Falcon*. (R)
5. Students will copy sentences neatly and correctly. (H)

Materials

LAR
SAP
Lovey Dove and the Falcon
Writing Skills Workbook page is available

Teaching

1. Use the LAR page. Step students through it. **There are different parts to stories. Stories have characters. There is an order to the story, the story sequence. There are other things we can talk about. These are called story elements. They are things every story should have. Look at the workbook page. In the color boxes are story elements. Below the boxes are descriptions from the story. We'll match the numbers to the story elements.**

   Conflict: **Most stories have a conflict. A conflict many times happens between a character that is the hero (the good character) and a character that is a villain (the bad character). The conflict is the struggle a character faces. It can be against another character, like in *Lovey Dove and the Falcon.* Sometimes the struggle is within the character, for example the character might be afraid of the dark. The conflict would be between the character and fear. A conflict can also be something in nature, such as the weather. A character may be trying to survive a storm at sea in a small life raft.**

   In Lovey Dove and the Falcon, two characters are heroes. One character is the villain. Write their numbers in the circles.

   Background: **The background is information you learn in the story about things that took place before the story. It can also be extra information that helps you understand why things work together. There are two pieces of background information in the list. Write their numbers in the circles.**

   Plot: **The plot is what happens in the story. It includes the order of events. Find a sentence that tell what Burton was planning to do at the beginning of the story. Write the number in one of the plot circles. Find a sentence that tells something Lovey Dove did. Write that number in the other plot circle.**

   Setting: **Where did the story take place? Write the number in the circle.**

   Climax: **The climax is the high part of the story. It's the part that leaves you wondering what will happen next. Find the sentence that is the climax to the story. Write the number in the circle.**

   Resolution: **Usually there is a part of the story where you find out how the conflict was solved. This is usually the ending of the story. It can tell what the characters learned. Find the sentence that tells how Burton the falcon changed at the end of the story. Write the number in the resolution circle. At the bottom of the page are six words: confused, smart, protector, motherly, strong, unpleasant. Match two of the words to each character. Write the words on the lines.**

2. Use the SAP page. **Match the spelling words to the descriptions. Write the words on the lines.**

3. Students will write a story. Say: In the story *Lovey Dove and theFalcon*, Lovey Dove had a big friend. Who was it? (Sonny thebear) Lovey Dove raised Sonny from a cub. She had to teach him many things. Write a story about Lovey Dove and Sonny. How did she find him? What are things she taught him? She tried to teach him to fly. What happened?

4. Read the book *Lovey Dove and the Falcon* again. Next, have students look at the back of the book and answer the following questions about the word list. You may do this orally or have students write answers:

   What word is the opposite of covered? (uncovered)
   What word is a synonym for griping? (complaining)
   What word means to think of others? (considerate)
   What word means you can't think clearly? (confused)
   What word is something that grows in a garden? (onion)
   What words have the same vowels as the word *food*? (blood, cook, spoon)
   Which one has the same vowel sound? (spoon)
   What word has the word *other* in it? (another)
   What word has the word *loves* in it? (gloves)
   What word is the opposite of closed? (opened)
   What words are contractions? (can't, don't, I'm, you're)
   What words are they made up of?
   (can not, do not, I am, you are)
   What words are kinds of birds? (dove, falcon)

5. Use the handwriting sheet or have the children write the following:

   The falcon had sharp talons.
   Did the plug become unconnected?

LAR Answers

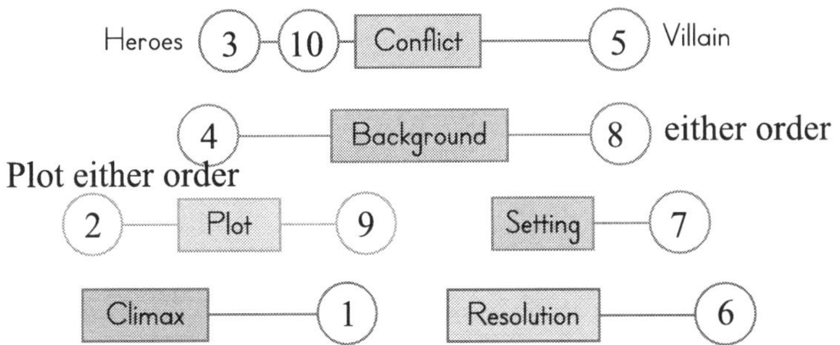

Lovey Dove: smart, motherly
Burton: confused, unpleasant
Sonny: protector, strong

SAP Answers

month	color
onion	another
falcon	love
mother	cover
shovel	confuse
nothing	above
welcome	company

Lesson 125

Lesson Objectives

1. Students will be tested on phonics concepts. (P)
2. Students will be tested on language concepts. (L)
3. Students will take a spelling test. (S)
4. Studetns will answer questions about *Lovey Dove and the Falcon.*
5. Students will read the story they have written. (R)
6. Students will copy a sentence neatly and correctly. (H)

Materials

LAR
Creative writing assignment from lesson 124
Assessment 125

Teaching

1. Use part A of the assessment as a phonics test. Have the students fill in the circles next to the words that complete the sentences.

2. Use part B of the assessment page. Students will circle all the nouns in the sentences.

3. Have students number their papers from 1 to 14. Give the following words as dictation.

   Spelling word list:

   1. month, 2. welcome, 3. shovel, 4. confuse, 5. color, 6. company, 7. nothing,

   8. cover, 9. above 10. onion 11. falcon, 12. another, 13. love, 14. mother

4. Use the LAR page.**Read the sentences on the workbook page. Number them in the order that they happened in the story.** Have students do the exercise without looking at the book. After finishing the assignment students may use their books to check or correct their answers.

   Bottom section: **Read the statements about the story. Are they true or false? Fill in the ovals to mark your answers.**

5. Have students take turns reading the books or stories that were written during the creative writing section of the previous lesson.

6. Use the handwriting sheet or have the children write the following:

   June is a lovely month.
   What color are doves?

Assessment Answers

Phonics Test:

1. talons
2. blood
3. confused
4. community
5. Welcome

Language Test:

1. **Sonny** lost the old **compass**.
2. The **onions** grew in the small **garden**.
3. **Mammoths** had large **tusks**.
4. The **oven** was made by that **company**.
5. **Mother** is done working on the **computer**.

LAR Answers

8
3
10
5
1
7
9
2
6
4

4. true **false**

5. true **false**

Lesson 126

Lesson Objectives

1. Students will read words that end with -tion. (P)
2. Students will spell words correctly. (S)
3. Students will practice vocabulary skills. (L)
4. Students will prepare to read the story *The Foozles of Loopation.* (R)
5. Students will copy sentences neatly and correctly. (H)

Materials

LAR
SAP
The Foozles of Loopation
Writing Skills Workbook page is available

Word List: action, affection, attention, auction, carnation, caution, celebration, commotion, competition, completion, condition, connection, decoration, direction, emotion, formation, fraction, hesitation, information, instruction, irritation, lotion, mention, motion, nation, notion, occupation, portion, position, proportion, question, relation, relaxation, sensation, station, vacation

Teaching

1. There are many more words that could be added to this list. Not all the words may be in the child's speaking vocabulary. Most phonics concepts have already been introduced at this point. The next step in phonics mastery is recognizing "chunks" of words. Morphology, that is recognizing familiar parts (syllables) in longer words that have meaning. Many of the remaining lessons in this curriculum will be designed to do this.

   In this lesson the syllable –tion will be introduced. Write the letters tion. Have students try to pronounce it. Next, write the letters shun. Tell students that tion is pronounced shun.

   If a single (not part of a vowel digraph) a, e or an o proceeds tion, the vowel sounds are long. (nation, completion, notion)

   If an i proceeds tion, it is short. (position) There are no words in the list where tion is proceeded by a single u or e.

   Vowel digraphs do not change sound. (caution)

2. Use the SAP page. Have students read and spell each word. Spelling list: station, nation, question, fraction, action, information, celebration, mention, vacation, direction, condition, commotion, solution, location

   Top section: **Sort the words by the number or syllables.**

   Bottom section: **Write the spelling words that have the root words.**

3. Use the LAR workbook page. C**hoose the word from the list that matches the meaning. Write the words on the lines.**

4. *The Foozles of Loopation* focuses on words with the syllable tion. In addition to those words, the following words may be new to students and will require some instruction: **foozle, Loopation, McGotion, straight, through.** The words and pronunciation guide is at the bottom of the LAR workbook page.

   The word *foozle:* It's a nonsense word. The oo makes the oo sound of moose.
   The word *Loopation:* It's also a nonsense word. The oo makes the same long sound as in *loop*. The a is long.
   The word *McGotion*: It's a last name. Mc is mic (or mac). The first o is long.
   The word *straight*: The letters aigh make the long a sound.
   The word *through*: The letters ough make the oo sound as in moose.

   You may also review the following words: learned, bulldozer, critters, enough, tomorrow

   Also put additional emphasis on words that end with tion.

   Introduce the story: Ask a student to read the title of the book. **What is the name of this story?** *(The Foozles of Loopation)* **What is a foozle?** Answers may vary. It's a made-up creature.
   As you read the book you'll learn about foozles and a place called Loopation.

   Students will read the words on the back of the book out loud.
   Students will silently read as much of the story as they can in the time allowed.

5. Use the handwriting sheet or have the children write the following:

   Our family is going on vacation.
   We will drive across the nation.

LAR Answers

1. irritation
2. attention
3. carnation
4. occupation
5. hesitation
6. commotion
7. affection
8. emotion

SAP Answers

Two syllables
station nation question fraction
action mention

Three syllables
vacation direction condition
commotion solution location

Four syllables
information celebration

action	location
direction	celebration
information	solution

The Foozles of Loopation

Second Grade Phonics & Reading

Book 23
Lessons 126 to 130

The Foozles of Loopation

Written and illustrated by
Brian Davis

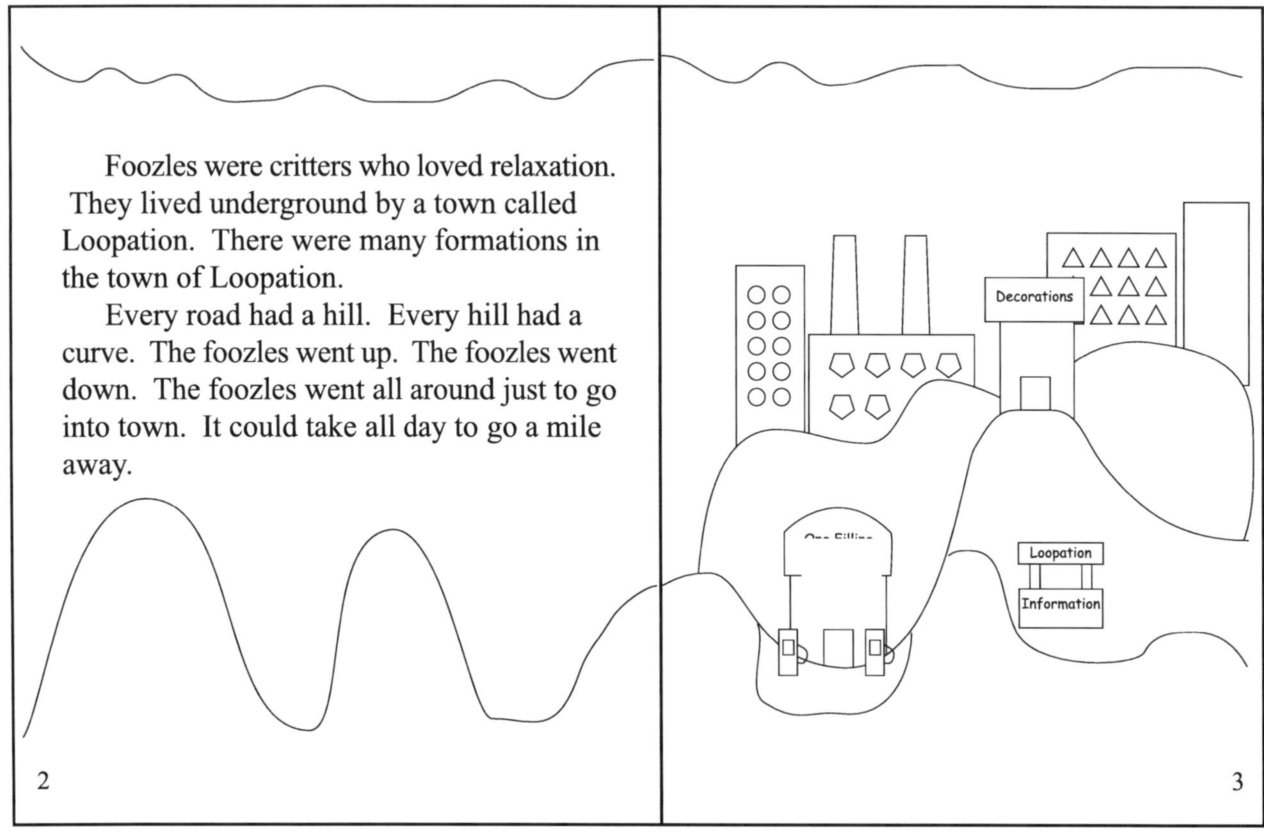

Foozles were critters who loved relaxation. They lived underground by a town called Loopation. There were many formations in the town of Loopation.

Every road had a hill. Every hill had a curve. The foozles went up. The foozles went down. The foozles went all around just to go into town. It could take all day to go a mile away.

2

3

The Foozles of Loopation

They had great affection for their walnut shell cars. They loved to drive. But, they never got far.

Every direction they drove was a hill and a curve. To drive very fast took a great deal of nerve.

Driving to work, they used great caution. They would arrive in time to leave for vacation.

They hopped back into their walnut shell cars. They drove up the hills. They drove down. The foozles drove all around.

They all gassed up at the one filling station. Each night they left the town of Loopation.

4

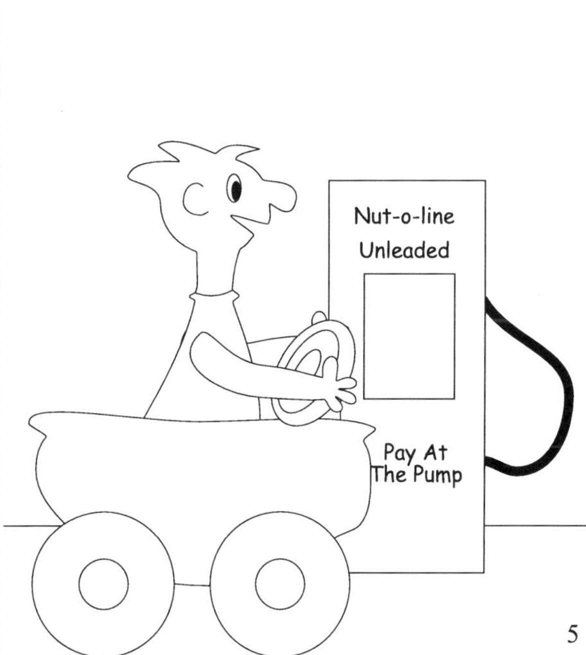

5

One foozle drove the other way. Lou McGotion didn't work in the day. Each night Lou McGotion hopped into his walnut shell car.

He drove up. He drove down. He drove all around. Lou McGotion drove into town.

The streets were quiet in the town of Loopation. Lou gassed up his car at the one filling station.

His job was to check on the road conditions. His boss always left a sheet of directions.

Next, Lou was ready to go into action. To do his job well, Lou had to know fractions.

6

7

The Foozles of Loopation

One day the directions were not too clear. As Lou read them he said, "Oh dear."

Lou's boss had writing that was not too great. Lou couldn't read a number. Was it three? Was it eight?

Lou tried the phone. The boss was on vacation. Lou didn't know the vacation location.

"I'll do my best," sighed Lou.

He hopped on a bulldozer. Lou put on his orange vest. He started the motor. Lou headed out west.

8

9

He rolled to the place the directions had mentioned. Making a new road had been his intention. That's when he really had a question.

He wished he could read that one last fraction. He wasn't quite sure how to take action.

On the hill was a store that sold decorations. On the curve was a booth that gave information.

To make a new road, he would have to plow one. He had to choose which should be gone.

Just then, a thought popped into his head. He could drive his bulldozer right straight ahead.

Lou McGotion was done as quick as a wink. He looked at his work. Lou just had to blink.

"This is the best road ever. That's what I think."

Lou got back into his walnut shell car. He drove out of town. It didn't take long. He didn't go far.

Lou was ready for a little relaxation. "I think tomorrow I'll take a vacation."

10

11

The Foozles of Loopation

The foozles drove into town the next day. They didn't go up. They didn't go down. They didn't go all around. The foozles drove straight into town.

They all arrived before it was eight. Not a single foozle was late.

This caused a very great commotion. "What should we do now?" was the big question. Not a single foozle had even a notion.

12

13

They sat in their cars not sure what to do. The foozles waited until the workday was through.

They sat and they waited. There was night. There was day. Not a single foozle drove away.

Lou McGotion came back from vacation. It had been a good night of relaxation.

There was a big crowd in the town of Loopation. Lou thought it was some huge celebration.

His boss soon got his attention. "I don't think you knew my intentions."

"I'm sorry," said Lou, "for this great irritation. If only I'd had enough information. This whole thing was caused by one unclear fraction. I know I must take some other action."

14

15

The Foozles of Loopation

Lou got on his bulldozer. He made a great mound. He dozed up a loop that went up and down. All the foozles drove out of town. Their walnut shell cars went upside down.

"That's more like it," the foozles all said. "A walnut shell car is not a good bed."

"We'll be home in time to go to work," smirked the decoration store clerk.

Lou McGotion learned a lesson that day. In Loopation a straight line is the long way.

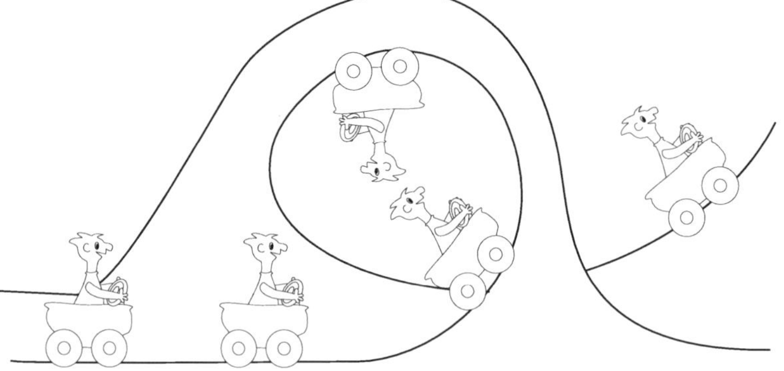

16

The Foozles of Loopation word list:

action
affection
arrive
attention
bulldozer
caused
caution
celebration
clear
commotion
conditions
critters
crowd
curve
decorations
direction
eight
enough
every
foozle

formations
fractions
gassed
information
intention
irritation
learned
leave
location
loop
Loopation
McGotion
mentioned
motor
mound
nerve
never
night
notion
number

phone
plow
question
quiet
relaxation
smirked
station
straight
thought
through
tomorrow
town
unclear
underground
upside
vacation
walnut
who
workday
writing

Lesson 127

Lesson Objectives

1. Students will find long vowel sounds in words. (P)
2. Students will write the meanings of words ending with tion. (L)
3. Students will review spelling words. (S)
4. Students will read the story *The Foozles of Loopation.* (R)
5. Students will copy sentences neatly and correctly. (H)

Materials

LAR
SAP
The Foozles of Loopation
Writing Skills Workbook page is available

Teaching

1. Use the top of the LAR workbook page. Have students circle the long vowel sounds in the words. Underline the words that have no long vowel sounds.

2. Write the word *unlocked.* Ask students to read the word and tell what it means (not locked). Ask how the prefix un changed the word. (It made it the opposite.) **In the word unlocked, the syllable *un* meant not. The syllable *tion* also has a meaning in some words. It means to do or act. The root word is a verb. The syllable tion turns the words into nouns.**

   Use the bottom of the LAR page. Have students use roots of words + ing to write definitions. For example 1: Relaxation – An act of relaxing.

3. Use the SAP workbook page. Top section: **Proofread the sentences. Write them correctly on the lines.**

   Bottom section: **Each box contains two spelling words. Can the other words be made from the spelling words? Answer yes or no.**

4. Students will read pages 1 to 8 out loud. Next, ask the following questions:

   Where did the foozles live? (by a town called Loopation)
   Why did it take a long time to drive in Loopation? (There were many hills and curves.)
   What were the cars made of? (walnut shells)
   How much work did most foozles do? (none)
   What did they do instead of working? (drive around and go on vacation)
   Who worked at night? (Lou McGotion)
   Why was Lou confused? (His directions were not clear.)
   What did Lou use at work? (a bulldozer)
   Why couldn't Lou contact his boss?
   (He didn't know the vacation location.)

5. Use the handwriting sheet or have the children write the following:

   We did not follow the directions.
   We stopped to get information.

LAR Answers

Top

formation	notion	completion
vacation	station	condition
caution	emotion	carnation

Bottom

2. An act of instructing.
3. An act of celebrating.
4. An act of hesitating
5. An act of irritating
6. An act of connecting.

SAP Answers

The Fourth of July is a celebration of our nation.
We needed directions to the location of the vacation house.

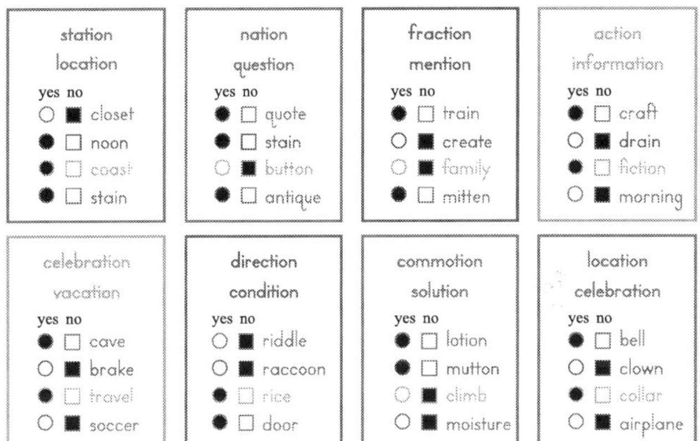

Lesson 128

Lesson Objectives

1. Students will use review verbs. (L)
2. Students will combine sentences. (L)
3. Students will review spelling words. (S)
4. Students will read the story *The Foozles of Loopation.* (R)
5. Students will copy sentences neatly and correctly. (H)

Materials

LAR
SAP
The Foozles of Loopation

Teaching

1. Ask students to define verbs. (They tell what nouns are doing. They show action.) Have students read this sentence: The white cow chewed the green grass. Ask students which word is a verb. (chewed)

   Use the top of the LAR workbook page. **Read the sentences. Fill in the circle above all the verbs.**

2. Use the bottom section of the LAR workbook page. **Combine two sentences into one. Write the new sentences on the lines.**

3. Use the SAP page. Top section: **Fit the spelling words into the grid. Start with the clues spaces, the letters m and o.**

   Bottom section: **Read each sentence. Words are underlined. Write the spelling word that can take the place of the words and change the meaning of the sentence the least.**

4. Review the first half of the book *The Foozles of Loopation*. Next, read the second half of the book. After completing the story ask the students the following questions:

   What two things were Lou going to bulldoze? (decoration store, information booth)
   What did he do instead? (He drove straight ahead.)
   What happened the next day? (The foozles got to work on time.)
   Why did they get to work on time? (The straight road made it a short drive.)
   Why didn't the foozles know what to do? (They had never gotten to work on time.)
   What did they do instead? (Nothing, they just sat there.)
   How did Lou McGotion solve the problem? (He made a big loop.)
   Which way was really the better way? (answers vary) **Why?**
   Why do you think the foozles couldn't change? (answers vary)

5. Use the handwriting sheet or have the children write the following:

   We saw formations in the cave.
   They looked like decorations.

LAR Answers

1. We hung the decorations to celebrate her birthday.
2. The train stopped at the station so people could hop on.
3. Dad asked for directions from a man walking by the street.
4. The lotion spilled on the floor and made it slippery.
5. We added the two fractions to find the answer.

Wording can vary. Sample answers:

The green gloves are in the box.

The sliced onion made tears in my eyes.

SAP Answers

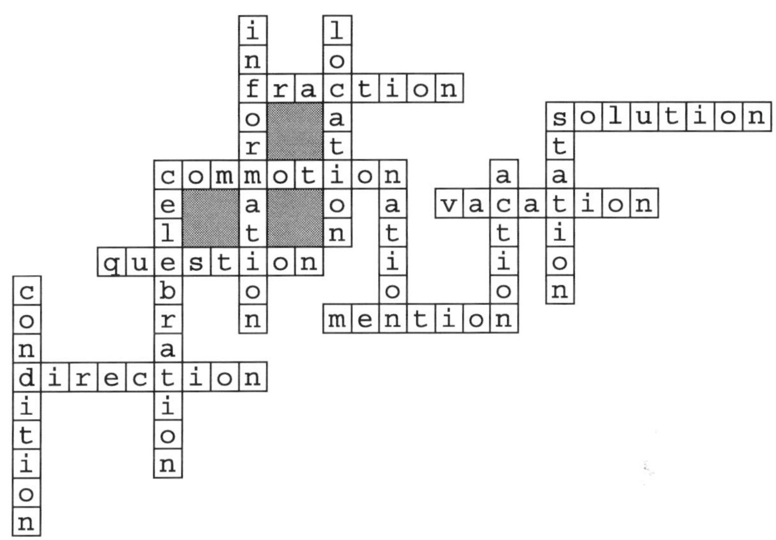

1. commotion
2. fraction
3. celebration
4. mention
5. location

Lesson 129

Lesson Objectives

1. Students will find the main idea of a paragraph. (L)
2. Students will review spelling words. (S)
3. Students will write a story. (CW)
4. Students will read the story *The Foozles of Loopation.* (R)
5. Students will copy sentences neatly and correctly. (H)

Materials

LAR
SAP
The Foozles of Loopation

Teaching

1. Use the LAR page. **Every paragraph has a main idea. The main idea is a sentence that best describes what the whole paragraph is about. A paragraph usually has a main idea with other sentences that give more details to the main idea.**

   Read the first paragraph on the workbook page about an auction. Allow students to read, then continue the discussion. **There are four choices to the side that state the main idea. Let's look at the choices. Which one is the main idea?** (There are great deals at auctions.)

   Dad bought a computer doesn't tell what the whole paragraph is about. I have a box of decorations also doesn't tell what the whole paragraph is about.

   The last choice wasn't even really a part of the paragraph.

   Read the other three paragraphs and find the main idea.

2. Use the SAP page. **Match the spelling words to the descriptions.**

3. Students will write a story. Say: In the story *The Foozles of Loopation,* what kind of animals were foozles? They were creatures that were just made up. How would you describe foozles? What did they look like? How did they act?

   Have students write their own stories with made-up "critters", or another story about foozles.

4. Read the book *The Foozles of Loopation* again. Next, have students look at the back of the book and answer the following questions about the word list. You may do this orally or have students write answers:

   What words mean something that tells you what to do? (direction, information)
   What is something that needs an answer? (question)
   What word has the short i sound right before t-i-o-n? (conditions)
   What words have the long a sound spelled with 4 letters? (eight, straight)
   What word is something that is hung at parties? (decoration)
   What ends with the f sound spelled with gh? (enough)
   What word means not clear? (unclear)
   What word is a machine that build roads? (bulldozer)
   What word means the day after today? (tomorrow)
   What words are compound words?
   (bulldozer, underground, workday)
   What word means something that is a bother? (irritation)

5. Use the handwriting sheet or have the children write the following:

   We used caution at the beach.
   The lotion kept us from burning.

LAR Answers

There are great deals at auctions.

I like getting flowers.

Police work involves lots of action.

Knowing fractions is important.

SAP Answers

solution	vacation
question	mention
celebration	comotion
direction	information
fraction	station
location	action
nation	condition

Lesson 130

Lesson Objectives

1. Students will be tested on phonics concepts. (P)
2. Students will be tested on language concepts. (L)
3. Students will take a spelling test. (S)
4. Students will answer questions about the story. (R)
5. Students will read the story they have written. (R)
6. Students will copy a sentence neatly and correctly. (H)

Materials

LAR
Creative writing assignment from lesson 129
Assessment 130
The Foozles of Loopation

Teaching

1. Use part A of the assessment as a phonics test. Have the students fill in the circles next to the words that complete the sentences.

2. Use part B of the assessment page. Write the word for the definitions.

3. Have students number their paper from 1 to 14. Give the following words as dictation.

   Spelling word list: **1. action, 2. station, 3. mention, 4. fraction, 5. nation, 6. direction, 7. question, 8. vacation, 9. commotion 10. celebration 11. condition, 12. information, 13. location, 14. solution**

4. Use the LAR page and the *The Foozles of Loopation* reading book. **Complete each set of rhyming sentences from the story. Find the sentences in the book and fill in the missing words.**

   On the bottom section, read the statements about the story. Are they true or false? Fill in the oval to mark your answer.

5. Have students take turns reading the books or stories that were written during the creative writing section of the previous lesson.

6. Use the handwriting sheet or have the children write the following:

   Our station wagon broke down.

   It caused us some irritation.

Assessment Answers

Phonics Test:

1. directions
2. question
3. lotion
4. decorations
5. affection

Language Test:

1. relaxation
2. irritation
3. celebration
4. hesitation
5. instruction

LAR Answers

Page 2	Loopation
Page 4	station
Page 6	fractions
Page 8	location
Page 14	information

1. ● (false)
2. (true) ●
3. ● (false)
4. (true) ●
5. ● (false)

Lesson 131

Lesson Objectives

1. Students will read words that end with -ly. (P)
2. Students will recognize adverbs. (L)
3. Students will spell words correctly. (S)
4. Students will prepare to read the story *What is Blizzy?* (R)
5. Students will copy sentences neatly and correctly. (H)

Materials

LAR
SAP
What is Blizzy?
Writing Skills Workbook page is available

Word List: angrily, boldly, bravely, bubbly, carefully, carelessly, certainly, closely, coldly, completely, constantly, happily, harshly, jointly, joyfully, kindly, lately, lightly, likely, loosely, lovely, meanly, merrily, mildly, monthly, noisily, oddly, pleasantly, powerfully, proudly, quickly, quietly, rarely, really, sadly, scraggly, secretly, selfishly, Shelly, shortly, shyly, simply, sleepily, slightly, slowly, softly, strangely, suddenly, sweetly, swiftly, terribly, tightly, unkindly, unlikely, unselfishly, weakly, wobbly, yearly

Teaching

1. There are many more words that could be added to this list. Most of the time when ly is added to a root, the word becomes an adverb. Sometimes the words are also adjectives (<u>bubbly</u> water, <u>unlikely</u> hero).

   The ly, sounds like lee in these words. When adding ly to some words, the roots change as follows:

   The le is dropped on words that end with le (terrible, terribly).
   Silent e on long vowel words is not dropped (brave, bravely).
   The y is changed to i on two-syllable words that end with y (happy, happily)

   Use the top of the LAR workbook page. Have students apply the rules. **Add ly to the words.**

2. Review the term adjective. Ask students to define an adjective. (An adjective describes a noun.) Say: **There are words that describe verbs too. They are called adverbs.** Write the sentences: The horse ran swiftly. The horse ran slowly.

   In both sentences the horse ran. Was the horse running the same way in each sentence? Maybe the horse got hurt and had a problem running in the second sentence. Using adverbs told us more about the way the horse was running.

   Use the bottom of the LAR workbook page. **Add an adverb to each sentence. Choose the words from the list.**

3. Use the SAP page. Have students read and spell each word. Spelling list: completely, terribly, happily, unlikely, sweetly, lovely, slowly, suddenly, rarely, quickly, carefully, secretly, softly, noisily

   Top section: **Sort the words by the number or syllables.**

   Bottom section: **Write the spelling words that have the root words.**

4. *What is Blizzy?* focuses on words with the suffix –ly. The following words may be unfamiliar to students: journey, moment, zebra. The words and pronunciation guide are at the bottom of the page.

   The word *journey:* our makes the ur sound, ney has the long e sound.
   The word *moment:* The o is long, the e is short.
   The word *zebra*: The e is long.

   Introduce the story: Ask a student to read the title of the book. **What is the name of this story?** *What is Blizzy?* **What do you think Blizzy is?** Answers may vary. **In the story Blizzy is not sure what she is. Read the story to find out why she is confused.**

   Students will read the words on the back of the book out loud.
   Students will silently read as much of the story as they can in the time allowed.

5. Use the handwriting sheet or have the children write the following:

   The rain fell constantly.
   The bubbly spring swiftly flowed.

LAR Answers

Top

simply giggly humbly bubbly
bravely likely closely completely
happily noisily sleepily angrily

Middle

Answers vary.

SAP Answers

1. carefully	4. lovely
2. completely	5. noisily
3. happily	6. quickly

1. rarely	5. suddenly
2. secretly	6. sweetly
3. slowly	7. terribly
4. softly	8. unlikely

happily The y changed to i.
terribly The le was dropped.
rarely It didn't change.

What is Blizzy?

Second Grade Phonics & Reading

Book 24
Lessons 131 to 135

What is Blizzy?

Written and illustrated by
Brian Davis

Blizzy was born in a toy company. Blizzy was the last toy made that day. Many tigers had been quickly stuffed and stitched.

The lady had to work quickly. The tigers needed to be shipped. The next day she would make zebras. The lady grabbed a piece of cloth.

She accidentally grabbed the zebra cloth. "This will certainly do," she said.

The lady quickly stitched up Blizzy. She swiftly tossed Blizzy into a box. She rapidly taped it up. It was completely dark in the box.

Blizzy had landed softly. The box was full of tigers. It was tightly packed. "At least I'm not squashed," Blizzy growled softly.

2

3

What is Blizzy?

"Who's there?" said a voice sleepily.

"My name is Blizzy. I'm a tiger," Blizzy growled softly.

"We're all tigers," the voice said loudly. "You may call me Siggy. Your tail is tickling my nose. Would you kindly move it?"

"Sorry," said Blizzy. She carefully tucked her tail under her paw. "If you talk noisily, will people hear you?" asked Blizzy.

"The people can't hear you," answered Siggy. "Only a boy or girl who loves you can hear."

"Oh," said Blizzy happily. "I must get me one of these boys or girls. I will enjoy talking to them."

"We all will," smiled Siggy happily. "First, we must go on a journey."

4

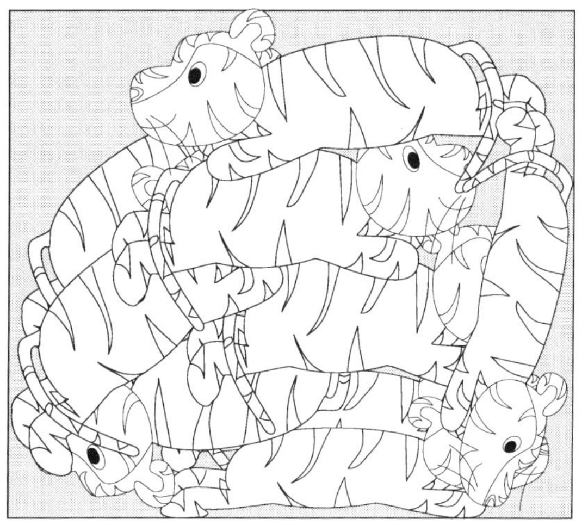

5

The box of tigers moved strangely for two days. Finally, the box was opened up. The tigers were quickly pulled from the box. They were carefully placed on a shelf.

Blizzy's eyes were not used to the light. Her legs were wobbly. But, Blizzy was really excited.

"Where are we?" Blizzy asked joyfully.

Siggy's eyes were completely closed.

"We're in a very bright toy store," answered Siggy.

Both tigers slowly opened their eyes. That's when Blizzy saw that she was very different. All the other tigers saw this too. They stared at her oddly.

"What are you?" asked Siggy.

"I'm a tiger," Blizzy growled shyly.

"Tigers are orange and black. You're simply not orange," said Siggy.

6

7

What is Blizzy?

Blizzy looked closely at her paws. There was not one speck of orange.

"Then what am I?" Blizzy growled softly.

Just then a child picked Blizzy up.

"Can I have the funny zebra?" the little boy asked.

"Not today," said the mother.

The mother put Blizzy with the zebras. The zebras looked at Blizzy meanly.

"Don't even think of biting us," a zebra named Stripes said harshly.

8

"I don't bite," growled Blizzy shyly. "I'm already stuffed." Then she thought a moment. "Do I look like something that bites?"

"You look like a very short zebra," another zebra loudly laughed.

Suddenly, Blizzy was pulled off the shelf.

9

"Look at the baby zebra," said the little girl.

"I don't think that's a zebra. Is that the one you want, Shelly?" asked her mother.

Shelly lovingly looked into Blizzy's eyes.

"Do you want to go home with me?" Shelly asked softly.

"Yes, yes, yes, " Blizzy happily growled.

"She wants me to buy her," Shelly told her mom.

"She can hear me," Blizzy thought joyfully. "She must love me."

Blizzy rode in a sack to her new home.

"I am so happy," thought Blizzy, "but, I want to know what I am. I'm slightly too short for a zebra. I'm not orange like a tiger."

10

11

What is Blizzy?

That night, Blizzy snuggled comfortably.

"I love you, Shelly," said Blizzy quietly.

"I love you too," Shelly answered sweetly.

Soon, Shelly was asleep. That's when Blizzy heard something. It was someone softly sobbing.

"Who are you?" asked Blizzy. "Why are you sad?"

"I'm Teddy," a voice sadly answered. "I used to get to snuggle with Shelly. I am her little teddy bear."

"Oh," Blizzy softly sighed. She honestly felt sad for Teddy. But, it also made her feel good. Shelly chose her instead of Teddy.

It was simply confusing. Then, Teddy said something else. It confused her even more.

"I hardly see why anyone would want a skunk. You even have a scraggly tail. It's way too thin."

12

Blizzy was terribly upset. "Am I a skunk?"

"I think so," Teddy angrily answered, "a skunk with a scraggly tail. You are black and white. Skunks have stripes."

13

Blizzy didn't sleep at all that night. She was terribly concerned. She didn't want to suddenly get scared. Blizzy didn't want to make an unpleasant smell.

"I don't want to be a skunk. I'm not even a good skunk. I have a scraggly tail."

"Good morning, Blizzy," Shelly said happily. "I'm going to show you to all my friends."

Shelly put a nice little hat on Blizzy. She looked at Blizzy sweetly.

"You look so cute," said Shelly.

"Do I smell OK?" Blizzy growled shyly.

"You're so funny," laughed Shelly. "Of course you smell OK."

Blizzy was still secretly afraid.

"Shelly doesn't know I'm a skunk," thought Blizzy.

"Maybe Teddy would like to go instead," Blizzy said hopefully.

14

"I want my friends to meet you," said Shelly. "We're going to the zoo. Maybe we'll see a zebra like you."

"Or a skunk like me," Blizzy sadly thought.

15

What is Blizzy?

Blizzy rode in a backpack. It could have been fun. Blizzy was just trying not to stink. Suddenly, the backpack was opened. Shelly gently picked up Blizzy.

"Now I know what you are," Shelly said joyfully.

"Oh no," said Blizzy. "I'm sorry I'm a skunk. I'll honestly try not to stink."

Shelly giggled loudly. "You're not a skunk. Look in the window."

Blizzy looked closely at the window. Inside some baby animals were playing.

"They look just like me," Blizzy said joyfully. "What are they?"

"The sign says they are tigers. They are white Bengal tigers."

"I am a white Bengal tiger," Blizzy growled proudly.

"You're my white Bengal tiger," Shelly said happily.

16

What is Blizzy? word list:

accidentally	friends	orange	squashed
angrily	giggled	paw	stitched
another	growled	people	strangely
answered	happily	proudly	stripes
backpack	hardly	quickly	stuffed
Bengal	harshly	quietly	suddenly
biting	honestly	rapidly	sweetly
black	hopefully	sadly	swiftly
Blizzy	inside	scraggly	terribly
bright	instead	secretly	thought
buy	journey	Shelly	tickling
carefully	joyfully	shipped	tiger
certainly	kindly	shyly	today
child	laughed	Siggy	unpleasant
comfortably	loudly	simply	upset
company	maybe	skunk	very
completely	meanly	sleepily	we're
concerned	moment	slightly	where
confusing	morning	slowly	white
enjoy	mother	snuggled	window
excited	noisily	softly	wobbly
finally	opened	something	zebra

Lesson 132

Lesson Objectives

1. Students will correct adverbs in sentences. (L)
2. Students will use words that end with –ly as adjectives. (L)
3. Students will review spelling words. (S)
4. Students will read the story *What is Blizzy?* (R)
5. Students will copy sentences neatly and correctly. (H)

Materials

LAR
SAP
What is Blizzy?

Teaching

1. Use the top of the LAR workbook page. **Read the sentences. One word in each sentence needs an –ly suffix. Find the words. Add the suffix ly. Write them on the lines.**

2. Review adverbs and adjectives. Most –ly words are adverbs. Some are used as adjectives.

   Use the bottom of the LAR workbook page. **Choose one of the words from the list to use as an adjective. Write the words on the lines.**

3. Use the SAP page. Top section: **Read the sentences. Words are underlined. Replace the words with spelling words that change the meaning of the sentence the least.**

   Bottom section: **Complete the analogies with spelling words.**

4. Students will read pages 1 to 8 out loud. Next, ask the following questions:
   What kind of cloth was Blizzy made from? (zebra cloth)
   What do you think zebra cloth looks like? (white with black stripes)
   Why couldn't people hear the tigers? (The people had to love the tigers.)
   Where were the tigers shipped? (to a toy store)
   How was Blizzy different? (She was black and white, not orange.)
   What did the little boy think Blizzy was? (a zebra)
   Why wouldn't Blizzy bite? (She was stuffed.)
   Why do you think the zebras were mean to Blizzy? (They didn't want to be bit.)
   Did the little boy buy Blizzy? (No)

5. Use the handwriting sheet or have the children write the following:

   The man bravely climbed the tree.
   The scraggly kitten purred softly.

LAR Answers

Top

1. humbly
2. suddenly
3. unselfishly
4. quietly
5. sweetly

Bottom

1. lovely
2. yearly
3. wobbly
4. wiggly
5. motherly

SAP Answers

1. lovely
2. happily
3. suddenly
4. completely
5. terribly
6. rarely
7. noisily

happily	unlikely
slowly	lovely
rarely	secretly

Lesson 133

Lesson Objectives

1. Students will use recognize adverbs. (L)
2. Studetns will match opposites. (L)
3. Students will review spelling words. (S)
4. Students will read the story *What is Blizzy?* (R)
5. Students will copy sentences neatly and correctly. (H)

Materials

LAR
SAP
What is Blizzy?
Writing Skills Workbook page is available

Teaching

1. Review adverbs.

   Use the top of the workbook page. **Read the sentences. Fill in the circles above the adverbs.**

2. Use the bottom of the workbook page. **Read each sentence. Complete the sentence choosing a word from the box that is the opposite of the words under the lines.**

3. Use the SAP page. Top section: **Use the shape code to decode the spelling words.**

   Bottom section: **Move words in each sentence to turn it into a question. Write the questions on the lines.**

4. Review the first half of the book *What is Blizzy?* Next, read the second half of the book. After completing the story ask the students the following questions:

   Who bought Blizzy? (a girl named Shelly)
   Why was Shelly able to hear Blizzy? (She loved the Blizzy.)
   Who was sad that Blizzy was bought? (Teddy)
   Why? (He didn't get to snuggle with Shelly.)
   What did Teddy call Blizzy? (a skunk)
   What did Teddy mean by calling Blizzy's tail scraggly? (It wasn't thick like a skunk's.)
   Why was Blizzy afraid of being a skunk? (She didn't want to stink.)
   Where did Shelly take Blizzy? (to the zoo)
   What did Shelly and Blizzy see at the zoo? (white Bengal tiger cubs)

5. Use the handwriting sheet or have the children write the following:

   I rocked the baby carefully.
   She still cried loudly.

LAR Answers

1. The money was greatly needed.
2. The string was tied tightly.
3. I sleepily answered the telephone.
4. Shelly knocked softly on the door.
5. Joe watched the baking cake closely.

1. joyfully
2. rarely
3. proudly
4. powerfully
5. quietly

SAP Answers

unlikely quickly lovely
suddenly softly happily
slowly noislily secretly
rarely sweetly terribly
completely carefully

Was Blizzy suddenly tossed softly into a box?

Is it unlikely that the car will be fixed quickly?

Lesson 134

Lesson Objectives

1. Students will match events to settings. (L)
2. Students will review spelling words. (S)
3. Students will write a story. (CW)
4. Students will read the story What is Blizzy? (R)
5. Students will copy sentences neatly and correctly. (H)

Materials

LAR
SAP
What is Blizzy?

Teaching

1. Use the LAR page. **The story, *What is Blizzy?* happens in five different settings. The five settings are in the ovals on the workbook page. A list of ten events are numbered to the side. Write the numbers for the events in the squares to match the setting.**

2. Use the SAP page. **Match the spelling words to the descriptions.**

3. Students will write a story. Say: **The story *What is Blizzy?* is about a toy. What is your favorite toy? Write a story about it. It can be a real story telling about how you got your toy and why you like it. It can be a made up story like the story about Blizzy.**

4. Read the book *What is Blizzy?* again. Next, have students look at the back of the book and answer the following questions about the word list. You may do this orally or have students write answers:

   What words are colors? (black, orange, white)
   Besides -ly what other suffixes can you find? (ing, ed) **Find examples of words with the ing and ed suffixes.** (concerned, confusing, excited, giggled, growled, laughed, opened, shipped, snuggled, squashed, stitched, tickling)
   Find the second word in the first column. What letter changed when -ly was added? (y changed to i, angry - angrily)
   What words are kinds of animals? (skunk, tiger, zebra)
   Are the words quickly and rapidly antonyms (opposites) or synonyms? (synonyms)
   What two words in the second column are synonyms? (giggled, laughed)
   What word is something that smells unpleasant? (skunk)
   What words are compound words? (backpack, something)
   What word means a long trip? (journey)
   Find the word that is the opposite of the fourth word in the second column. (sadly)

5. Use the handwriting sheet or have the children write the following:

   Shelly sang the song sweetly.
   I listened to her joyfully.

LAR Answers

Numbers can be switched from left to right

SAP Answers

secretly	quickly
carefully	completely
happily	softly
slowly	unlikely (can be switched)
noisily	suddenly
rarely	terribly
lovely	sweetly

Lesson 135

Lesson Objectives

1. Students will be tested on phonics concepts. (P)
2. Students will be tested on language concepts. (L)
3. Students will take a spelling test. (S)
4. Students will answers questions about *What is Blizzy?* (R)
5. Students will read the story they have written. (R)
6. Students will copy a sentence neatly and correctly. (H)

Materials

LAR
Creative writing assignment from lesson 134
Assessment 135
What is Blizzy?

Teaching

1. Use part A of the assessment as a phonics test. Have the students fill in the circles next to the words that complete the sentences.

2. Use part B of the assessment page. Circle the adverbs.

3. Have students number their papers from 1 to 14. Give the following words as dictation.

   Spelling word list:

   1. rarely, 2. sweetly, 3. quickly, 4. terribly, 5. lovely, 6. suddenly, 7. slowly, 8. happily,

   9. carefully 10. unlikely 11. secretly, 12. completely, 13. noisily, 14. softly

4. Use the LAR page. **Read the sentences on the workbook page. Number them in the order that they happened in the story.** Have students do the exercise without looking at the book. After finishing the assignment students may use their books to check or correct their answers.

   Bottom section: **Read the satements about the story. Are they true or false? Fill in the ovals.**

5. Have students take turns reading the books or stories that were written during the creative writing section of the previous lesson.

6. Use the handwriting sheet or have the children write the following:

   The truck suddenly stopped.
   It followed a car too closely.

Assessment Answers

Phonics Test

1. gently
2. noisily
3. quickly
4. swiftly
5. kindly

Language Test

1. bravely
2. carefully
3. quickly
4. constantly
5. loosely

LAR Answers

4
7
1
8
6
10
2
9
3
5

1. true **false**
2. **true** false
3. **true** false
4. true **false**
5. **true** false

Lesson 136

Lesson Objectives

1. Students will read words with the prefix re. (P)
2. Students will recognize pronouns. (L)
3. Students will spell words correctly. (S)
4. Students will prepare to read the story *Ruff Returns*. (R)
5. Students will copy sentences neatly and correctly. (H)

Materials

LAR
SAP
Ruff Returns
250

Word List: react, recall, recess, recite, reclaim, recline, record, recount, recover, recruit, redecorate, redeem, redouble, reduce, reduction, refill, refinish, reflect, reflex, refresh, refrigerate, refund, refuse, regain, regret, rehearse, rejoice, rejoin, relate, relax, relay, release, relief, relieve, relive, rely, remain, remake, remark, remember, remote, remove, renew, renumber, repair, repay, repeat, repent, rephrase, replace, replant, replay, reply, report, reprint, request, require, resign, respect, respond, result, resume, retell, retire, retrace, retreat, return, reveal, revenge, reverse, review, revue, reward, rewind

Teaching

1. There are many more words that could be added to this list. The e in the prefix re makes the long e sound (remix) in some words. In some words it makes a short i sound (recite). A few have both pronunciations. The way the e is pronounced can change the meaning of the word. Recover with a long e means to cover again. Recover with the short i means to get back.

   There are no rules for telling the difference by looking at the word. Once students are familiar with decoding the word, they will choose the correct pronunciation based upon their speech patterns. We suggest that the long e and short i both be introduced so that students are aware of the differences, but allow students flexibility in pronunciation. Students will not be asked to make the distinction in the exercises in this curriculum.

   Teacher's Note: If re is combined with another consonant in the same syllable, the e has the short e sound (reptile). No words in the above list fit this category.

   Tell students that in some words the prefix re means *to do again*. Use the top of the LAR workbook page. **Write words beginning with *re* that matches the meanings.**

2. Introduce the term pronoun. Ask students to find the word noun in pronoun. **Pronouns are like nouns. They are people, places, or things. Pronouns take the place of nouns.** Introduce the pronouns he, she, it, they, and them. **Sometimes we use pronouns instead of nouns to make writing more interesting. Repeating the same words, close together, doesn't sound as well when we read it.**

   Write the sentences: Mary saw a whale. Mary liked the whale. Have students read the sentences. Say: Now I will rewrite the second sentence using pronouns. She liked it.

   Who is she? (Mary) What is it? (whale)

   Use the bottom of the workbook page. Have students rewrite the sentences. Replace the underlined words with pronouns.

3. Use the SAP page. Have students read and spell each word. Spelling list: completely, rely, repair, refill, relax, reward, recount, remember, replace, require, remove, remain, relief, recess, return

   Top section: **Sort the words by the number of letters.**

   Bottom section: **Add suffixes to the spelling words.**

4. Ruff Returns focuses on words with the prefix re.

   Introduce the story: Ask a student to read the title of the book. **What is the name of this story?** *(Ruff Returns)* **What happened in the last Ruff story?** Answers may vary. He built an airplane. **In this story Ruff thinks he sees a crime being committed. Read the story to find out what he does about it.**

   Students will read the words on the back of the book out loud.
   Students will silently read as much of the story as they can in the time allowed.

5. Use the handwriting sheet or have the children write the following:

   Father relaxed in the chair.
   He required some rest.

LAR Answers

Top

1. recount
2. refill
3. repay
4. rewind
5. replant

Bottom

1. He
2. it
3. them
4. She
5. They

SAP Answers

4 letters
rely

5 letters
relax

6 letters
repair refill reward remove
remain relief recess return

7 letters
recount replace require

8 letters
remember

replacing removed
relied
remaining relaxed

Ruff Returns

Book 25
Lessons 136 to 140

Ruff Returns

Written and illustrated by
Brian Davis

Ruff was replanting Violet for the night. He had just tucked in her roots. Ruff glanced out the window.

"That's very strange," remarked Ruff.

He stared across the street. Ruff watched his neighbor's house. Two people were removing something. It was his neighbor's recliner. Ruff was relieved to see his neighbor, Mr. Rebus.

"Oh, Mr. Rebus must be wanting to relax outside."

Ruff said goodnight to Violet. He went to bed.

2

3

Ruff Returns

The next day, Violet woke Ruff up.

"Some men are taking the recliner!" Ruff responded. "We don't have time to report it to the police."

Ruff and Violet ran outside. The truck was pulling away with the recliner.

"We've got to return the recliner," said Ruff. "I need my super wagon."

Ruff had replaced some parts of the wagon. He had used airplane parts to repair it. Ruff removed the cover from the wagon.

He pushed the remote control. The wagon responded. Ruff was relieved. Sometimes it didn't start. Ruff and Violet reclined in the wagon.

4

5

Ruff and Violet followed the truck. It removed all kinds of things. The men picked up things at the side of the road.

"We must make them return these things," said Ruff.

He followed the truck to the city dump.

"Please remove those things from the truck," said Ruff.

"OK," said the man. "It's all yours."

Ruff was relieved. He didn't want to have to bite the man.

"I think he regretted taking it," Ruff told Violet. "We won't report him to the police."

Ruff loaded up his wagon.

"We've got to return this stuff," remarked Ruff. "Can you remember the houses it came from?"

6

7

Ruff Returns

Ruff and Violet just had to guess. They retraced their steps. Ruff returned something to every house. He just didn't remember what to return.

Ruff was relieved to unload his wagon. He remembered what to leave at the last house. Ruff unloaded the recliner.

"Mr. Rebus will be relieved to see this," remarked Ruff.

Tom arrived home from work.

"Tom will be glad we returned things. We might even get a reward," rejoiced Ruff.

Violet and Ruff returned home. They greeted Tom.

8

9

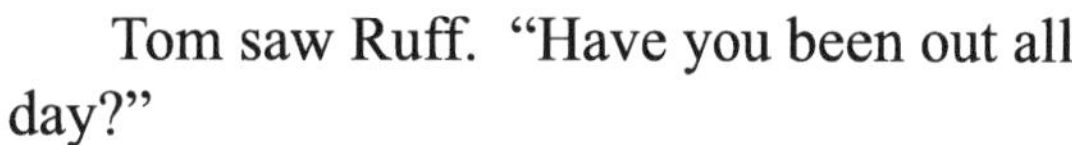

Tom saw Ruff. "Have you been out all day?"

Ruff responded by nodding his head.

"Somebody put trash all over the neighborhood," remarked Tom. "People will be mad when they get home. Do you remember seeing anything?"

Ruff didn't recall seeing anyone with trash. Ruff was excited about his day. He told Tom about replacing all the stuff.

"Maybe I'll get a reward," said Ruff.

"You returned all the things?" Tom repeated.

"Yes," answered Ruff.

"Oh no," said Tom. "That was junk people didn't want. The truck was removing it for them. Those were things that were replaced."

10

11

Ruff Returns

A few neighbors had seen Ruff. They had watched him return things. Everyone knew Ruff had replaced the junk. Tom's phone started ringing.

"How will I respond to these people?" moaned Tom.

He answered the phone.

"Please don't report Ruff," Tom requested.

"I think he should be repaid for what he did," said the phone caller. "I refuse to be quiet about this. It needs to be reported."

The phone caller hung up. Tom turned to Ruff.

"You are in big trouble. That lady was going to report you. You need to retrieve all the junk, Ruff. Return it to the junkyard."

Ruff returned to each house. The junk was gone.

12

13

Soon the street was full of reporters. They knocked on Tom's door.

"Is this Ruff's home?" asked the reporter.

Tom didn't want to reply. A lady came up to Tom.

"I reported Ruff. He left an old lamp at my house."

"He will return it to the junkyard," said Tom.

"No," said the lady. "I like the lamp. I can repair it. Ruff is such a good dog. I wanted the reporters to know about Ruff. We don't need to fill up the junkyards. These things can be reused. We respect what Ruff did."

Everyone refused to return the junk. They were very happy that Ruff had returned things.

14

15

Ruff Returns

Mr. Rebus relaxed in his recliner. It remained in his yard. He watched the crowd leave. No reporters remained. Mr. Rebus waved to Tom and Ruff.

"Thank you, Ruff," said Mr. Rebus. "I regretted getting rid of the recliner. I was redecorating. Now, I think I'll redecorate it, too. It was a relief to see it tonight. You have a remarkable dog, Tom."

"You are remarkable," Tom repeated to Ruff. "You should get a reward. How about a nice big bone?"

Returning things had made Ruff very hungry.

"My tummy could use refueling," replied Ruff. But, Ruff refused. "I don't need a reward for helping others."

"OK," said Tom. "I'll give you a great big bone because I love you."

That was something Ruff couldn't refuse.

16

Ruff Returns word list:

answered	phone	remarked	responded
anything	police	remember	retraced
arrived	recall	remote	retrieve
control	recliner	removed	return
couldn't	redecorating	repaid	reused
cover	refueling	repair	reward
every	refuse	repeated	something
excited	refused	replacing	strange
glanced	regretted	replanting	super
goodnight	rejoiced	replied	tonight
junkyard	relax	reply	trouble
lady	relief	report	unload
neighbor	relieved	reporters	Violet
neighborhood	remained	requested	wagon
outside	remarkable	respect	watched

Lesson 137

Lesson Objectives

1. Students will complete sentences using words that begin with re. (L)
2. Students will match pronouns to nouns. (L)
3. Students will use spelling words in sentences. (S)
4. Students will read the story *Ruff Returns*. (R)
5. Students will copy sentences neatly and correctly. (H)

Materials

LAR
SAP
Ruff Returns
Writing Skills Workbook page is available

Teaching

1. Use the top of the LAR workbook page. **Read the sentences. A word in each sentence is missing. Have students complete the sentences. Choose words from the list.**

2. Review pronouns. Review he, she, it, they, and them. Use the bottom of the LAR workbook page. **Read the pairs of sentences. Match the nouns to the pronouns.**

3. Use the SAP page. **Complete each set of sentences with the spelling words in each box.**

4. Students will read pages 1 to 8 out loud. Next, ask the following questions:

   What did Ruff see out the window? (He saw someone moving a recliner.)
   What happened to the recliner the next morning? (Some men took it.)
   What worked by a remote control? (Ruff's super wagon)
   What problem did Ruff have when he decided to return the things? (He didn't remember where they came from.)
   Why was Ruff relieved that the man gave him the things on the truck? (He didn't have to bite the man.)
   What was the last thing returned? (the recliner that belonged to Mr. Rebus.)

5. Use the handwriting sheet or have the children write the following:

   Tammy repaired the bike.
   She replaced the chain.

LAR Answers

Top

1. replaced
2. repay
3. recliner
4. remote
5. reverse

Bottom

1. Jerry, book
2. baby, balloons
3. children, flowers

SAP Answers

relax	recess
replace	repair
relief	rely
remember	refill
reward	return
require	remain
recount	removed

Lesson 138

Lesson Objectives

1. Students will use recognize parts of speech. (L)
2. Students will recognize incomplete sentences. (L)
3. Students will review spelling words. (S)
4. Students will read the story *Ruff Returns*.(R)
5. Students will copy sentences neatly and correctly. (H)

Materials

LAR
SAP
Ruff Returns

Teaching

1. Review pronouns, nouns, verbs, adjectives, and adverbs. Tell students that the following are also pronouns: I, we, me, us, you, him, her.

   Use the top of the LAR workbook page. **Read the sentences. A word is underlined. Fill in the circle that tells how the underlined word was used.**

2. Use the bottom of the LAR page. **Are the sentences complete or incomplete? Fill in the circle. Add parts to the incomplete sentences and write complete sentences on the lines.**

3. Use the SAP page. Top section: **Each box contains two spelling words. Can the other words be made from the spelling words? Answer yes or no.**

   Bottom section: **Proofread the sentences. Write them correctly on the lines.**

4. Review the first half of the book *Ruff Returns*. Next, read the second half of the book. After completing the story ask the students the following questions:

   What did Tom say happened to the neighborhood? (Somebody put trash in it.)
   What did the lady who called say she was going to do? (Report Ruff.)
   What happened when Ruff went back to the houses? (The junk was gone.)
   What happened to it? (The people kept it.)
   What was Mr. Rebus going to do with his chair? (redecorate it)
   Why didn't Ruff want a reward? (He didn't need it for helping others.)
   Why didn't he need it? (answers vary – It feels good to help others.)
   Why did Tom give Ruff a bone? (Tom loves Ruff.)
   Why do you think this story was called Ruff Returns? (Because Ruff returned things.)
   What do you think might happen the next time a neighbor wants to get rid of something? (answers vary)

5. Use the handwriting sheet or have the children write the following:

   I will rehearse my lines.
   I hope I remember them.

LAR Answers

Top
1. pronoun
2. adjective
3. adverb
4. pronoun
5. verb

4. no

5. yes

SAP Answers

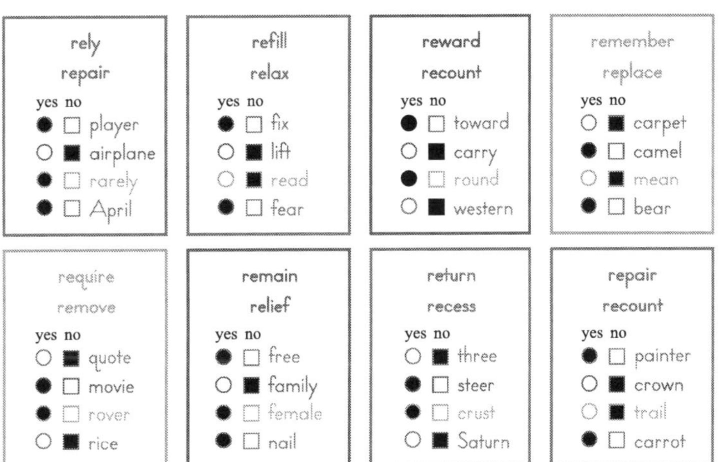

Did you remember to remove the wrapper?

We had extra time at recess as a reward.

Lesson 139

Lesson Objectives

1. Students will find the main idea. (R)
2. Students will review spelling words.(S)
3. Students will write a story. (CW)
4. Students will read the story *Ruff Returns*. (R)
5. Students will copy sentences neatly and correctly. (H)

Materials

LAR
SAP
Ruff Returns

Teaching

1. Use the LAR page. **Read each paragraph and find the main idea.**

2. Use the SAP page. **Match the spelling words to the descriptions. Write the words on the lines.**

3. Students will write a story. Say: **In the story Ruff Returns, Ruff helps people in an unexpected way. What do you think would have happened if the people were angry at Ruff? Write a story about a time that you tried to help someone. It can be a true story or it can be made up. Maybe the people you helped really liked what you did. Maybe it didn't turn out as well as you planned. The story could be about something that you would like to do someday to help others.**

4. Read the book *Ruff Returns* again. Next, have students look at the back of the book and answer the following questions about the word list. You may do this orally or have students write answers:

   What word means used again? (reused)
   What word means unusual? (remarkable)
   What word means to say no to something? (refuse)
   What words have the same vowel sound and vowel digraph as thief? (relief, relieved, retrieve)
   What word is a contraction? (couldn't)
   What word means to fix something? (repair)
   What word is a chair? (recliner)
   What word is the opposite of forget? (remember)
   What word is the opposite of load? (unload)
   What words are compound words? (anything, goodnight, junkyard, neighborhood, outside, something)
   What word is someone who tells the news? (reporter)

5. Use the handwriting sheet or have the children write the following:

   Cats react to barking dogs.
   They retreat to tall trees.

LAR Answers

I'm looking forward to recess.

You can return the candy.

It's been fun preparing for the play.

I lost my baseball glove.

SAP Answers

relax	refill
remain	require
return	reward
replace	rely
repair	recount
remove	remember
recess	relief

Lesson 140

Lesson Objectives

1. Students will be tested on phonics concepts. (P)
2. Students will be tested on language concepts. (L)
3. Students will take a spelling test. (S)
4. Students will answer questions about the story. (R)
5. Students will read the story they have written. (R)
6. Students will copy a sentence neatly and correctly. (H)

Materials

LAR
Creative writing assignment from lesson 139
Assessment 140
Ruff Returns

Teaching

1. Use part A of the assessment as a phonics test. Have the students fill in the circles next to the words that complete the sentences.

2. Use part B of the assessment page. Read the pairs of sentences. Answer the questions about the pronouns. Write the answers on the lines.

3. Have students number their papers from 1 to 14. Give the following words as dictation.

   Spelling word list:

   1. remove, 2. reward, 3. replace, 4. refill, 5. recount, 6. remain, 7. relax,

   8. rely, 9. relief, 10. require, 11. repair, 12. remember, 13. return, 14. recess

4. Use the LAR workbook page. Top section: **Read the questions. Write answers on the lines. Use complete sentences. The first question is an example.**

   Bottom section: **Are the statements about the story *Ruff Returns* true or false? Fill in the ovals.**

5. Have students take turns reading the books or stories that were written during the creative writing section of the previous lesson.

6. Use the handwriting sheet or have the children write the following:

   Kate reviewed for the test.
   She did not regret it later.

Assessment Answers

Phonics Test

1. rewind
2. repaired
3. respect
4. remark
5. relax

Language Test

1. Libby, fish
2. Dan, books
3. Jill

LAR Answers

1. Mr. Rebus owned the recliner.
2. Ruff and Violet rode in a wagon.
3. Tom told Ruff to take the junk back.
4. Ruff gave the lady a lamp.
5. Ruff couldn't refuse the great big bone.

1. true **false**

2. true **false**

3. **true** false

4. true **false**

5. **true** false

Lesson 141

Lesson Objectives

1. Students will read words with the suffix -ment. (P)
2. Students will practice vocabulary skills. (L)
3. Students will spell words correctly. (S)
4. Students will read *Jonathan's Musical Instrument*. (R)
5. Students will copy sentences neatly and correctly. (H)

Materials

LAR
SAP
Jonathan's Musical Instrument
Writing Skills Workbook page is available

Word List: Agent, agreement, announcement, apartment, basement, cement, comment, compartment, compliment, content, department, different, element, enjoyment, excitement, experiment, garment, instrument, lament, moment, monument, movement, ornament, parent, payment, present, prevent, repent, silent, statement, treatment

Teaching

1. The main emphasis in this lesson is words with the syllable ment. Words that end with –ent were also included in the list. The end –ment indicates a state of being or action.

   Have students read the following words, then add the letters –ment at the end:

   announce, base, excite, move, pay, state.

   Use the top of the LAR workbook page. **Add the parts of words. Write the word on the lines.**

2. Use the bottom of the LAR workbook page. **Read the definitions. Use the definitions to find the correct words to complete the sentences.**

3. Use the SAP page. Have students read and spell each word. Spelling list: silent, apartment, compliment, present, different, parent, agreement, basement, garment, moment, excitement, instrument, enjoyment, payment

   Top section: **Sort the words in each box in alphabetical order.**

   Bottom section: **Add suffixes to the spelling words. All of the words end with two consonants, so you won't need to change the root words before adding the suffix.**

4. *Jonathan's Musical Instrument* focuses on words that end with -ent. The following words may also be new to students: music, musical, harmonica, salesperson.

   Introduce the story: Ask a student to read the title of the book. **What is the name of this story?** Jonathan's Musical Instrument. **What happened in some of the other Jonathan stories?** Answers may vary. **In this story Jonathan wants to play a musical instrument. What instrument do you think he'd want to play? Let's read the story to find out.**

   Students will read the words on the back of the book out loud.
   Students will silently read as much of the story as they can in the time allowed.

5. Use the handwriting sheet or have the children write the following:

   The girl lives in that apartment.
   The chair is in the basement.

LAR Answers

Top

1. apartment
2. enjoyment
3. instrument
4. ornament

Bottom

1. lament
2. compliment
3. garments
4. prevent
5. announcement
6. ornament
7. contents
8. agent

SAP Answers

1. agreement	5. different
2. apartment	6. enjoyment
3. basement	7. excitement
4. compliment	

1. garment	5. payment
2. instrument	6. present
3. moment	7. silent
4. parent	

silently complimented
presenting
differently parented

Jonathan's Musical Instrument

Second Grade Phonics & Reading

Book 26
Lessons 141 to 145

Jonathan's Musical Instrument

Written and illustrated by
Brian Davis

My name is Jonathan. I really like music. One day my parents were in the living room.

"I have an announcement," I said. "I would like to play an instrument."

My parents were silent for a moment.

"I want to play for your enjoyment," I said.

"You're always thinking of others," my dad commented. "But, I would be content if you were silent."

I think he was teasing.

"I think you should be older," said my mom. "Instruments cost a lot of money."

"I will make the payments," I said.

My dad laughed, "You need money to make payments. This is the agreement. You will make the payments."

"Great," I said. Dad didn't remember my ten dollars. It had been a birthday present.

2

3

Jonathan's Musical Instrument

"Do you want to go to the department store?" asked my mom.

"To get an instrument?" I asked.

My mom picked up some clothes.

"I have to return these garments."

"They look like shirts to me," I said.

Mom smiled, "Garments are clothes. I need a different size. You may stay here. Rosie wants to play dolls with you."

"I think you need me. I'll help you get the right garments," I said.

4

5

We went to the department store.

Mom said, "I think I'll try on some garments."

At that moment, I knew I had made a mistake. Mom wouldn't be content with just trying on one blouse. This could take hours. Mom tried on a blouse.

"How do I look?

"You look like a movie star," I complemented her. "Can we go now?"

"In a moment," said my mom. "I want to look in one more department."

"Oh no," I lamented. "Maybe I should have played dolls with Rosie."

6

7

Jonathan's Musical Instrument

Mom surprised me. We went to the musical instrument department.

"Am I getting a present?" I asked.

"No," said my mom. "But, you need to know how much they cost. You will buy the instrument. Remember the agreement?"

I smiled. I remained silent. I had ten dollars. It had been a birthday present. I could play for my parent's enjoyment today!

We walked to the music department. It just took a moment. I had a feeling of excitement. I saw many different instruments.

"Look at the drums," I said. "That's a great instrument."

Mom looked at the drums. She sighed. They cost a lot of money. I wouldn't be able to buy them today. I think she was sad.

8

9

"I have ten dollars. Can I buy a musical instrument?" I asked the salesperson.

"You can't buy an instrument for ten dollars," my mom commented. "You just need to see how much they cost."

"We have lots of instruments for ten dollars," commented the salesperson. "We have bells. We have whistles. We even have harmonicas."

"A harmonica!" I was overcome with excitement. "That's what I want."

"Oh no," my mom lamented.

I think she wanted me to play drums. I couldn't make payments on the drums.

10

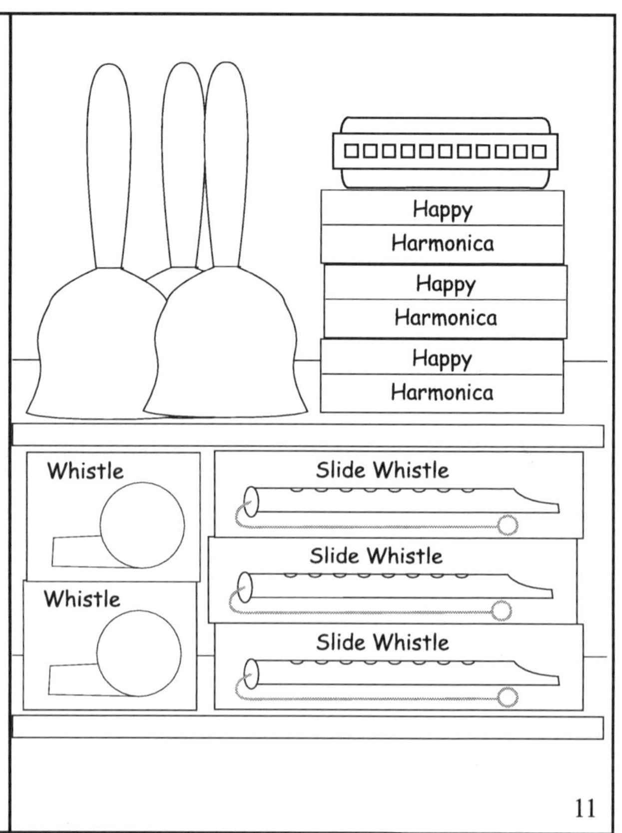

11

Jonathan's Musical Instrument

I played it all the way home. I wasn't silent for a moment. It was all for my mom's enjoyment.

"I bought my own musical instrument. This music is a present for you," I commented to my mom. "I don't play well yet," I said. "That shouldn't prevent me from trying. Isn't that right, mom?"

"Right," my mom groaned.

I think she wanted a harmonica too. Maybe I would get her one as a present. We could both play for enjoyment.

12

13

We got home. I hopped out of the car. Dad was in the yard.

"I have an announcement," I said. "I have a real instrument."

My parents looked at each other.

"I thought we had an agreement," said my dad. "Why did Jonathan get a present?"

"I bought it," I commented. "That was our agreement. I didn't make payments. It cost less than ten dollars."

I pulled the harmonica from my pocket. I played it loudly. I was getting better.

14

15

Jonathan's Musical Instrument

Rosie heard the music.

"I have an announcement," said Rosie. "I want to play a musical instrument too."

I turned to my parents.

"Please prevent Rosie from getting an instrument. She'll never be silent."

Dad smiled, "It's for your enjoyment. I think you should teach her. You can practice every day in the basement."

"That's right," commented my mom. "She does have ten dollars."

I put my harmonica away.

"Hey, Rosie," I yelled, "Let's play with dolls instead."

16

Jonathan's Musical Instrument
word list:

agreement	garments	others
always	harmonica	overcome
announcement	hours	parents
basement	instead	payment
birthday	instrument	pocket
blouse	isn't	present
bought	lamented	prevent
commented	laughed	really
complemented	loudly	remained
content	mistake	remember
department	moment	salesperson
different	money	silent
dollars	movie	teasing
drums	music	thinking
enjoyment	musical	until
every	older	whistles
excitement		

Lesson 142

Lesson Objectives

1. Students will combine sentences using *and.* (L)
2. Students will review spelling. (S)
3. Students will read the story *Jonathan's Musical Instrument.* (R)
4. Students will copy sentences neatly and correctly. (H)

Materials

LAR
SAP
Jonathan's Musical Instrument

Teaching

1. Write the sentences: We went to a barn. I saw a calf. Have students read the sentences. Say: **We can make these two sentences into one sentence. If you were just telling somebody about going to a barn and seeing a calf, you would probably say something more like: We went to a barn, and I saw a calf.**

   What word did I add? (and)

   Use the top of the LAR page. **When we make new words by putting two words together, what are they called?** (compound words) **If we combine the words base and ball, we make the compound word, baseball. When we put two sentences together, we call them compound sentences.**

   Look at the sample in the book. The marmot came out of the tall grass. We watched it for an hour. What is the compound sentence? (The marmot came out of the grass, and we watched it for an hour.) **Notice that the word *and* has a comma before it.**

   Use the bottom of the LAR workbook page. **Read the pairs of sentences. Write compound sentences for each pair.**

2. Use the SAP page. Top section: **Fit the spelling words into the grid. There are two clue spaces, the letter m and the letter f.**

   Bottom section: **Proofread the sentences. Write them correctly on the lines. Look for spelling and punctuation errors.**

3. Students will read pages 1 to 8 out loud. Next, ask the following questions:

   What was Jonathan's announcement? (He wanted to play an instrument.)
   What agreement did he make with his parents? (Jonathan would buy the instrument.)
   Where did Jonathan and his mom go? (To a department store)
   What did Jonathan's mother return? (Some garments - shirts)
   Why do you think Jonathan wanted to leave the clothes department? (answers vary)
   What was the first musical instrument Jonathan saw? (drums)
   Why did Jonathan think his mom sighed? (Because he couldn't get them that day.)
   Why do you think she sighed? (answers vary)

4. Use the handwriting sheet or have the children write the following:

   Sam likes different kinds of foods.
   His parents like to cook outside.

SAP Answers

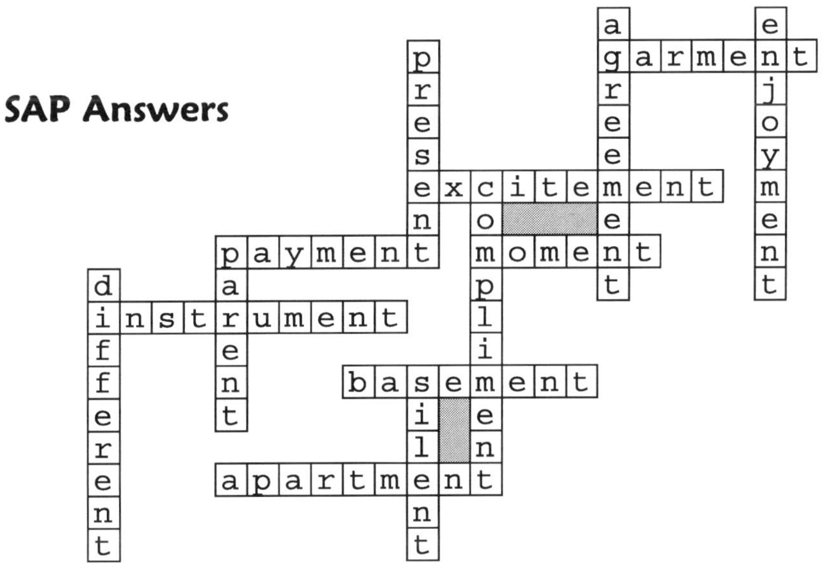

There was much excitement about the new instruments.

We will make a payment for the basement apartment.

LAR Answers

1. My sister plays an instrument, and my brother can sing.
2. Ken has an apartment, and his dog lives in the basement.
3. Mom found the box of ornaments, and Dad put up the tree.

Lesson 143

Lesson Objectives

1. Students will make compound sentences using *but* and *or*. (L)
2. Students will review parts of speech.
3. Students will review spelling words. (S)
4. Students will read the story *Jonathan's Musical Instrument*. (R)
5. Students will copy sentences neatly and correctly. (H)

Materials

LAR
SAP
Jonathan's Musical Instrument
Writing Skills Workbook page is available

Teaching

1. Review compound sentences. **Today you will use the words *but* and *or* to make compound sentences. When we combine two sentences what happens to the first period?** (It is changed to a comma.) Use the top of the LAR workbook page. **Read the pairs of sentences. Use or for the first two sentences. Use but to combine the second two sentences.**

2. Write the sentence: She neatly placed the old garments in the box. Write numbers 1 to 5 above the following words (see the bottom of LAR page 134 for an example): She, neatly, placed, old, box. **Read the sentence. Notice the numbers above the words. Which number is above the noun?** (5, box) **Which number is above the verb?** (3, placed) **Which number is above the adverb?** (2, neatly) **Which number is above the adjective?** (4, old) **Which number is above the pronoun?** (1, She)

   Bottom of the LAR workbook page. **Read the sentences. Match the parts of speech to the words by writing the number on the lines.**

3. Use the SAP page. Top section: **What spelling words can make the small words? Write their numbers on the lines. There will be a spelling word for every set of lines.**

   Bottom section: **Fill in the missing vowels to spell the spelling words.**

4. Review the first half of the book Jonathan's Musical Instrument. Next, read the second half of the book. After completing the story ask the students the following questions:

   Did Jonathan's mom think he could buy an instrument? (No)
   Why not? (It cost too much.)
   What instruments did the salesperson show Jonathan? (bells, whistles, harmonicas)
   Why was Jonathan overcome with excitement? (He wanted a harmonica.)
   What did Jonathan do on the way home? (play the harmonica)
   Why did Jonathan think his mother groaned? (She wanted a harmonica.)
   Why do you think she groaned? (answers vary)
   Who made an announcement at the end of the story? (Rosie.)
   Why didn't Jonathan want Rosie to play an instrument? (She would never be silent.)
   What did the dad say Jonathan could do to help Rosie? (teach her to play an instrument)
   Why do you think Jonathan decided to play dolls with Rosie? (answers vary)

5. Use the handwriting sheet or have the childrenwrite the following:

   We put ornaments on the tree.
   The children were silent.

LAR Answers

Top

1. I could ride with my parents, or I could ride with my grandparents.
2. I complimented Mom on her cooking, but she didn't hear me.

Bottom

4 noun 2 verb 1 adverb 3 adjective

3 noun 4 verb 5 adverb 2 adjective 1 pronoun

5 noun 3 verb 2 adverb 4 adjective 1 pronoun

SAP Answers

Top

yet 13,14 ape 2,6,14
nice 3,11 grant 7,9 drift 5
is 2,12 bee 8 jet 13 green 7 mice 11
nest 1,4,8 mom 3,10
pen 2,3,4,6,14 line 1,3
rent 2,4,5,6,7,9,12

Bottom

excitement compliment silent
apartment garment moment
instrument present basement
agreement different payment
enjoyment parent

Lesson 144

Lesson Objectives

1. Students will find the main idea of a paragraph. (L)
2. Students will review spelling words. (S)
3. Students will write a story. (CW)
4. Students will read the story *Jonathan's Musical Instrument*. (R)
5. Students will copy sentences neatly and correctly. (H)

Materials

LAR
SAP
Jonathan's Musical Instrument

Teaching

1. Use the LAR workbook page. **Read each paragraph and find the main idea.**

2. Use the SAP workbook page. **Match the spelling words to the descriptions.**

3. Students will write a story. **What instrument did Jonathan learn to play in the story, *Jonathan's Musical Instrument*? Do you play an instrument? Would you like to play an instrument someday? Write a story about playing an instrument.**

   Options: 1. Students may write a non-fiction book about instruments instead.
   2. Students may make a musical instrument. Use boxes, rubber bands, or any other materials. Write a book to show how it was made.

4. Read the book ***Jonathan's Musical Instrument*** again. Next, have students look at the back of the book and answer the following questions about the word list. You may do this orally or have students write answers:

   What means to tell something important? (announcement)
   What word means just for fun? (enjoyment)
   What word is an adverb that ends with ly? (loudly)
   What words have to do with buying something? (bought, money, dollars, payment, salesperson)
   What word means the underground part of a house? (basement)
   What words are musical instruments? (harmonica, whistles)
   What word is a contraction? (isn't)
   What word is a synonym of joking? (teasing)
   What word is the opposite of allow? (prevent)
   What word is the opposite of loud? (silent)

5. Use the handwriting sheet or have the children write the following:

   A dog lives at the fire department.
   I play music for enjoyment.

LAR Answers

The Washington Monument is tall.

George Washington was a great leader.

It's fun to shop in December.

SAP Answers

payment	different
parent	enjoyment
compliment	moment
apartment	basement
instrument	agreement
present	excitement
garment	silent

Lesson 145

Lesson Objectives

1. Students will be tested on phonics concepts. (P)
2. Students will be tested on language concepts. (L)
3. Students will take a spelling test. (S)
4. Students will answer questions about the story. (L)
5. Students will read the story they have written. (R)
6. Students will copy a sentence neatly and correctly. (H)

Materials

LAR
Creative writing assignment from lesson 144
Assessment 145

Jonathan's Musical Instrument

Teaching

1. Use part A of the assessment as a phonics test. **Fill in the circles next to the words that complete the sentences.**

2. Use part B of the assessment page. **Read the pairs of sentences. Write a compound sentence for each pair.**

3. Have students number their papers from 1 to 14. Give the following words as dictation.

   Spelling word list:

   1. basement, 2. different, 3. silent, 4. agreement, 5. garment, 6. compliment, 7. excitement,

   8. present, 9. instrument 10. payment, 11. moment, 12. parent, 13. apartment, 14. enjoyment

4. Use the LAR page. **Write answers to the questions. Use complete sentences. On the bottom section, read the statements. Are they true or false? Fill in ovals to mark answers.**

5. Have students take turns reading the books or stories that were written during the creative writing section of the previous lesson.

6. Use the handwriting sheet or have the children write the following:

   I was filled with excitement.
   I liked the musical instrument.

Assessment Answers

Phonics Test

1. apartment
2. enjoyment
3. payments
4. basement
5. instrument

Parenthesis lists acceptable answers.

1. The new boy was silent, (but,and) the rest of the class talked loudly.
2. I will go to the department store, (and, or) I will go to the park

LAR Answers

Suggested answers.
Wording may vary.

1. They went to a department store.
2. Rosie wanted to play with dolls.
3. Jonathan bought a harmonica.
4. It had been a birthday present.
5. He wanted them to practice in the basement.

4. **true** false

5. true **false**

Lesson 146

Lesson Objectives

1. Students will practice vocabulary skills. (L)
2. Students will spell words correctly. (S)
3. Students will prepare to read the story *Hound Dog Hoedown.* (R)
4. Students will play a game with compound words. (R)
5. Students will copy sentences neatly and correctly. (H)

Materials

LAR
SAP
Question Word poster
Dog Pound Compound Game and playing pieces
Hound Dog Hoedown
Writing Skills Workbook page is available

Word List: Barnyard, hoedown, sidewalk, sidekick, skateboard, homework, schoolwork, grown-up, handcuffs, himself, herself, keyboard, quicksand, someday, sixteen, somewhere, themselves, therefore, without, bagpipe, bedroom, blackboard, eighteen, footstool, footstep, know-how, punchbowl, haystack, bedtime, nighttime, hayloft, pitchfork, washtub, horseshoe, hushpuppies, cornbread, hayride, applesauce, background, backwoods, blacksmith, blackbird, campfire, catfish, crawfish, doorway, earthworm, homestead, friendship, greyhound, hardship, lighthouse, livestock, pinecone, playground, raindrops, withdraw, yourself, buckshot, bug-eyed, bullfrog, bull's-eye, icehouse

Teaching

1. Use the LAR workbook page and a blank piece of paper. **Read about the words. Write the definitions for the words in the word list. You should be able to write definitions from the paragraphs on the page.**

   Use the Question Word poster. **Write three questions about the words on the page. Begin the questions with question words.**

2. Use the SAP page. Have students read and spell each word. Spelling list: bedtime, raindrops, keyboard, earthworm, lighthouse, without, horseshoe, playground, yourself, friendship, sidewalk, bullfrog, skateboard, footstool

   Top section: **Sort the words in each box in alphabetical order.**

   Bottom section: **Look at the list of five compound words. They have one of the words that make up a compound word in the spelling list. Write the spelling words that have one of the same words.**

3. *Hound Dog Hoedown* focuses on compound words. The following words may also be new to students: earthworms, Bumpkin, guests, opossum, parlor, youngins'. The word bass on page 10 is pronounced with the long a sound. It is a homograph of bass, a kind of fish.

   The book captures some of the dialect of the characters. Typically, the final g on ing endings is dropped. An apostrophe appears in its place (fiddlin'), just like contractions use apostrophes to indicate that letters have been dropped. Not every word was changed to match the dialog, so the reader wouldn't get too distracted.

   Introduce the story: Ask a student to read the title of the book. **What is the name of this story?** *(Hound Dog Hoedown)*. **What is a hoedown?** Answers may vary. **A hoedown is a big party. You will find a synonym for hoedown in the story. Read to see if you can discover what it is.**

   Students will read the words on the back of the book out loud. Students will silently read as much of the story as they can in the time allowed.

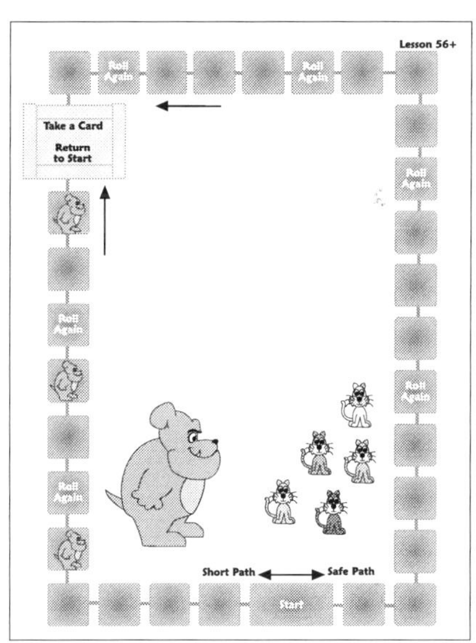

4. Play the Dog Pound Compound game after adding the crates from the second sheet of crates. The directions are on the game board.

5. Use the handwriting sheet or have the children write the following:

   Can I ride the skateboard?
   I will stay on the sidewalk.

SAP Answers

1. bedtime	5. friendship
2. bullfrog	6. horseshoe
3. earthworm	7. keyboard
4. footstool	

1. lighthouse	5. skateboard
2. playground	6. without
3. raindrops	7. yourself
4. sidewalk	

bedtime horseshoe
without
yourself sidewalk

LAR Answers

Wording may vary.

gristmill: a place to grind grain
parlor: a room in a house for friends
washtub: a tub for washing clothes
washboard: a wavy piece of metal used to scrub clothes
blacksmith: someone who works with metal
anvil: a table for hammering metal

The Hound Dog Hoedown

Second Grade Phonics & Reading

Book 27
Lessons 146 to 150

Hound Dog Hoedown

Written and illustrated by
Brian Davis

Something was going on in the barnyard. Buckshot the hound dog stared bug-eyed.

"Look at all the decorations," he said to his sister, Bumpkin.

"It's just grand," Bumpkin commented.

"Look out below, youngins'," yelled their pappy. He peered out of the hayloft. "I'll be tossing down haybales."

"Are we havin' a wingding?" asked Buckshot.

"That's right," said their pappy. "We're having us a hoedown."

"Will you be fiddlin'?" asked Bumpkin.

"What's a hoedown without fiddlin'?" asked Pappy. "Now get your hoedown chores done."

2

3

The Hound Dog Hoedown

Buckshot and Bumpkin liked doing hoedown chores. The pups raced to the haystack. They each grabbed a pitchfork.

Buckshot and Bumpkin loaded a wagon with hay.

"That will make a mighty fine hayride," said Bumpkin.

Next, they ran to the gristmill.

"We'd like a bag of cornmeal, please," Bumpkin said to the miller.

"Is your momma making cornbread and hushpuppies?" asked the miller.

"Yes sir," said Buckshot. "It's for the hoedown. Are you coming?"

"I never miss a wingding," smiled the miller.

4

5

Next, they went to the pond. Buckshot dug for earthworms.

"I'll soon catch us a mess of catfish," said Buckshot.

Bumpkin waded into the creek. "I've got half a bucket of crawfish, already."

"Yum, yum," said Buckshot.

They took the food back to the barnyard. Their momma was coming out of the house. She carried a large punchbowl.

"Help me carry the blackbird pies, Buckshot."

"I'll get the applesauce," said Bumpkin.

Momma hound and her pups put the food on the table.

"Blackbird pies, yum, yum," said Pappy. "We'll be ready for the hoedown, soon. I'd best be putting on my dancing overalls."

The four hound dogs headed for the house.

6

7

The Hound Dog Hoedown

A mother opossum had a burrow right under the table.

"Did someone say hoedown?" she asked sleepily.

Opossums sleep in the day. She thought she may have been dreaming. Then, she smelled the crawfish.

She climbed out of the burrow. The mother opossum looked around. She saw a table of food. The opossum saw haybale benches. She looked at all the decorations.

"It looks like they'll be having a mighty big hoedown. My babies won't sleep a wink. Hounds will be stomping and fiddlin' all day long. I must prevent this wingding."

Then the mother opossum had an idea.

8

9

The guests started arriving. The bullfrog singers came all the way from the swamp. They could croak some lively tunes.

"Where's your brother Hopper?" asked Bumpkin.

"He's back at the swamp. He can't sing today," said the bullfrogs. "He has a frog in his throat."

The band was in the barnyard. The old greyhound played the washtub bass. Joe the bulldog clicked his toenails on the washboard.

"Go get your fiddle, Pappy," said the old greyhound. "We're having us a wingding."

Pappy sent Buckshot to the house to get the fiddle.

10

11

The Hound Dog Hoedown

The fiddle wasn't in his parent's bedroom. It wasn't in the icebox. It wasn't in the parlor. The fiddle was nowhere to be found.

"I'll look in the barnyard," thought Buckshot.

The pup looked in the haystack. All he found was one of his momma's sewing needles.

"She's been looking for this," thought Buckshot.

The pup went into the barn. He looked in the hayloft. He even asked the livestock.

"Have you seen Pappy's fiddle?"

They all said no. Pappy came into the barn.

"What's going on, Buckshot? We can't have a hoedown without a fiddle."

"I can't find hide nor hair of it," said Buckshot.

12

13

The guests looked all over for the fiddle. The old greyhound searched the backwoods.

"This looks like a fiddle thief hideout," thought the greyhound.

The greyhound looked up into the treetops.

"Probably a squirrel took it," said the greyhound. "Them squirrels are nuts for fiddles."

The greyhound didn't see the quicksand. He stepped right into it.

"Help," howled the greyhound. "I'm sinking in quicksand."

The guests were too far away.

"What's all that howling?"grumbled the mother opossum. "My babies are going to wake up."

She scurried into the backwoods. The greyhound was up to his armpits in quicksand.

14

15

The Hound Dog Hoedown

"Why are you howling?" asked the opossum. "You're going to wake my babies."

"I'm sinking," answered the greyhound. "I'm howling for help."

The opossum scurried up a tree. She walked on a branch over the quicksand. The opossum hung by her tail.

"Hand me your paws," said the opossum.

She pulled out the greyhound. They walked back to the barnyard.

"Oh no," said the opossum. Her children were munching on cornbread and crawfish. "Your howling woke them up."

"Well it's nighttime now. Aren't they supposed to be awake?" asked the greyhound.

A little opossum was tugging a fiddle. "This was in our burrow."

"I think we're ready for that hoedown now," said the mother opossum.

They had a mighty grand wingding all night long.

16

Hound Dog Hoedown word list:

applesauce	cornmeal	hushpuppies	quicksand
aren't	crawfish	icebox	scurried
armpits	dancing	lively	sewing
arriving	decorations	livestock	sleepily
babies	earthworms	mighty	someone
backwoods	fiddle	miller	something
barnyard	fiddlin'	momma	stomping
bedroom	greyhound	needles	supposed
blackbird	gristmill	nighttime	swamp
Buckshot	grumbled	nowhere	table
bug-eyed	guests	opossum	thief
bullfrog	haybales	overalls	toenails
Bumpkin	hayloft	pappy	treetops
burrow	hayride	parent's	washboard
catfish	haystack	parlor	washtub
chores	hideout	pitchfork	wingding
commented	hoedown	prevent	without
cornbread	howled	punchbowl	youngins'

Lesson 147

Lesson Objectives

1. Students will correct sentences using compound words. (P)
2. Students will review parts of speech. (L)
3. Students will use spelling words in sentences. (S)
4. Students will read the story *Hound Dog Hoedown*. (R)
5. Students will copy sentences neatly and correctly. (H)

Materials

LAR
SAP
Hound Dog Hoedown

Teaching

1. Write the nonsense sentence: I stood on the keystool to reach the footboard. **Read the sentence. What's wrong with it?** (The parts of the compound sentences are switched.) **How should the sentence read?** (I stood on the footstool to reach the keyboard.)
   Use the top of the LAR workbook page. **Read the nonsense sentences. Rewrite the sentences correctly.**

2. Review the terms noun, pronoun, verb, adjective, and adverb. Use the bottom of the LAR workbook page. **Read the sentences. A word is underlined. Write how the word is used on the line (noun, verb, adjective, adverb).**

3. Use the SAP page. Top section: **Fit all the words into the grid. There is one clue space, the letter g.**

   Give the following examples before assigning the bottom section. Write the pairs of words: racehorse snowshoe, sideways spacewalk, earthquake silkworm, bulldog leapfrog. **Read these silly phrases. We can combine parts of them to make spelling words. What spelling word can you find using the first phrase, racehorse snowshoe?** (horseshoe) Repeat with the other phrases: sidewalk, earthworm, bullfrog.

   Bottom section: **Find the spelling word in each phrase. Write the spelling word on the lines.**

4. Students will read pages 1 to 8 out loud. Next, ask the following questions:

   What was Pappy tossing? (Haybales)
   What are the pup's names? (Buckshot and Bumpkin)
   What is someone who works at a gristmill called? (A miller)
   What did the pups catch in the water? (Crawfish, catfish)
   Do you know what a crawfish is? (It's a kind of lobster that lives in ponds and streams)
   What are hushpuppies? (Deep fried balls of cornmeal)
   What animal wasn't excited about a hoedown? (The opossum)
   Why? (Because she wanted her babies to sleep.)

5. Use the handwriting sheet or have the children

   write the following:

   An opossum was in the hayloft.
   I think it is somewhere else now.

Lesson 147

LAR Answers

Top
1. We caught the catfish with the earthworm.
2. I did my homework at nighttime.
3. The raindrops soaked the playground.

Bottom
1. pronoun
2. noun
3. adjective
4. adverb
5. verb

SAP Answers

```
             s
             keyboard
        b    a##e
        u    t##d
footstool    earthworm
        l    b  i i
        f    o  m t
   raindrops a  e h
        o    r    o
    playground    u
     i#o          t
     g#u
     horseshoe
     t s
     h e
     o l
     u friendship
     s
  sidewalk
```

friendship keyboard

playground

footstool

Lesson 148

Lesson Objectives

1. Students will review parts of speech. (L)
2. Students will recognize incomplete sentences. (L)
3. Students will use spelling words in sentences. (S)
4. Students will read the story *Hound Dog Hoedown*. (R)
5. Students will copy sentences neatly and correctly. (H)

Materials

LAR
SAP
Hound Dog Hoedown
Writing Skills Workbook page is available

Teaching

1. Use the top of the LAR page. **Read the sentences. Match the numbers to the parts of speech.**

2. Use the bottom of the LAR page. **Read the sentences. Are they complete or incomplete? Fill in yes if the sentence is complete. Fill in no if it is incomplete. Add parts to the incomplete sentences and write them on the lines.**

3. Use the SAP page. **Complete the pairs of sentences with the words in each box.**

4. Review the first half of the book *Hound Dog Hoedown*. Next, read the second half of the book. After completing the story ask the students the following questions:

   Why couldn't Hopper sing? (He had a frog in his throat.)
   Who played bass? (The old greyhound)
   What was lost? (A fiddle)
   Who took it? (The mother opossum.)
   Why did she think it was okay to have the hoedown at night? (Her babies were awake.)
   What did Buckshot find in the haystack? (A sewing needle)
   Who got stuck in quicksand? (The old greyhound)
   Who saved him? (The opossum)
   Who did the greyhound think took the fiddle? (Squirrels)
   What were the baby opossums eating? (Cornbread and crawfish)

5. Use the handwriting sheet or have the children write the following:

   Tom bought a can of earthworms.
   He wants to catch a catfish.

LAR Answers

2 noun, 3 verb, 4 adverb, 1 adjective, 5 pronoun

1 noun, 2 verb, 3 adverb, 5 adjective, 4 pronoun

5 noun, 3 verb, 2 adverb, 4 adjective, 1 pronoun

1. yes ●
2. ● no
3. ● no
4. yes ●
5. ● no

SAP Answers

1. skateboard playground
2. bullfrog earthworm

3. yourself bedtime
4. raindrops sidewalk

5. without lighthouse
6. horseshoe footstool

7. without keyboard
8. bedtime friendship

Lesson 149

Lesson Objectives

1. Students will write dialogue. (L)
2. Students will review spelling words. (S)
3. Students will write a story. (CW)
4. Students will read the story *Hound Dog Hoedown*. (R)
5. Students will copy sentences neatly and correctly. (H)

Materials

LAR
SAP
Hound Dog Hoedown

Teaching

1. Use the LAR workbook page to teach writing dialogue. The text from the page is reprinted below.

Writing Dialogue

Both of the stories in the boxes tell the same thing. One describes what is said. The other uses dialogue. It uses the exact words of the characters. This makes it easier to understand how the characters are expressing themselves. This makes the writing more interesting.

Use quotation marks to show when a character is speaking. Begin the quotation with a capital letter. Some of the words are not in quotation marks. These are words that aren't said by the character, but give you extra details, such as which character is talking.

Commas end the quotation if it is followed by other words unless it is an exclamation or a question. Use a question mark if the character is asking a question. Use an exclamation mark to show a character is excited. Periods replace commas if the dialogue is at the end of the sentence. The second quotation mark follows the ending punctuation of the dialogue.

Buckshot told his sister, Bumpkin, to look at all the decorations. She thought they were grand.

Suddenly, the pups heard their pappy shout. Pappy was getting ready to toss down some haybales. He warned the pups to stay out of the way.

"Look at all the decorations," Buckshot said to his sister, Bumpkin.

"It's just grand," Bumpkin commented.

"Look out below, youngins'," yelled their pappy. He peered out of the hayloft. "I'll be tossing down haybales."

On another piece of paper, write dialogue for these paragraphs. Add in more details if you would like.

Hopper the bullfrog asked his friends if they wanted to sing with him. The mudpuppy said she would love to sing. The catfish said he could sing bass. The crawfish offered to play the fiddle.

Soon, an oppossum came to listen. He thought the group was great. He suggested they make a recording. He thought their music would be very soothing. The animals were very excited. They talked about becoming rich and famous stars.

Continued on the next page.

Provide the student with dialogue punctuation examples. Write the following dialogue as an example.

"The kitten is so playful," said my sister. **Find the comma in the sentence. What is after the comma?** (the ending quotation mark) **The word *said* follows the quotation mark, so a comma was used.** Change the sentence to "Is the kitten playful?" asked my sister. **What punctuation mark would follow the word *playful*?** (A question mark) **If you wanted to show that the sister was excited when she spoke, what punctuation mark would follow the word playful?** (exclamation mark).

Change the sentence to: My sister said, "The kitten is so playful." **This time a comma follows the word *said* to show that there is a pause in the sentence. What is after the word *playful*?** (period) **Use a period unless it is a question or exclamation.**

You may also note that the first word that begins the dialog is capitalized. In the second example, the word *The* was capitalized even though it followed the word *said,* because it was the beginning of the dialogue.

2. Use the SAP page. **Match the spelling words to the descriptions. Write your answers on the lines.**

3. Students will write a story. **The story Hound Dog Hoedown used a lot of old fashioned words. Someday, our words might sound old fashioned. Pretend that you hop into a time machine. You go into the future. You're talking to someone, but they don't understand your old fashioned words. What words might be old fashioned? You can even make up new words for the future.**

4. Read the book *Hound Dog Hoedown* again. Next, have students look at the back of the book and answer the following questions about the word list. You may do this orally or have students write answers:

   What is something made from a fruit? (applesauce)
   What is a synonym for farm animals? (livestock)
   What word has the er sound spelled e-a-r? (earthworm)
   What word has the long o sound spelled with ow? (burrow, punchbowl)
   What word is something that flies? (blackbird)
   What word is a place with big grinding wheels? (gristmill)
   What word is something on your feet? (toenails)
   What word is a synonym of hoedown? (wingding)
   What words are things replaced by a washing machine? (washtub, washboard)
   What words end with ly? (lively, sleepily)

5. Use the handwriting sheet or have the children write the following:

   I lost my homework paper.
   I had it on the playground.

SAP Answers

skateboard	keyboard
bedtime	footstool
sidewalk	playground
lighthouse	earthworm
bullfrog	yourself
horseshoe	without
raindrops	friendship

LAR Answers

Answers vary

Lesson 150

Lesson Objectives

1. Students will be tested on phonics concepts. (P)
2. Students will be tested on language concepts. (L)
3. Students will take a spelling test. (S)
4. Students will read the story they have written. (R)
5. Students will copy a sentence neatly and correctly. (H)

Materials

LAR
Creative writing assignment from lesson 149
Assessment 150
Hound Dog Hoedown

Teaching

1. Use part A of the assessment as a phonics test. Have the students fill in the circles next to the words that complete the sentences.

2. Use part B of the assessment page. Number each set of compound words in alphabetical order from 1 to 3.

3. Have students number their papers from 1 to 14. Give the following words as dictation.

   Spelling word list:

   1. lighthouse, 2. playground, 3. earthworm, 4. yourself, 5. sidewalk, 6. keyboard,

   7. raindrops, 8. horseshoe, 9. bullfrog 10. bedtime 11. without, 12. friendship,

   13. skateboard, 14. footstool

4. Use the LAR page. **Write sentences to answer the questions on the top part. Read the statements on the bottom part and decide if they are true or false.**

5. Have students take turns reading the books or stories that were written during the creative writing section of the previous lesson.

6. Use the handwriting sheet or have the children write the following:

   A blacksmith hammers metal.
   He can make horseshoes.

Assessment Answers

Phonics Test

1. gristmill
2. bedtime
3. barnyard
4. playground
5. pinecone

Language Test

2 3 1	1 2 3

3 2 1	2 1 3	3 1 2

LAR Answers

Wording may vary

1. A wingding is a hoedown.
2. Pappy plays the fiddle.
3. The pups got a bag of cornmeal.
4. Pappy was going to wear dancing overalls.
5. She thought the hounds would stomp and dance.

5. true **false**

Lesson 151

Lesson Objectives

1. Students will read compound words and words with a silent u. (P)
2. Students will practice vocabulary skills. (L)
3. Students will spell words correctly. (S)
4. Students will read *The Bobcat Cowboy Jellybean Train Robbery.* (R)
5. Students will copy sentences neatly and correctly. (H)

Materials

LAR
SAP
The Bobcat Cowboy Jellybean Train Robbery
Writing Skills Workbook page is available

Word List: Silent u list: build, builder, building, built, disguise, guarantee, guard, guardrail, guess, guesswork, guest, guide, guidebook, guideline, guidepost, guilt, guiltless, guilty, guinea hen, guinea pig, guitar

Teaching

1. This list is made up of mainly three-syllable compound words and some four-syllable compound words. Some have been included in other lessons. Choose words from the list. Write parts of words and have students add the parts to make words. Have students write the words on a piece of paper.

   In addition to the compound words is a list of words with a silent u. All of them begin with g except words with the root word *build.* The a, i, or e following the silent u retain their own sounds in these words.

   Use the top of the LAR workbook page. **Read the words. They are spelled incorrectly. They need a silent u before the first vowel. Write the words correctly.**

2. Use the bottom of the LAR workbook page. Have students read the definitions. Students will choose the words that answers the questions. Write the words on the lines.

3. Use the SAP page. Have students read and spell each word. Spelling list: guess, business, guitar, penguin, league, fatigue, built, guardrail, anguish, building, tongue, guilty, disguise, guarantee. Make sure students know the meaning of each word.

   Look at the word *business.* The first vowel sound is spelled with u and i, but the s is in front of the i and the u is silent. The word looks like it has three syllables, but it only has two.

   Top section: **Sort the words by the number of syllables.**

   Bottom section: **Add suffixes to the words. Remember the spelling rules.**

4. *The Bobcat Cowboy Jellybean Train Robbery* focuses on compound words and words with silent u. The following words may also be new to students: poster, wonderful.

   Introduce the story: Ask a student to read the title of the book. **What is the name of this story?** *(The Bobcat Cowboy Jellybean Train Robbery).* **Have you read about the Bobcat Cowboys before? What happened in the last bobcat cowboy story? The bobcat cowboys weren't too successful at robbing a stagecoach. Read to find out how well they do at robbing a train.**

   Students will read the words on the back of the book out loud.
   Students will silently read as much of the story as they can in the time allowed.

5. Use the handwriting sheet or have the children write the following:

   The guidebook said to be careful.
   Rattlesnakes roam in the backwoods.

LAR Answers

Part A

1. builder
2. guinea
3. guard
4. guest
5. built
6. guide

Part B

1. guardrail
2. gingerbread
3. jellyfish
4. arrowhead
5. buttercups
6. guidelines

SAP Answers

One syllable
guess league built tongue

Two syllables
business guitar penguin fatigue
guardrail anguish building guilty disguise

Three syllables
guarantee

Suffixes
guessing guiltier
disguising
guaranteeing guardrails

The Bobcat Cowboy Jellybean Train Robbery

Written and illustrated by
Brian Davis

Sheriff Prairie Dog held the Rowdent Gulch newspaper.

"The Bobcat Cowboys are out of jail," read the sheriff. "Their mother, Bessybob Bobcat, paid their fine."

"Weren't they guilty of robbing the stagecoach?" asked Deputy Guinea Pig.

The guinea pig was new in town. Sheriff Prairie Dog had just hired him.

"That's right," said the sheriff. "We built a big goldfish. It disguised a steamboat."

The sheriff handed Deputy Guinea Pig an old wanted poster. The guinea pig put on his eyeglasses.

"They look like troublemakers," said Deputy Guinea Pig.

"They could come back," said Sheriff Prairie Dog. "We've got to tell everyone."

2

3

The Bobcat Cowboy Jellybean Train Robbery

"Are we going to rob another stagecoach?" asked Bubba.

Billybob laughed, "We're undertaking something much bigger. We're going to stickup a train."

"Won't that take a lot of glue?" asked Bubba.

"Hushup, Bubba," said Bobbybill. "Billybob has a plan. It's guaranteed to work."

"Thank you," said Billybob. "A trainload of jellybeans is heading to Rowdent Gulch. It will be here tomorrow. You'll stop the train, and I'll unhook the jellybean boxcar. Bobbybill will help unload it."

"What will we glue the train to?" asked Bubba.

"Hushup, Bubba," said Billybob.

4

5

The bobcats didn't see the woodpecker. He was standing on a telegraph pole. He tapped out a message to Sheriff Prairie Dog.

The sheriff read the message, "Bobcats are undertaking to rob the train. They want the jellybean shipment."

"This is awful," said Deputy Prairie Dog. "Where do you think they'll strike?"

The sheriff rubbed his head.

"My guess is Honeysuckle Pass. They can unhook the jellybean boxcar. It will roll away from the train. We'd better ride that way."

The sheriff and deputy rode to Honeysuckle Pass. They hid behind a rock. The bobcat cowboys were building something.

"We're outnumbered," said Deputy Guinea Pig.
"Is there anything we can do?"

"We've got to get more help," sighed Sheriff Prairie Dog.

The two lawmen rode back to town. The bobcat cowboys kept working.

6

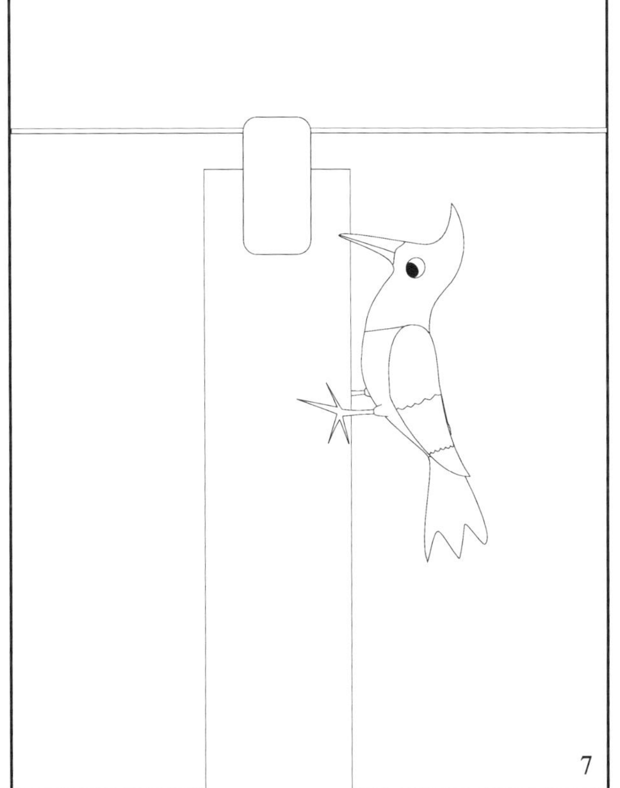

7

The Bobcat Cowboy Jellybean Train Robbery

"So how do we make the train stop?" asked Bubba.

"Easy," said Billybob. "We're building a Rowdent Gulch Free Guidebook stand."

"Everyone likes a free guidebook," said Bobbybill.

"Can they color it?" asked Bubba.

"Hushup, Bubba," said Billybob. "There isn't really a guidebook. It's a trick."

"Won't everyone be disappointed?" asked Bubba.

"Hushup, Bubba," said Bobbybill. "We're supposed to disappoint them. We're train robbers. It's our job."

"I thought we ran a guidebook stand," thought Bubba. "I'm kind of disappointed."

8

9

The next day, the Jellybean Express chugged along. The rodents of Rowdent Gulch waited at Honeysuckle Pass. They hid behind rocks watching the Bobcat Cowboys.

The sheriff had telegraphed the jellybean bank. There were no jellybeans on the train.

Billybob and Bobbybill left Bubba at the guidebook stand. Bubba waited until they were out of sight. Bubba took down the guidebook stand sign. He put up his own sign.

It read, "Bubba's Marshmallow Hamburgers."

The train was coming. It slowed down climbing the hill to Honeysuckle Pass. The train came to a stop at Bubba's hamburger stand.

10

11

The Bobcat Cowboy Jellybean Train Robbery

Billybob and Bobbybill were about to steal the jellybeans. Just then, all the rodents from Rowdent Gulch lined up at Bubba's stand.

The line was as long as the train. The bobcats knew they would be caught if they took the jellybeans.

Bubba was having a good time.

"How would you like your marshmallow hamburger? With or without pineapple?" Bubba asked a muskrat.

"With pineapple," said the muskrat.

"That will be four jellybeans," said Bubba.

The muskrat bit into the pineapple, marshmallow hamburger.

"This is wonderful!" said the muskrat.

Everyone loved the hamburgers. The line kept getting longer.

12

13

The jellybeans Bubba charged were piling up.

"There might be jellybean thieves around," thought Bubba. "I need a safe place for these."

That's when Bubba saw Deputy Guinea Pig.

"Deputy," Bubba called. "Can you find a safe place for my jellybeans?"

Deputy Guinea Pig thought for a moment. "I guess you can put them on the train. We can haul them to the bank."

Soon, Bubba had filled up the boxcar. Billybob and Bobbybill had waited for all the rodents to leave. They had fallen asleep in their hideout. They woke up just as the last rodents were leaving.

14

15

"Quick, let's steal the jellybeans," said Billybob.

The bobcats unhooked the boxcar. It rolled down the hill. Billybob opened the boxcar door.

"Put your hands up," said Sheriff Prairie Dog.

Deputy Guinea Pig put handcuffs on Billybob. "You're under arrest for stealing Bubba's jellybeans."

"Bubba's jellybeans?" asked Billybob.

"He asked us to guard them," said Deputy Guinea Pig.

Bubba hopped out of the boxcar. "I sold pineapple, marshmallow hamburgers. I didn't give away free guidebooks. You couldn't color them. Everyone would have been disappointed."

"Who would want a pineapple, marshmallow hamburger?" asked Billybob.

Bobbybill nibbled a pineapple, marshmallow hamburger.

"Hushup, Billybob. These are good," said Bobbybill.

16

The Bobcat Cowboy Jellybean Train Robbery word list:

another	everyone	lawmen	stagecoach
anything	eyeglasses	marshmallow	steamboat
arrest	glue	message	stickup
asleep	goldfish	moment	telegraph
awful	guaranteed	muskrat	thieves
Bessybob	guard	newspaper	tomorrow
Billybob	guidebook	outnumbered	trainload
bobcat	guilty	pineapple	troublemakers
boxcar	guinea	poster	undertaking
Bubba	gulch	prairie	unhooked
building	hamburgers	rodent	unload
cowboys	handcuffs	Rowdent	wanted
deputy	hideout	sheriff	weren't
disappointed	Honeysuckle	shipment	wonderful
disguised	jellybeans	something	woodpecker

Lesson 152

Lesson Objectives

1. Students will correct sentences using compound words. (P)
2. Students will review parts of speech. (L)
3. Students will review spelling words. (S)
4. Students will read The *Bobcat Cowboy Jellybean Train Robbery.* (R)
5. Students will copy sentences neatly and correctly. (H)

Materials

LAR
SAP
The Bobcat Cowboy Jellybean Train Robbery

Teaching

1. Write the nonsense sentence: My pinemother sliced the grandapple. **Read the sentence. What is wrong it?** (The parts of the compound sentences are switched.) **What's the correct sentence?** (My grandmother sliced the pineapple.)

   Use the top of the LAR workbook page. **Read the nonsense sentences. Rewrite the sentences correctly.**

2. Review the terms noun, verb, adjective, and adverb. Use the bottom of the LAR workbook page. **Read the sentences. A word is underlined. Have students write how the word is used on the line.** (noun, verb, adjective, adverb)

3. Use the SAP page. Top section: **Each box contains two spelling words. Can the other words be made from the spelling words? Answer yes or no.**

   Bottom section: **Proofread the sentences. Write them correctly on the lines.**

4. Students will read pages 1 to 8 out loud. Next, ask the following questions:

   Why wasn't Deputy Guinea Pig in the first story? (He was new in Rowdent Gulch.)
   How did the Bobcat get out of jail? (Bessybob paid their fine.)
   What did Bubba think they were going to put on the train? (glue)
   Why? (To stick it up.)
   What was on the train that the bobcats wanted? (jellybeans)
   What telegraphed the sheriff? (a woodpecker)
   What was the bobcat's plan for stopping the train?
   (They pretended to be giving away free guidebooks.)

5. Use the handwriting sheet or have the children write the following:

   Mr. Kent works for the newspaper.
   His office is in that building.

LAR Answers

Top

1. I saw bumblebees by the blackberries
2. Somebody ate my hamburger.
3. The jellybean tasted like pineapples.

Bottom

1. adjective
2. noun
3. verb
4. adverb
5. pronoun

SAP Answers

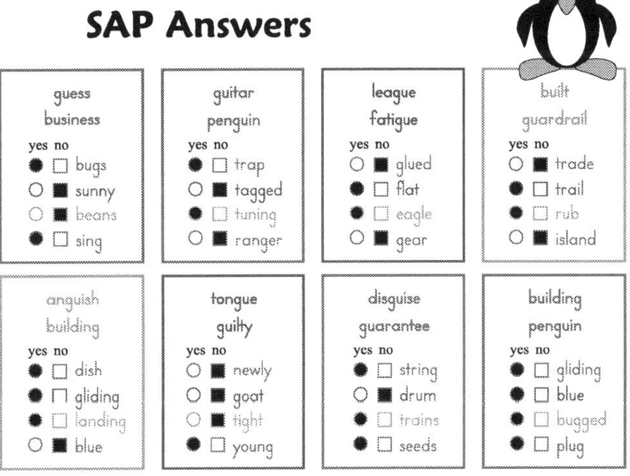

The penguin wore a funny disguise.
Can you guess what is in that building?

Lesson 153

Lesson Objectives

1. Students will find the main idea of paragraphs. (L)
2. Students will review spelling words. (S)
3. Students will complete analogies with spelling words. (S & L)
4. Students will read *The Bobcat Cowboy Jellybean Train Robbery.* (R)
5. Students will copy sentences neatly and correctly. (H)

Materials

LAR
SAP
The Bobcat Cowboy Jellybean Train Robbery

Teaching

1. Use the LAR page. **Read the paragraphs. Find the main ideas and fill in the circles.**
2. Use the top of the SAP page. **Read the sentences A word is underlined. Write the spelling word that can take the place of the underlined word and change the sentence the least.**
3. Use the bottom of the SAP page. **Complete the analogies with spelling words.**
4. Review the first half of the book *The Bobcat Cowboy Jellybean Train Robbery.* Next, read the second half of the book. After completing the story ask the students these questions:

   Why weren't there jellybeans on the train? (The sheriff had warned them.)
   How did Bubba change the guidebook stand? (He made it into a hamburger stand.)
   How do you think a pineapple, marshmallow hamburger would taste? (answers vary)
   Why couldn't the bobcats rob the train right after it stopped? (There were too many rodents around.)
   Did the rodents like the hamburgers? (yes)
   What was Bubba afraid would get stolen? (jellybeans)
   Why do you think he thought robbers were in the area? (answers vary)
   Who stole his jellybeans? (Billybob and Bobbybill)
   Did they know the jellybeans were Bubba's? (no) **Do you think they would have done something different it they had known?** (answers vary)

5. Use the handwriting sheet or have the children write the following:

   We ate hamburgers at the table.
   My sister liked the tablecloth.

LAR Answers

It's interesting being a scientist.

Bubba's stand was very successful.

The guidebook was confusing.

We used all our senses on a hike.

SAP Answers

1. built
2. building
3. guarantee
4. disguise
5. business
6. guess
7. guardrail

Analogies

guitar	anguish
tongue	guilty
penguin	fatigue

Lesson 154

Lesson Objectives

1. Students will review story elements. (L)
2. Students will review spelling words. (S)
3. Students will read the story. (R)
4. Students will copy sentences neatly and correctly. (H)

Materials

LAR
SAP
The Bobcat Cowboy Jellybean Train Robbery
Writing Skills Workbook page is available

Teaching

1. Use the LAR workbook page. Guide the students through the page.

   Write numbers to match the story elements. Let's start with the conflict. Who are the heroes and the villains? Write the numbers in the circles. (Heroes 6, 7 Villains 4)

   Background is information that is given in the story about the past. It doesn't take place in the story, but it is talked about to give the reader a clearer understanding. Write the two statements that give background information. (It will not matter which side the numbers are written in for the rest of the story elements.) (Background 3, 9)

   The plot is what happens in the story. Find the two sentences that give an overall idea of what happens in the story. Fill in the circles. (Plot 2, 11)

   The setting is where the story takes place. Fill in the number for the setting. (Setting 1)

   The climax is the high point of the story where you wonder what will happen next. It's near the end of the story. What two sentences are about the climax? (Climax 8, 12)

   The resolution is the ending of the story. It gives more information about what happened after the climax. Find the two sentences that tell what happens at the very end of the story. (Resolution 5, 10)

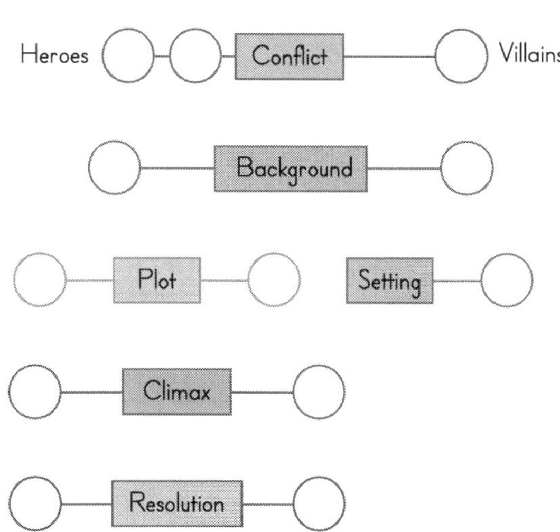

1. Honeysuckle Pass.
2. Bobcats plan to steal jellybeans.
3. The bobcats robded a stagecoach.
4. Bobcat Cowboys
5. The jellybeans belonged to Bubba.
6. Sheriff Prairie Dog

7. Deputy Guinea Pig
8. The sheriff surprises two bobcats.
9. A steamboat is disguised as a goldfish.
10. Bobbybill enjoyed a hamburger.
11. The sheriff must stop a train robbery.
12. Billybob opened a boxcar door

2. Use the SAP workbook page. **Match the spelling words to the descriptions. Write your answers on the lines.**

3. Read the book *The Bobcat Cowboy Jellybean Train Robbery* again. Next, have students look at the back of the book and answer the following questions about the word list. You may do this orally or have students write answers:

   What is something usually made of beef? (hamburger)
   What words have a silent u as the second letter? (building, guaranteed, guard, guidebook, guilty, guinea)
   What word is the opposite of hooked? (unhooked)
   What two words are homophones? (rodent, Rowdent)
   What words are things Bubba put on hamburgers? (pineapple, marshmallow)
   What compound word has a silent u? (guidebook)
   What word has a silent u in the middle of it? (disguise)
   What word has the most letters? (troublemakers)
   What word is a part of a train? (boxcar)
   What word is a bird? (woodpecker)

4. Use the handwriting sheet or have the children write the following:

   The guitar is fun to play.
   Your fingernail can strum it.

LAR Answers

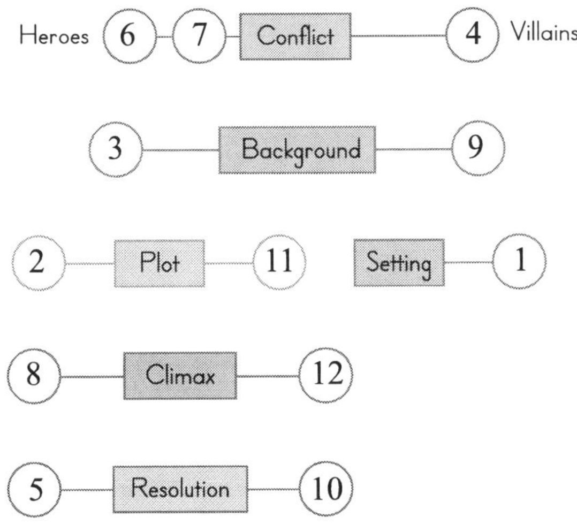

SAP Answers

tongue	penguin
guess	guilty
guardrail	business
league	anguish
guitar	disguise
guarantee	building
fatigue	built

Lesson 155

Lesson Objectives

1. Students will be tested on phonics concepts. (P)
2. Students will be tested on language concepts. (L)
3. Students will take a spelling test. (S)
4. Students will answer questions about the story. (R)
5. Students will copy a sentence neatly and correctly. (H)

Materials

LAR
Assessment 155
The Bobcat Cowboy Jellybean Train Robbery

Teaching

1. Use part A of the assessment as a phonics test. Have the students fill in the circles next to the words that complete the sentences.

2. Use part B of the assessment page. Students will make five compound words from the words in the list.

3. Have students number their papers from 1 to 14. Give the following words as dictation.

   Spelling word list:

   1. built, 2. guess, 3. anguish, 4. guitar, 5. building, 6. disguise, 7. guardrail, 8. league,

   9. guilty 10. business 11. tongue, 12. guarantee, 13. penguin, 14. fatigue

4. Use LAR page 146. **Read the questions. Write complete sentences for answers. At the bottom of the page, write another question about the story, *The Bobcat Cowboy Jellybean Train Robbery.* Write the answer to your questions on the last lines.**

5. Use the handwriting sheet or have the children write the following:

   My grandfather built a skyrocket.
   It is louder than a firecracker.

LAR Answers

Wording of answers may vary.

1. Bubba started a hamburger stand.
2. Bubba charged four jellybeans.
3. It tapped it on a telegraph line.
4. Bubba wanted to color the guidebooks.
5. The train stopped at Honeysuckle Pass.

Assessment Answers

Phonics Test

1. guidelines
2. eyeglasses
3. building
4. jellybeans
5. grasshopper

Language Test
any of the following
in any order

fingernail
guidebook
rattlesnake
newspaper
bumblebee
gingerbread

Lesson 156

Lesson Objectives

1. Students will review words where o makes the u sound and words where u is silent. (P)
2. Students will review compound sentences. (L)
3. Students will review spelling words. (S)
4. Students will copy sentences neatly and correctly. (H)

Materials

LAR
SAP

Lessons 156 to 158 will review phonics and language concepts taught in lessons 121 to 155. There will be no reading book or creative writing assignment given. Students may read books from previous weeks or have students try reading library books. Compound words will not be reviewed, but will be included on the test. **Lessons 159 and 160** will be set aside for the fourth unit test.

Review Word List

From Lesson 121: above, another, become, beloved, blood, collide, color, come, comfort, comfortable, commend, community, company, compass, compare, compete, complain, complete, computer, conclude, confuse, connect, consider, control, cover, done, dove, falcon, from, front, glove, love, lovely, mammoth, month, mother; none, nothing, of, onion, other, oven, shove, shovel, some, somewhat, somewhere, someone, sometime, something, son, ton, undone, welcome

From Lesson 151: build, builder, building, built, disguise, guarantee, guard, guardrail, guess, guesswork, guest, guide, guidebook, guideline, guidepost, guilt, guiltless, guilty, guinea hen, guinea pig, guitar

Teaching

1. Choose words from the two lists. Write a few words from the lesson 121 list. Ask students to find the letter that made the short u sound in each word.

   Use the top of the LAR workbook page. **Read the sentences. Letters are missing in the words. Fill in the missing vowels.**

2. Review conjunctions and, but, and or. Remind students to use a comma before conjunctions in compound sentences.

   Bottom of the LAR workbook page: **Combine the sentences using conjunctions.**

3. Use the SAP page. Have students read and spell each word. Spelling list: welcome, another, question, direction, unlikely, sweetly, remember, replace, agreement, basement, friendship, sidewalk, waterfall, building, guitar

   Top section: **Sort the words by the number of syllables.**

   Bottom section: **Add suffixes to the words. Remember the spelling rules.**

4. Use the handwriting sheet or have the children write the following sentences:

   The falcon spied the guinea hen.
   They are building a glove company.

LAR Answers

Part A

1. Someone left the computer running.
2. Mother built a comfortable chair.
3. The car collided with the guardrail.
4. The compass guided us in the woods.
5. The falcon made a nest on the building.

Part B

1. The man played a guitar, and his son played the banjo.
2. The children built a sand castle, but the sea washed it away.
3. We can look in the guidebook, or you can ask for help.

SAP Answers

Two syllables

welcome question sweetly
replace basement friendship
sidewalk building guitar

Three syllables

another direction unlikely
remember agreement waterfall

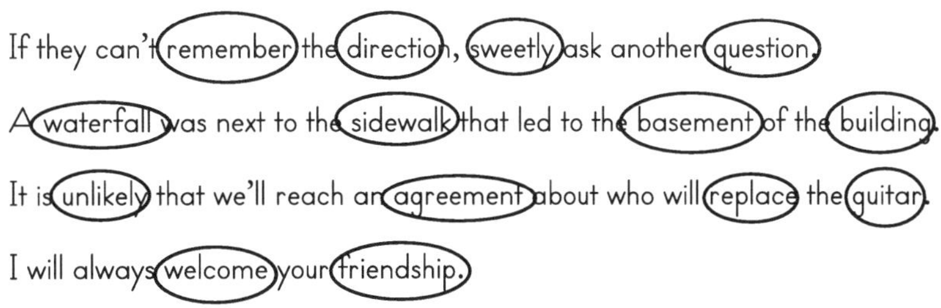

Lesson 157

Lesson Objectives

1. Students will review words that end with –tion and -ment. (P)
2. Students will review incomplete sentences. (L)
3. Students will review spelling words. (S)
4. Students will copy sentences neatly and correctly. (H)

Materials

LAR
SAP

Review Word List

From Lesson 126: action, affection, attention, auction, carnation, caution, celebration, commotion, condition, decoration, direction, emotion, formation, fraction, hesitation, information, instruction, irritation, lotion, mention, motion, nation, notion, occupation, portion, position, proportion, question, relation, relaxation, sensation, station, vacation

From Lesson 141: Agent, agreement, announcement, apartment, basement, cement, comment, compliment, content, department, different, element, enjoyment, excitement, experiment, garment, instrument, lament, moment, monument, movement, ornament, parent, payment, present, prevent, repent, silent, statement, treatment

Teaching

1. Choose words from both list. Write the words without the final syllable (tion or ment). Have students choose the correct ending. Use the top of the LAR workbook page. **Complete the words by adding the final syllable** (tion or ment).

2. Use the bottom of the LAR page. **Read the sentences. If a sentence is complete, fill in the yes circle. If it is incomplete, fill in the no circle. Add parts to the incomplete sentences to make them complete. Write the sentences on the lines**

3. Use the SAP page. Top section: **Find the spelling words that have the letters to spell the shorter words. Write the words on the lines.**

   Bottom section: **Are the words spelled correctly? Fill in yes or no.**

4. Use the handwriting sheet or have the children write the following sentences:

   The teacher asked a different question.
   We hung ornaments for the celebration.

LAR Answers

Top

1. vacation	2. excitement
3. movement	4. celebration
5. question	6. department
7. emotion	8. agreement

1. yes (filled) no
2. yes (filled) no
3. yes no (filled)
4. yes (filled) no
5. yes no (filled)

SAP Answers

building	another
question	waterfall
sidewalk	agreement
unlikely	guitar
friendship	basement
replace	welcome
sweetly	
remember	direction

yes ■ unlikly	● no replace	yes ■ guitare	yes ■ builbing	● no direction
yes ■ replase	● no sweatly	● no question	● no unlikely	● no building
yes ■ waderfall	yes ■ bacement	yes ■ agreament	yes ■ sidewolk	● no another
yes no quetsion	yes ■ welcome	yes ■ freindship	yes ■ anuther	● no basement
● no friendship	● no waterfall	yes ■ remenber	● no sweetly	yes ■ wellcome
yes ■ direcion	● no sidewalk	● no agreement	yes ■ freindship	● no guitar
● no remember	● no guitar			

Lesson 158

Lesson Objectives

1. Students will review the prefix re- and the suffix -ly. (P)
2. Students will review parts of speech. (L)
3. Students will review spelling words. (S)
4. Students will copy sentences neatly and correctly. (H)

Materials

LAR
SAP

Teaching

1. Use the top of the LAR workbook page. **Add either re or ly to the root words. Write the words on the lines.**

2. Review the parts of speech (nouns, pronouns, verbs, adverbs, adjectives). Use the bottom of the LAR workbook page. **Read the sentence. Tell how the listed words were used.** Repeat with the following sentence.

   The little boy loudly rejoiced when he found the little puppy.

3. Use the SAP page. Top section: **Fit the spelling words into the grid. Start with the two clue spaces, the letters t and c.**

   Bottom section: **Change the order of the words to make the two statements into questions.**

4. Use the handwriting sheet or have the children write the following sentences:

   We carefully recounted the pennies.
   Shelly felt bubbly at recess.

Review Word List

Lesson 131: angrily, boldly, bravely, bubbly, carefully, carelessly, certainly, closely, coldly, completely, constantly, happily, harshly, jointly, joyfully, kindly, lately, lightly, likely, loosely, lovely, meanly, merrily, mildly, monthly, noisily, oddly, pleasantly, powerfully, proudly, quickly, quietly, rarely, really, sadly, scraggly, secretly, selfishly, Shelly, shortly, shyly, simply, sleepily, slightly, slowly, softly, strangely, suddenly, sweetly, swiftly, terribly, tightly, unkindly, unlikely, unselfishly, weakly, wobbly, yearly

Lesson 136: react, recall, recess, reclaim, recline, record, recount, recover, recruit, redecorate, redeem, redouble, reduce, reduction, refill, refinish, reflect, reflex, refresh, refrigerate, refund, refuse, regain, regret, rehearse, rejoice, rejoin, relate, relax, relay, release, relief, relieve, relive, rely, remain, remake, remark, remember, remote, remove, renew, renumber, repair, repay, repeat, repent, rephrase, replace, replant, replay, reply, report, reprint, request, require, resign, respect, respond, result, resume, retell, retire, retrace, retreat, return, reveal, revenge, reverse, review, revue, reward, rewind

Not Listed: Compound words from Lessons 146 to 155

LAR Answers

Top

1. selfishly
2. reflect
3. replace
4. suddenly
5. refund
6. replant
7. lovely
8. pleasantly

Bottom

1. noun
2. adverb
3. adjective
4. pronoun
5. noun
6. verb
7. adjective
8. verb

SAP Answers

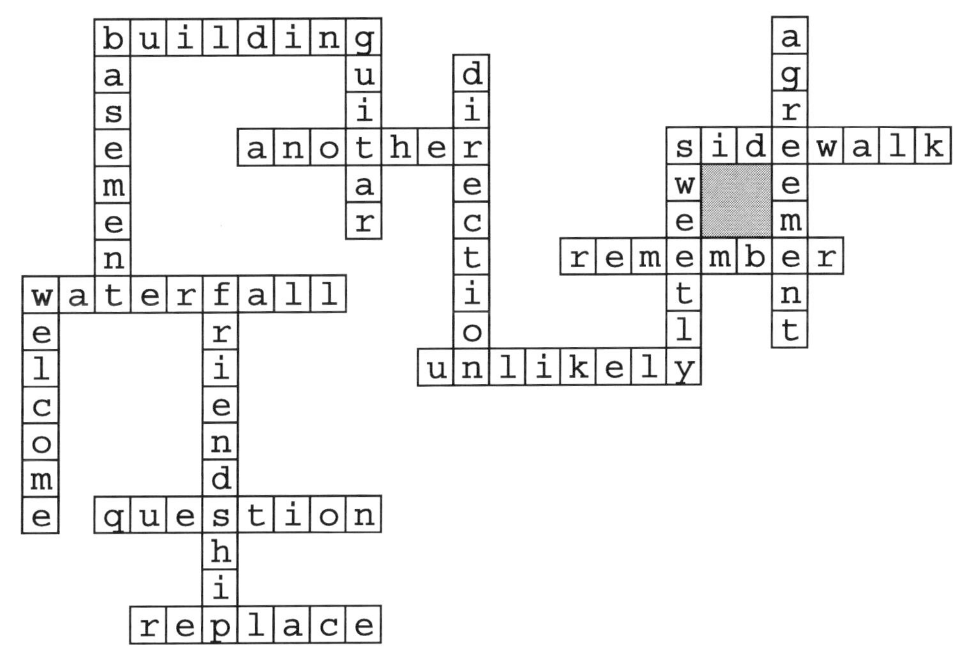

Did you remember to put the guitar in the basement?

Will the ranger replace the sign with directions to the waterfall?

Lesson 159

Lesson Objectives

1. Students will be tested over phonics concepts.
2. Students will review spelling words.
3. Students will copy sentences neatly and correctly. (H)

Materials

Test 4, pages 1 and 2
SAP

Test Directions:

1. **Phonics Test:**

   Part 1: Students will write the words that answer the questions.

   Part 2: Some words in the sentences are mixed up. Rewrite the sentences correctly.

   Part 3: Add tion, ment, ly or re to the words to complete them.

2. **Spelling**

   Use the SAP page. **Match the spelling words to the clues. Write your answers on the lines.**

3. Use the handwriting sheet or have the children write the following sentences:
   The speaker welcomed another question.
   Will they replace the sidewalk?

Test 4

Spelling Answers

sidewalk	
basement	question
waterfall	friendship
welcome	building
direction	sweetly
unlikely	replace
guitar	remember
another	agreement

Test Answers

Phonics Test

Page 1

Part 1

1. basement
2. redecorate
3. slowly
4. disguise
5. vacation
6. newspaper
7. parents
8. question
9. instrument
10. quietly

Page 2

Part 2

1. The rattlesnake hid underground.
2. Grandmother ate the applesauce.
3. A bumblebee landed on the windowsill.
4. The policeman spoke into the microphone.
5. The jellybean tasted like a strawberry.

Part 3

1. tightly	2. renumber	3. information
4. enjoyment	5. condition	6. remember
7. treatment	8. return	9. garment
10. monthly		

Lesson 160

Lesson Objectives

1. Students will be tested over language concepts.
2. Students will take a spelling dictation test.
3. Students will copy sentences neatly and correctly. (H)

Materials

Test 4, pages 3 and 4

Test Directions:

1. **Language Test:**

   Part 4: Read the sentences. Write how the listed words were used in the sentences (nouns, pronouns, verbs, adverbs, adjectives).

   Part 5: Read the sentences. Are they complete or incomplete?

   Fill in ovals, yes if it is complete, no if it is not complete.

   Part 6: Read the pairs of sentences. Combine the sentences using a conjunction (and, but, or).

   Part 7: Read the pairs of sentences. Answer the questions about pronouns.

2. **Spelling Dictation Test:** Have students number their paper from 1 to 15.

   1. building, 2. agreement, 3. another, 4. question, 5. unlikely, 6. replace, 7. guitar, 8. basement, 9. sweetly, 10. welcome, 11. remember, 12. friendship, 13. waterfall, 14. direction

3. Use the handwriting sheet or have the children write the following sentences:

   The building had a nice basement.
   The book gave directions for guitar playing.

Language Test

Test Answers

Page 3

Part 4

1. adjective 2. adverb
3. verb 4. pronoun
5. adjective 6. verb
7. noun 8. adverb
9. noun 10. pronoun

Part 5

1. ● (no)
2. (yes) ●
3. ● (no)
4. ● (no)
5. (yes) ●
6. (yes) ●
7. ● (no)
8. (yes) ●
9. ● (no)
10. (yes) ●

Page 4

Part 6

1. The basketball bounced off the goal, and it broke a window.
2. You like pineapple, but I like applesauce.
3. Tom can slice the onion, or he can fix the oven.

Part 7

1. grandfather 2. eyeglasses
3. Shelly
4. Mother 5. dove
6. people 7. Dad

Made in the USA
Monee, IL
07 June 2023

35180332R00151